CYBERCOGNITION

LEE HADLINGTON

Sara Miller McCune founded SAGE Publishing in 1965 to support the dissemination of usable knowledge and educate a global community. SAGE publishes more than 1000 journals and over 800 new books each year, spanning a wide range of subject areas. Our growing selection of library products includes archives, data, case studies and video. SAGE remains majority owned by our founder and after her lifetime will become owned by a charitable trust that secures the company's continued independence.

Los Angeles | London | New Delhi | Singapore | Washington DC | Melbourne

CYBERCOGNITION

LEE HADLINGTON

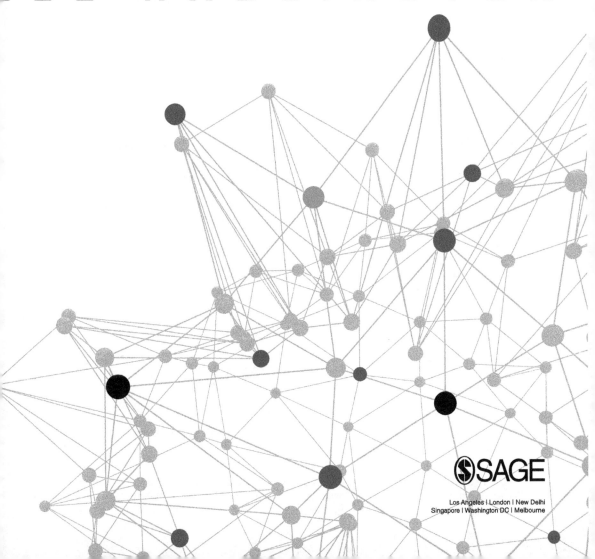

$\circledS$ SAGE

Los Angeles | London | New Delhi
Singapore | Washington DC | Melbourne

Los Angeles | London | New Delhi
Singapore | Washington DC | Melbourne

SAGE Publications Ltd
1 Oliver's Yard
55 City Road
London EC1Y 1SP

SAGE Publications Inc.
2455 Teller Road
Thousand Oaks, California 91320

SAGE Publications India Pvt Ltd
B 1/I 1 Mohan Cooperative Industrial Area
Mathura Road
New Delhi 110 044

SAGE Publications Asia-Pacific Pte Ltd
3 Church Street
#10-04 Samsung Hub
Singapore 049483

Editor: Luke Block
Editorial assistant: Lucy Dang
Production editor: Imogen Roome
Copyeditor: Neil Dowden
Proofreader: Leigh C. Timmins
Indexer: Elske Janssen
Marketing manager: Lucia Sweet
Cover design: Wendy Scott
Typeset by: C&M Digitals (P) Ltd, Chennai, India
Printed and bound by
CPI Group (UK) Ltd, Croydon, CR0 4YY

© Lee Hadlington 2017

First published 2017

Library of Congress Control Number: 2016954335

British Library Cataloguing in Publication data

A catalogue record for this book is available from the British Library

ISBN 978-1-4739-5718-3
ISBN 978-1-4739-5719-0 (pbk)

At SAGE we take sustainability seriously. Most of our products are printed in the UK using FSC papers and boards. When we print overseas we ensure sustainable papers are used as measured by the PREPS grading system. We undertake an annual audit to monitor our sustainability.

To Mrs Denise, for all the help with the proof-reading (and the inherent abuse that accompanied it)

To Nadia, for being the most supportive office mate I could ever hope for and the endless supply of chocolate

To my Mom and Dad who never really knew what I was doing, but were always there to support me

To Steph … for being the most valuable baseline for my ramblings and for being there when it all became a little bit too much

CONTENTS

ABOUT THE AUTHOR

Dr Lee Hadlington has been a Senior Lecturer at De Montfort University since 2006 after completing his PhD at Wolverhampton University. Originally coming from a background in applied cognitive psychology, he has developed a research profile in the area of cyberpsychology. His main focus of interest is exploring the way in which humans use cognition in the online environment as well as the potential for digital technology to change the underlying processes that we use in daily life. Associated with his work in the area of cyberpsychology is a keen interest in exploring key aspects of technology-enabled crime. He has also worked extensively with a variety of organisations exploring aspects of insider threat, susceptibility to cybercrime and attitudes towards cybersecurity. The aim of this research is to help identify potential indicators that could highlight a susceptibility to cybercrime alongside an examination of how individual differences play a role in risky cybersecurity behaviours.

The author also attempts to hide his mild Haribo addiction from his co-workers on a daily basis and has a 14-year-old cat that still believes she is a kitten. When not trapped behind a desk or teaching his lovely students he likes nothing better than to throw himself around various forest trails on his trusty mountain bike, much to the annoyance of dog walkers, ramblers and his army of minions that have to wash his bike/clothes.

PREFACE

Whilst on a research-related jolly to London to visit an organisation I was working with I had the fortune to be standing on a crowded tube, in rush hour with a colleague. In my position as a psychologist and general all-round nosey individual I began to scan the carriage for something that would distract me from (a) the rather noxious smell of perfume, deodorant and old shoes that was inhabiting my nose and (b) my inherent dislike of crowded spaces. A scene that, to this day, I still recount began to catch both my eye and my intellectual curiosity. A mother was standing over a pushchair wilfully transfixed by something on her smartphone. Meanwhile, her daughter sat mesmerised by her mother's interactions with the aforementioned device, occasionally pausing to quickly scan the environment in front of her to see if there was anything slightly more interesting. When this process failed, the child's facial expression changed somewhat suddenly, and all of a sudden she began grasping at the air uttering the words, 'iPad, Mommy … iPad, Mommy'. Sure enough, without actually saying a word and taking her eyes of the smartphone, the mother rummaged around in a jumble of bags that lay behind the pushchair and produced an iPad. Once received the child began to gleefully swipe, shake and poke to her heart's content while the mother continued on her quest to wear the screen of the smartphone out by the sheer power of staring.

I had previously explored some aspects of human cognition online as part of a funded research project, but my experience on the tube in London started me on a path that resulted in this book. I started to think about the way in which we all seemed to be drifting in a trance-like state in a world that was subsumed by digital technology, and where the interactions I had viewed on the tube were becoming the norm, not the exception. As I started to delve a little deeper into the subject matter, I started to notice more and more how digital technology was impacting on our daily lives. I sat in coffee shops noticing that people were sitting down and automatically taking out their smartphones and placing them on the tables in front of them; on nights out, friends would be more interested in posting the perfect selfie to Facebook than they were in actually engaging in socialisation; couples out for a romantic meal would sit next to each other, often communicating through the medium of WhatsApp to find out what the other was ordering; people walking blindly across roads or into street furniture whilst being preoccupied with posting what they had for breakfast on Twitter. Now before we get into name calling, I do have mates and my name isn't Billy – I just observed these things whilst I was alone, and it is something that once you notice you find it hard to switch off.

I wanted to start to understand the impact digital technology was having in terms of both its depth and breadth, not just in the context of social and developmental issues but also the processes that govern these, the cognitive processes that underlie them. More and more I became interested in the way we deploy our existing cognitive skills whilst we are engaged in the use of digital technology. My secondary concern was the one that actually served to drive me to complete this book, and that was if we are using digital technology on such a massive scale, could it be actually changing the way in which we think? The question didn't really present itself as being something simple or straightforward, and even now I am still finding new information that adds to the story that is being told here. It isn't until you actually sit down and commit words to screen that you realise the enormity of the issue as well as the complexity that underlies such a question. The key to this book is that the story is just beginning, and I want it to be seen as a first attempt to draw most of the strands of research on this topic together in one place. If the reader takes anything away at the end, it should be the understanding that more work is needed in this area and more research needs to be conducted so further tales can be told. The question of whether digital technology is impacting on the way in which we think seems even more poignant when we consider the interaction viewed on the London tube several years ago; it is the younger and developing generation that is being immersed in a technological environment that no one else will have experienced before. Now this isn't about being judgemental, or implementing a nanny-state where the time spent on the Internet is strictly governed; it is more about being responsible and acquiring as much information as possible about both the positives and negatives for engaging in the use of digital technology.

If you are expecting a stuffy, aloof and humourless exploration of our interactions with digital technology that is devoid of anecdotal evidence and a feverish attempt to engage the reader … you had better step away from this book and leave quietly. However, if you like the sound of an alternative approach to the former, have an interest in the area of cyberpsychology and want to start to understand the current themes that guide our exploration of cognition online, then, reader, you have come to the right place.

1

EXPLORING THE CONCEPT OF CYBERSPACE

Learning Aims and Objectives

This chapter will:

- introduce the key aims for the material covered in the book;
- present a clear outline for the key concepts and terminology that will form the building blocks for later discussion;
- explore the concept and present definitions of cyberspace;
- highlight the notion that cyberspace is a wholly psychological construct.

Overview

It is important to make a statement about the primary aims of this book right from the very start so that (a) you are clear on its contents and the scope of the discussion within and (b) you don't spend your money unnecessarily! There are two key aims of this book. The first is to explore the cognitive processes we are deploying when we are online and whether these differ substantially from the ones that we deploy when offline. The secondary aim is an exploration of how engaging in the online environment is affecting us on a psychological level, particularly in terms of changing our cognitive processes, altering the way in which our memory functions and how we pay attention. Therefore the exploration set out in this book is as much about how we are processing information when online as it is about how technology is affecting the way in which we do this. What this book will not do is spend pages and pages discussing the finer details of the technology that subsumes our experiences online. It should be stated that the important aspect here is not the technology itself (this has been the focus of many discussions, papers and reports), but the impact the use of such tools is having upon the human element within that system.

There will be a short introduction to the key concepts, but hopefully these will serve as a guide to those who have the most basic of understanding in all concepts related to the online world.

Cybercognition is a term that I use to describe the cognitive activities humans conduct in cyberspace, whether it is through digital media, smartphones, computers or tablet devices (Hadlington et al., 2013). The term is intended to cover a topic that has two distinct levels, and attempts to bridge a perceived gap with what we traditionally view as cognition in an offline environment. In the first instance the term is used to explore the concept of cognition in the online digital environment, with the aim of understanding how such mechanisms are being deployed in this sphere. Second, it also aims to encapsulate the possibility that being engaged in these activities could be actively changing the way in which we use certain aspects of cognition, whether this be a perceived negative or positive. The term includes an exploration of all areas underpinning human cognition alongside the context of any digital environment, as well as the associated interactions with new and emergent technologies that give us access to it. What is presented here is the sum of our current knowledge related to our interactions with technology and its sphere of influence on these cognitive capabilities (see 'Cybercognition in the Real World' box). The impact of this has a wide-ranging set of implications across elements of learning, memory, attention, problem-solving and decision-making, to highlight just a few. It is important to note that the effect the use of this technology is having on our cognitive processes should not be seen as wholly negative, with a great deal of assistive technology providing scaffolding capacities for aspects such as learning as well as aiding those who have severe learning difficulties or dementia and memory impairment (Carrillo et al., 2009; DePompei et al., 2008; LoPresti et al., 2008; O'Neill et al., 2014).

CYBERCOGNITION IN THE REAL WORLD: TRANSACTIVE MEMORY

Previous work by researchers Sparrow et al. (2011) noted a trend for individuals to remember less factual information (or semantic memory) in favour of a more defined memory for where to find this information. Essentially they noted a growing reliance on the notion that 'Google knows', with their research showing that the majority of participants in their study were using the Internet as another form of social or transactive memory. There are pros and cons to this: essentially, as our brains are having to remember less information there is more space for us to fill with other things, but if we lose access to the Internet as a source of information, we lose the capacity to access those facts we might need.

Humans have always shown the potential to evolve alongside new and emerging technologies, with such technological advancements providing mechanisms for an associated shift in cognition. One of the key reasons why this issue is such a point of concern for people in modern society is the speed at which technology is developing. In the words of Whittle (1997), cyberspace:

> represents one of the most significant advances the world has ever witnessed in providing humankind with a vehicle to access data and information ... The development of language, the invention of the printing press, the creation of libraries, the advent of the mass media – all have played pivotal roles in advancing civilization; but none has had the explosive impact and potential of cyberspace. (p. 30)

Whittle explores the ways in which cyberspace and our interactions within it can change the very shape of our laws, businesses, cultures and education. However, the question that is neglected in discussion is the one that is key to our very existence as well as our everyday functioning: are our cognitive capabilities evolving at a fast enough rate to allow us to keep up with the demands of cyberspace? This is where the basis for this book begins.

The Internet, the World Wide Web and Cyberspace

This is not a preamble to a post-modern interpretation of the unique Narnia universe created by C. S. Lewis, but rather an exploration of the key elements or 'levels' that can be viewed in the context of the online world. These levels can be conceptualised in terms of how abstracted they are, from the very physical to the more intangible. This section aims to provide a clearer introduction to some of the basic terminology that will frame the discussion throughout the rest of the book. An assumption is often made that we are all aware of the key differences between the Internet, the World Wide Web (WWW) and cyberspace. However, in reality, although many people engage with the online digital environment, I suspect that very few actually understand that there is a difference in what these terms refer to. It could be argued that buying cheese online or surfing the web looking for humorous pictures of cats doesn't really need a deeper understanding of such nuances in the terminology. You don't necessarily have to know how to build a computer in order to use it, but as for you, my intrepid reader, brace yourself and prepare to be amazed! Many mistakenly assume that all of the three elements discussed above are one and the same, but the further exploration outlined in the following section will make it clear that they are not.

The Internet

In the context of this book the label of 'Internet' (note the use of the capital 'I' in this instance) is used to describe the globally interconnected network of computers. The use of the term 'internet' (lower-case 'i') is a generally accepted reference to the 'internetwork' that originated in the early days of the Internet, and makes reference to a more localised system of interconnected computers, such as a local intranet (Praziale et al., 2006). The Internet is a technological structure that has a physical presence, with wires, connectors, Ethernet cables and the shiny devices we all adore and worship. The Internet is the thing that allows information to be transmitted around the world in a matter of seconds through the use of computer code.

The World Wide Web (WWW)

The term 'Internet' is something that is often confused with the World Wide Web, with the latter being the information-sharing platform that is built *on top* of the Internet. The WWW affords the capacity for any normal individual, not versed in the joys of programming and HTTP, the freedom to navigate around, collect information and post amusing pictures of food on Instagram, Twitter and Facebook. The Internet is merely the system that allows the WWW to exist, and without the Internet there would be no WWW. In contrast, the Internet existed long before Sir Tim Berners-Lee developed the WWW and could still exist if the WWW disappeared overnight. The important aspect for us as humans is that the WWW affords us elements of social, cultural and cognitive interaction that would be difficult or impossible for many individuals. The distinction between the two systems, although not inherently important for understanding the impact that technology is having on human cognition, is important if we are to assign how aspects of these technologies are impacting upon us.

Cyberspace

Cyberspace is something slightly different from elements such as the Internet and the WWW. When we are talking about cyberspace we are making reference to the psychological environment in which individuals are engaging in interactions, experiences, thoughts and emotions whilst being online. The WWW is purely a tool for individuals to explore and share information, and only when this is taken one step further and the individual begins to interact with that information does that environment become our 'cyberspace', the online environment where we live to exchange ideas and experiences.

Whittle (1997) presents some clear outlines of what cyberspace is and should be viewed as, and his work has been fundamental in driving other researchers to explore how we view this environment. Predominantly Whittle sees the notion of cyberspace as being virtual in nature, but also something that can be both real and artificial at the same time. At the same time Whittle also likens our experience of cyberspace to being in a trance-like state that we may enter into when we become fully engrossed in the thing that we are doing, such as reading, surfing or writing. In Whittle's view the realm of cyberspace should be considered the 'digital complement' to the atomic or physical offline world.

Cyberspace is also viewed as being something that is accessed through some form of physical device that has an element of artificial processing built into it, be it a smartphone, laptop or tablet PC. The actual access point, in any context, is irrelevant, but without this access device Whittle states that there is no difference between cyberspace and communication within an offline environment. The device being used will define the nature of the individual's experience within cyberspace, and according to Whittle these devices appear as the 'window' through which we view and enter cyberspace.

Finally, cyberspace allows individuals and groups to interact and communicate, as well as the ability to share creative output outside of the constraints of time and physical space. Importantly, Whittle noted that without this essential element of interaction the concept of cyberspace becomes obsolete. Similarly the notion of interaction in the context of cyberspace is viewed as being a qualitatively different phenomenon from what we experience in the offline environment, where it might be indirect, delayed or separated by distance (this also fits into the psychological concepts outlined by Suler (2005; which will be discussed below) which will be discussed below). Whittle notes that individuals create an illusion of immediacy in the context of online interactions as there are no limiting factors to force responses, and they can happen where both time and place are shifted.

Whittle actually presented two definitions of the concept of cyberspace, the earlier one being a working concept that was modified to use more understandable terms. The final definition presented by Whittle is one that will be used to encapsulate the digital environment in which the later concepts related to cognition will be discussed, so it is presented here in its entirety:

Cy*ber*space (sī-bûr-spās) n.

1. A fictional, psychic space where minds fuse in a trance-like "consensual hallucination".

2. The conceptual world of networked interactions between individuals and their intellectual creations and everything associated with such networks and interactions.

3. The state of mind shared by people communicating using digital representations of language and sensory experience who are separated by time and space but connected by networks of physical access devices. (Whittle, 1997: 9)

There are some important points to this definition, with the initial point making reference to the first author to use the term cyberspace as William Gibson in the sci-fi novel *Neuromancer*. The shared experience of being online within cyberspace is likened to being in a trance-like state, a shared experience that the individuals subject themselves to willingly. The description unwittingly suggests an almost drug-induced experience, with aspects of addiction and problematic use being realised in the present. Whittle's first concept also makes reference to the concept of 'psychic', again drilling the notion home that cyberspace is a psychologically created environment. In the second point raised by Whittle we have the interactivity of cyberspace as well as the exchange of ideas therein, a process that is again driven by the cognition of the individual. The last sub-definition relates to a shared, non-physical digital construct that is brought into being through the use of language and other forms of representation (e.g. digital media such as video clips). Here the emphasis is on a shared experience that can occur amongst as well as between individuals. This experience is also able to occur even though the individuals taking part may not share the same physical or chronological space. However, the networks of digital devices that build cyberspace allow everyone who is connected to them the freedom to engage that same digital environment.

There is an important point to note when we explore Whittle's conceptualisation of cyberspace, and that is that at each point the experiences and interactions are driven by our cognitive processes. As will become more apparent in the next section, the importance of psychology in the context of understanding cyberspace is inescapable. Cyberspace is not a physical thing, so as such is something that is constructed solely through our ability to represent complex ideas and formulate plans within our heads.

The Internet as a Psychological Construct

When we talk about 'construction' in the context of the offline work, we might create images of an army of builders furiously at work on some monolithic structure (or in my experience the construction of a chicken shed). The online environment is no different in terms of being constructed; however, the building blocks that are used to create it are wholly psychological in nature. For example, the power to simulate, imagine, engage and transfer our thoughts, feelings and actions have no physical equivalent, but can be conveyed through the medium of cyberspace. Cyberspace is not virtual reality – virtual reality is a technology-driven environment that presents a reality through the use of technology without any direct involvement from a human (Steuer, 1992). Cyberspace, on the other hand, is the reverse of virtual reality – it is our experiences and thoughts that create the digital environment, and without these cyberspace would not exist. It is accepted that the tools and devices we use to get online are inherently physical in nature, but the interactions that are contained within cyberspace have no clear physical tangibility outside of that created environment. In order to interact with information and individuals within cyberspace we have to use a variety of cognitive processes to engage with, manipulate and reason about the information we are being presented with – which is why the psychology of cyberspace is so inherently important for everyone who is using it (and abusing it!). Cyberspace affords the end user the unique opportunity to consume digital media at a pace that can far outstrip our capacity to actually digest and process that information in the same manner we can do in the offline world. It also provides us with a pervasive lure, and can always provide us with something that is new, interesting and novel (Small and Vorgan, 2008). This level of stimulation never actually diminishes, even though we may appear to be experiencing similar activities over and over again, and for some researchers it has been suggested that it is this process that could be linked to an aspect of digital addiction that has become prevalent in today's digital culture (Small and Vorgan, 2008). (This aspect will be discussed in Chapter 11.)

Our experiences within cyberspace are governed by key psychological principles that provide us with a starting point to begin to explore how individuals are interacting with new and emerging digital technology. The affective element of our online experiences and interactions relates directly to the psychology of motivation and emotion. When discussing the affective elements of cyberspace the focus is to explore the feelings and emotions that the individual is experiencing whilst being online. Here the individual may experience a set of similar emotional norms across all elements of cyberspace, but in other individuals there may be a change in their emotions according to what they are experiencing and where they have experienced it. Our experiences within cyberspace can also have consequences in our offline world, particularly when we are looking at emotional and motivational factors.

QUESTION TO CONSIDER

When someone is 'defriended' on Facebook could this affect their ability to concentrate offline?

In research conducted by Baumeister et al. (2002) the link between social isolation and the impact this could have upon cognitive processes was explored. It was noted that those people who were led to believe they would lead a socially isolated life had large reductions in intelligent thought, more specifically in terms of speed and accuracy of task performance. So there is an offline precedence that suggests that our emotive experiences online could impact on our cognitive processes offline. The individual may become upset, anxious, angry and distracted from their normal everyday activities directly as a result of something that has happened online. There are some more obvious malicious activities that individuals can experience online that can also impact directly on our self-esteem and psychological well-being. The emotional and psychological consequences of behaviours such as cybercrime, cyberstalking and cyberbullying are still being explored by researchers (e.g. Slonje et al., 2013). Some researchers have noted that the differences between cyberbullying and offline, face-to-face bullying are qualitative in nature, meaning that technology has actually created a new mechanism for individuals to abuse the vulnerable (see Dooley et al., 2009). In a similar vein, aspects of 'cyberslacking' impact on our ability to motivate and focus in our offline lives, again demonstrating the affective legacy set by the Internet on our daily lives (O'Neill et al., 2014; Vitak et al., 2011). Yet another avenue for our activities within cyberspace to leach out and taint our offline experiences includes elements of cybercrime, something that has been addressed in the research literature (for the interested reader, Wall, 2007, provides an excelllent coverage of these issues in more depth). It is from this perspective that the importance of exploring the impact technology is having upon our ability to freely engage in experiences within cyberspace without the fear of incurring psychological harm and upset becomes more apparent. Human cognition in terms of processes such as memory, attention, learning and problem solving do not occur in isolation and are interlaced with the affective elements that govern our day-to-day existences.

QUESTIONS TO CONSIDER

Can you easily remember information if you are upset or angry?

Do you pay more attention to disturbing images that you might accidentally stumble on whilst surfing the web?

Does seeing emotive aspects online make them more memorable, and does this in turn affect your later decisions?

This interplay between cognition and emotion is a critical one to understand and accept, particularly when we are exploring elements related to how we engage with cyberspace. Research has demonstrated that both positive and negative emotional stimuli can impact significantly on our ability to process information (Blair et al., 2007). Kensinger (2007) conducted a review of the research exploring the impact negative emotions can have on memory. Overall she noted that negative emotions associated with an event served to enhance the subjective vividness of the memory, but also an increased likelihood of remembering some of the event details. It is apparent that when we are discussing the psychological impact of digital technology it is disingenuous to believe that our emotions and cognitive processes are always acting in isolation.

To underestimate the influence that psychology has upon our experiences within cyberspace is very easy. Psychology is a driving force that serves a pivotal role in generating and maintaining our experiences online, and without aspects of cognition acting in conjunction with the emotional and motivation elements mentioned earlier our experiences within cyberspace would be meaningless. Aspects of cognition allow us to remember pieces of information as well as giving us the capacity to tie together individual episodes of our online lives so that the information we are gathering makes sense. We also need to be able to communicate effectively online to ensure our messages are getting across without being misunderstood and misinterpreted, again something that relies heavily on aspects of cognition. To keep track of our metaphysical position within cyberspace and to navigate around the myriad online websites and endless links also requires a capacity not only to remember where we are, but also to identify where we have been and where we need to go in order to achieve the current goal for being online. Such a process of online navigation, as will be discussed in Chapter 10, is an effortful process and relies heavily on a number of strategies that are developed over a period of time. Without the capacity to remember, such strategies would be lost and we too would become disorientated in a constantly evolving online ecosystem.

We could simply make the assumption that our experiences in the digital world are shaped by cognitive processes that are equitable to how we accomplish activities and actions in the offline environment. Such an assertion is perhaps erroneous in nature or may be misguided in the absence of clear empirical research, something that I hope will be driven further by this book and the material contained within. At present there is a growing body of research evidence that is beginning to make the comparison between how cognitive processes are being deployed in both the online and offline environments. However, such work is still very much in its infancy and even less is known about how the use of technology is changing such processes for better or worse. Many individuals may wish to ignore the fact that their active use of digital technology could be impacting on other aspects of their psychological functioning. Without descending into what could be categorised as some form of evangelic spiel warning against the horrors of the devil that is the web, it is apparent that many people just don't like to be made aware that their beloved piece of technology could be having a detrimental impact on their capacity to focus, learn and remember. When you do bring this information to the attention of people there is a great deal of sudden acceptance, and people are quick to point out that they are guilty of doing the very things that could cause them longer-term harm or put them in danger. However, these are the same people you will meet ten minutes later walking down the street glued to their iPhone just about to walk into the path of a passing lorry. Change is never easy, but the fact is that we are being changed at this precise moment in time by the very technology we are using, and for the most part we are blindly embracing such a change, not resisting it.

The Psychology of Cyberspace

According to Suler (2005) there are a set of underlying psychological components that are worthy of discussion here as they set the scene for some of the key elements that will be introduced later on in the book. As highlighted earlier, the nature of cyberspace means that it is a wholly psychological construct that lacks any real physical presence, although for people online those experiences and the interaction they are engaging in are just as real as those being undertaken in the offline environment. The individual can touch a tablet PC, type words using a keyboard or click on a link using a mouse, which would suggest some form of physicality attached to these experiences. However, these aspects are just tools that assist us in getting online, and it is the experiences that they afford us that remain metacognitive in nature – we know we are having them, but we cannot physically engage with them as we can in the offline world. In the same respect those emails, documents and posts that have accumulated online remain only as a partial record of our online interactions and not the interactions themselves. Details such as the way in which these documents were created and the interactions that lead to that final document are lost, hence missing out vital information that would be necessary to rebuild that actual iterative process.

Once the psychological components are removed from our engagement with cyberspace, whatever remains will just be a very basic collection of data. Without the capacity to analyse, interpret and interact with this material the essence of what cyberspace is becomes lost. Suler's (2005) exploration expands on these key points further and highlights the key psychological features that distinguish cyberspace from the offline environment. Each of Suler's (2005) psychological elements of cyberspace are discussed in more detail below.

Reduced sensations

Cyberspace is, as has been reiterated here several times already, a non-physical realm. The critical difference between the online interactions of the individual and those that are completed offline is the heavy reliance on a reduced number of senses. If an individual has a normal conversation with someone in a café or bar they are presented with an array of stimulation from the whole gamut of senses they have at their disposal. This may include aspects of smell, taste and touch as well as the relevant non-verbal cues that accompany human interaction. In contrast our capacity to communicate in the online environment can be presented as a fairly sanitised affair, with much of this peripheral information being lost due to the constraints placed upon us by the technology being used. Elements such as vocal intonation and finer nuances in terms of delivery are lost, meaning that a comment included in an email that was meant as sarcasm comes across as insulting and derogatory. Current advances in aspects of computer mediated communication (CMC) have presented the opportunity to access other senses for communication outside that of simple text. Those individuals familiar with the use of video conferencing will be all too aware this is a clear possibility, but there are still limits to how far this can go in emulating an offline experience. For example, there is little capacity for tactile feedback in an Internet-based video chat, so there is still a reduction in the amount of sensory feedback the individual can experience whilst being online.

Text

Irrespective of the advances made in the technology that delivers aspects of cyberspace to the individual, the typed word still remains the most dominant mechanism for communicating in the online world. Text is a fairly static form of communication and has the relevant disadvantage of being very basic in terms of its capacity to transfer the elements that stand outside of the actual plain of information contained within it. There is a skill in being able to transfer aspects such as feeling and empathy through the medium of text, with many individuals finding such a process difficult. However, Suler does note that text-based communication in the context of cyberspace still represents a powerful mechanism for self-expression and interpersonal communication. For the most part text and the written word constitute a relatively simple medium to produce, and as long as the message is targeted at the right populations (cultural and language boundaries accepted) it can be easily understood and open to a wide audience. Reading and producing text requires limited specialist knowledge on the individual, and for the most part humans possess the capacity to produce written language in some form or another, irrespective of their stage of development (this relates more directly to the age of the individual rather than the age of the race). It is also noted that communicating via text can also be a complex and cognitively demanding process, requiring the implementation of different mechanisms from simply talking and listening. According to Suler (2005) there is an aspect of construction, assessment, maintenance and perception associated with text-based communication in cyberspace. The individual has to be able to analyse what others are saying (based on limited knowledge of the other person sometimes) and then construct responses that accurately present their own ideals and beliefs. Text in its basic form can be a blunt instrument if care is not taken when using it, with the smallest mistakes (or that odd tired email) potentially leading to a completely different message being sent than the one originally intended.

Temporal Flexibility

In the context of cyberspace individuals are afforded two distinct patterns of communication linked into a temporal framework. There is concurrent communication where both individuals occupy the same space in time (but not necessarily the same location) and the dialogue occurs in real time. This pattern of communication is viewed as being *synchronous*. On the other hand communication can lie 'dormant' until the opposing end in the communication stream picks up the responses, with this forming an asynchronous communication pattern. In the latter there is no requirement for both parties to share the same temporal space in order for the communication to take place. The time taken to respond to communications can also depend directly upon the level of synchronicity afforded by the communication method. In the context of the asynchronous communication pattern there may be days or weeks available to mull over the contents of the message and prepare a response. In contrast, synchronicity gives the individual the capacity to respond in the magnitude of seconds or minutes. In all forms of online communication there is a greater capacity for a 'lag' between input and response, something that is not really evident in face-to-face offline forms of communication.

However, there might be other instances where the time we experience in cyberspace can appear to be more condensed, a process that is hypothesised to be a direct by-product of the dynamic environment in which individuals become immersed. For example, if you are a member of an online chat room for a period of several months you may become considered as a wiser and more senior member to whom individuals will delegate decisions and instil greater credibility compared with those members who have joined more recently. The underlying infrastructure associated with the Internet means that everything is in a constant state of flux, and this is also the same for the individuals who inhabit that environment. People can move from one aspect to another as they are searching for the next platform to engage with as their interest in the current one wains. On the other hand individuals may widen their interests outside the current area of focus, perhaps as a direct result of their experience with that media, meaning they want to go off and broaden their horizons in other chat rooms that appeal to that interest. Essentially time is a flexible construct in the context of cyberspace, where a week could be analogous to a month or more in terms of traditional offline engagement terms.

Flexibility of Identity

Cyberspace presents a unique opportunity for individuals to assume identities that can bear no similarity to our offline selves. If you explore Google (at your peril!) you can find any number of stories where people have purported to be something they are not online. Indeed, such a phenomenon has created its own movie and TV franchise in the form of the MTV documentary *Catfish*, which is replete with stories of how people have formed romantic attachments with people who often turn out not to be who they say they are. The crucial facet of cyberspace is that there is the lack of face-to-face interaction, which in turn allows the individual free reign to create whatever identity (or identities) they choose online. Such a process is being driven directly by the imagination and ingenuity of the individual. As an entity in cyberspace the individual is free to assume an identity or opinion that could match that of your offline persona, or it could be completely different. You can also engage directly in communication or become an invisible 'lurker', simply looking but not engaging. Such a process would perhaps be analogous to sitting next to a couple or group in a public place and just listening in on their conversation – the normal social conventions in the offline environment don't really match those of cyberspace. The concept of *trolling* is one aspect that is afforded a reality because of this notion of a flexible identity within cyberspace (Hardaker, 2010).

IN THE SPOTLIGHT: TROLLING

Trolling has gone through a variety of iterations since the term was first presented in the 1990s; originally it was used to describe a process by which an individual purposefully provoked another as part of mutual enjoyment (Bishop, 2014). However, in more recent years, the emphasis has changed considerably from one of enjoyment to that of abuse, and the mutual aspect has altered to that of the individual's own enjoyment. There have been several high-profile cases where individuals in the public eye have deleted or suspended social networking accounts due to the

(Continued)

(Continued)

activities of such trolls. In one instance the mother of murdered schoolgirl Sarah Payne was forced off Twitter due to a constant stream of abuse from trolls (www. telegraph.co.uk/news/uknews/crime/11237342/Sara-Payne-quits-Twitter-after-years-of-abuse.html). The daughter of the late and great actor Robin Williams, Zelda, was also the victim of online abuse after her father's suicide, which forced her to delete both her Instagram and Twitter accounts (www.telegraph.co.uk/news/celebritynews/11032371/Robin-Williamss-daughter-Zelda-quits-Twitter-after-being-trolled-over-fathers-suicide.html). Other high-profile names to have quit Twitter include the screenwriter Jane Goldman, 'superbrain' and all-round decent bloke Stephen Fry, as well as singers such as Nicki Minaj, Tom Clarke and Sinead O'Connor. (www.telegraph.co.uk/women/womens-life/11238018/Celebrity-Twitter-trolls-The-famous-people-whove-been-driven-off-social-media-by-abuse.html).

Trolling can also allow an individual the capacity to say whatever they like without fear of discovery and reprisal upon their offline self. The mask of anonymity may allow individuals the opportunity to express an opinion that they may otherwise be unable to discuss, or it may be that it allows them chance to abuse others online without actual consequences (Suler, 2005).

Altered Perceptions

According to Suler, when we engage in any activity in cyberspace it has the potential to alter our perceptions of reality and consciousness. He noted that when we are immersed in the digital environment there could be a phenomenon where we begin to feel a 'blending' of our minds with those with whom we are communicating. Suler suggested that this very process might ultimately lead people to engage in activities online for lengthy periods of time. For many people the interaction they engage in online affords them an opportunity to escape from the routine of their daily lives, in turn leading to the potential for aspects of addiction and chronic use (Suler, 2005).

Transcended Space

Digital technology affords individuals the flexibility to communicate and interact that no longer has to be confined by geographical boundaries. Communication technologies developed at each epoch in human history have served to decrease the metaphysical size of the world in which we live, with the advent of cyberspace making a small world even smaller. The capacity to transcend geographical boundaries means that we have greater freedom to seek out and interact with those who may share similar passions and interests to us.

QUESTIONS TO CONSIDER

How many people on the street in which you live would be interested in the same things that you are?

Now think about whether there are any groups on Facebook that might share some of your specific interests.

Transcending space allows support groups the capacity to reach a multitude of individuals who could have potentially missed out on vital support, interaction and information. However, as with everything, there are downsides to the aspect of transcended space, as it allows in those who have agendas outside of support and increases the capacity to attack individuals and groups without having to leave the comfort of their own home.

Equalised Status

The interesting thing about being in cyberspace is the concept that it offers everyone, irrespective of who they might be in the offline environment, a level playing field on which to get their opinions voiced and heard. This notion is something that Suler referred to as the 'net democracy' and presents a unique capacity for individuals from any walk of life the ability to get their message out. The importance of this is something that cannot be underestimated as previously this may have just been a capacity afforded to the privileged few, perhaps through published work or by being experts in their field. In cyberspace the status you have online becomes linked to the individual's popularity and that of their message. It also relates directly to the capacity that individual has for getting that message across effectively and efficiently using the media of the Internet. The obvious downside to this aspect of equalised status is that it raises problems for anyone searching for information online, as well as the associated credibility of that information (this point will be discussed further in Chapter 9).

Social Multiplicity

Cyberspace affords us with another unique capacity that lies outside of our normal offline lives. We have the potential to both engage in and maintain any number of online interactions and relationships, many of which can be condensed into a very short period of time. These multiple relationships can happen both synchronously and asynchronously, but more importantly they can be achieved without the other person in the relationship ever being aware that the messenger is involved in these other associations. For most of us the assumption is that we are the only one that is being communicated with and the messenger is solely focused on us. There are some obvious downsides to this aspect of cyberspace, with deception in online dating (e.g. Whitty, 2013; Whitty and Buchanan, 2012) being one of the more obvious examples. The online romance scam has recently emerged as part of this capacity for social multiplicity. In this fraud, criminals will seek out individuals via online dating sites and initiate a relationship with them with the primary aim of defrauding the victim of large amounts of money. As Whitty and Buchanan (2012) noted, the damage encountered by victims of this type of crime isn't just financial but also psychological, as many believe they are actually engaged directly in a relationship with someone whom they trust.

Recordability

QUESTIONS TO CONSIDER

When was the last time you sat down with your friends in a social environment and turned on a recording device so that you had a record of your interactions? When did you last pause mid-conversation to record the interactions you were having with your friends in your notebook or journal?

It would be very surprising to find anyone doing this in the offline world unless there was a specific requirement to do so (e.g. in the context of police interviews or research). Very rarely do we record our daily conversations, instead relying more upon our capacity to remember to provide us with the important aspects of our daily lives. In contrast, our interactions within cyberspace are presented as being different in terms of their sense of permanence. The technology that we use to exchange ideas and have online discussions also provides us with a unique opportunity to record and reflect upon these interactions long after they have happened. In essence, these online documents then become the record of the interactions themselves, offering a sense of permanence and detail that is lacking in the offline environment. Such a process can often cause a variety of issues, particularly where those interactions come to light in later life and where they no longer reflect the current views of the individual. This is more apparent in teenagers who have little regard for aspects of their digital privacy, leaving their online lives open to all to see for ever (Madden et al., 2007, 2013)

Media Disruption

The technologies through which we engage in our activities in cyberspace are never one hundred per cent reliable. We experience the annoying rolling circle that indicates the current stream we are watching is being buffered and then the fragility of mobile phone signals. The unreliability of technology means that our interactions can easily be disrupted due to failure, malfunction or damage. This can in turn have serious psychological consequences for the individual, again demonstrating the emotive aspect of cyberspace. Being cut off from cyberspace can lead to feelings of loss, anger and frustration, particularly when so many of us are dependent on technology to keep them connected and abreast of current events. This element is demonstrated in the emerging phenomenon of fear of missing out (FoMO; Przybylski et al., 2013), where an individual experiences psychological distress when they are unable to gain access to aspects of social media or the digital environment. The individual may also experience aspects of anxiety and withdrawal in situations where they fail to get a response to a message sent due to a failure in the Internet. FoMO will be discussed in more detail in Chapter 11 when we explore the impact of addiction to technology and its potential impact on cognition.

Summary

So what can we take from this introductory chapter? Well, the most important point to make is that cyberspace as a concept is not a static and technologically-driven environment. Instead technology should be seen as a secondary and almost redundant aspect to our experiences in cyberspace, with the digital devices being used simply as tools and access points; it is not the technology that is important, but more the experiences they afford us. Aligned with this is the essential ingredient that brings cyberspace into being – the aspect of human interaction. Cyberspace is a psychologically-driven environment that relies heavily upon the capacity of the individual to make sense of it using a number of cognitive processes. Without the capacity for individuals to have this meta-physical presence, cyberspace would be devoid of interaction and lack the depth of social interaction with which we are currently so familiar. It is only through our mental processes that cyberspace can become a reality.

So what next? In the next chapter we will be exploring the basic elements that make up human cognition, which will then lead us into an exploration of how we engage in these activities in cyberspace. Aligned to this is showing how being online may also be having an impact on how these cognitive processes are being deployed, with key findings from research being presented to support the changing face of human cognition in the light of digital technology. Again the material is not presented to shock, petrify and pander to the creation of a moral panic, but more to allow the reader a capacity to understand that technology, even when its use is taken for granted, can and will have an impact on us as human information processors.

2

THE HUMAN INFORMATION PROCESSOR

Learning Aims and Objectives

In this chapter you will:

- gain a basic understanding of the key concepts that drive the exploration of human cognition;

- explore the information-processing framework in the context of cognitive psychology;

- understand the machine–mind metaphor and its implications for understanding the way in which we think.

Overview

The aim of this chapter is to provide an introduction to the key concepts that govern our understanding of human cognition. The material here should be viewed as a basic reference point from which to start to explore the fundamentals of this massive area. These will in turn be discussed in more depth during the coming chapters alongside an exploration of recent research that has investigated how these processes are being used, or potentially altered due to our online lives. Importantly the aim isn't to cover every aspect of cognition, as this would require a whole book and there are many good books already in existence that can do this better than I could ever hope to. There are some fundamental principles that will guide the discussion, so this is where we shall begin.

What Are the Core Assumptions of the Cognitive Psychology Approach?

As the context for our exploration focuses directly on aspects of cognition it seems logical that we establish the ground rules from here on in. The exploration of human cognitive processes is the central focus of the cognitive psychologist, who for the most part is interested in exploring the myriad mental processes that subsume our daily activities. Ashcraft and Radvansky (2013) handily make reference to three clearly outlined assumptions that are core to the cognitive psychology paradigm:

1   *Mental processes do exist*: Cognitive psychology expresses a scientific interest in human mental activities and processes. The basic assumption, in contrast to other approaches such as that of *behaviourism*, is that mental processes do exist, and they are key in our understanding of human behaviour.

2   *Mental processes can be studied*: Cognitive psychologists believe that objective, scientific study of mental processes is a real possibility. They attempt to unravel complex questions using methods that are both scientific and reliable, and that can be repeated a number of times to yield the same results.

3   *Active information processors*: Humans are viewed as active information processors constantly searching their environment for new pieces of information to assimilate. This is in stark contrast to those who follow the behaviourist approach, viewing humans as being passive and inactive and waiting for a stimulus to occur.

I am interested in both exploring and understanding how the use of digital technology serves to shape our cognitive processes, as well as exploring the nature of those being deployed when we are online. So from this perspective the first two assumptions of cognitive psychology play a crucial role in this. If we don't acknowledge that mental processes exist, there is no point in talking about cognition and the impact technology is having upon them – we may as well not bother, go home and have a nice piece of cake and a cup of tea. In stark contrast to early behaviourist approaches exposed by individuals such as Watson (1913), Skinner (1974) and Thorndike (1898) who would ignore these mental processes, cognitive psychology can provide us with the basis to explore these. If we can explore them, they can be studied, measured and compared so we can get a feeling of whether and how digital technology is affecting these processes. The latter tenet of cognitive psychology is also critically important to us when we are exploring the impact of digital technology on cognition itself. Humans are not passive, and are hardwired to explore their environment as well as the unique stimulus contained within it. The Internet and digital technology now offer an infinite number of ways for the human to engage in information processing, and our engagement and clamour for new experiences is perhaps one of the fundamental reasons why the Internet engages us so much.

The Mind–Machine Analogy

We often use analogies to make more complex activities or actions easier to understand by using a real-world example to help. Psychologists are no different and often use various analogies to describe abstract concepts or processes that underpin our day-to-day activities. Cognitive psychology adopted the *mind–machine analogy* to help map human cognitive processes onto the functioning of a system or computer. The underpinnings of this approach had their foundation in the early work of pioneering theorists such as Shannon and Weaver (1949), who had begun to explore how mathematical models could be used to understand the operation of communication systems. Known as *information theory*, this provided the basis for the information-processing approach to human cognition that we know and love today. The important thing about information theory is that it began to make psychologists change the way they viewed human cognition in a pretty radical way. The emerging view was that mind could be treated as an information processing system, akin to the communication systems proposed in Shannon and Webster's work. From this perspective any stimulus we encounter is viewed as an *input* that goes into an internal system. This internal representation of that stimulus can then be encoded in a number of ways and moved around the system. The movement around the system could lead to the potential for further operations to be conducted on the information, which could in turn lead to an output from the system. Such an output in the context of human cognition would be a directly observable behaviour that we could measure and record.

At around the same time Shannon and Weaver were exploring the concept of information theory, another development provided a further potential source of analogy. In the early 1950s, as a progression from early developments made during the Second World War as part of the Allied efforts to break the code of Axis forces, scientists developed the early antecedents to our digital age. Many of the concepts we now take for granted in the context of computer technology were just being designed and built. During this time a variety of psychologists saw the applicability of such new technology to the functioning of the human mind and, combined with the work by Shannon and Weaver, the potential to use the new and exciting realm of computers as a way of visualising how our mind works was born.

If we take apart the mind–machine analogy and use the notion of a computer as the 'machine' element, the computer is seen to have a series of functionally separate components that perform specific jobs. The analogy to human cognitive processing should be fairly obvious, but the idea is that these separate components can be mapped onto mental processes with the basic premise that different parts of the mind are dedicated to different tasks, such as appreciating music, doing mental arithmetic and understanding language. The basic elements of the computer metaphor are highlighted in 'The Basics of the Computer Metaphor' focus box, with the most important aspect being that control can be programmed into the system. This aspect of 'control' could in turn be linked to the mental process of learning (we need to learn how to do things, so these are essentially programs) and this information also needs to be stored and retrieved at some point (Quinlan and Dyson, 2008). This notion of programmed control also brings with it another aspect that is central to the computational metaphor of the mind but also human cognition – that of a need to store and retrieve data that is represented in an internal memory system.

Some cognitive psychologists take the analogy one stage further and have explored the operations of programmable computers and that of the human mind (e.g. Johnson-Laird, 1983; Pinker, 1997). In the instances where such strict comparisons have been made, researchers suggest that the actual *computational processes* being conducted by computers can also be linked to mental processes (Fodor, 1980).

FOCUS BOX: THE BASICS OF THE COMPUTER METAPHOR

So let's take this one step further with an exploration of the key components that make up the computer metaphor as it relates to human cognitive processes. Quinlan and Dyson (2008) identified the key components as follows:

- The central processing unit (CPU) contains an arithmetical unit (which allows it to perform calculations to produce an output) and a control unit (which allows it to integrate information from a number of sources and identify which processes to carry out and when).

- The program memory is the memory that is related to the processes being conducted by the CPU, so may include a program for a complex calculation.

- The data memory is the memory for information that is needed to perform a calculation or to store the result of the calculation so this can be used later on.

- The data bus is essentially a shuttle that transfers information from one point to another and is controlled directly by the CPU according to the current demands of the system.

The Formality Condition

QUESTION FOR CONSIDERATION

Given the evidence from research, is the mind nothing more than a biological computer?

Cognitive psychologists have explored this question in some detail and many have expressed a degree of caution when jumping to conclusions about making parallels between humans and biological computers (Fodor, 1980). If we accept the computational metaphor of the human mind, then it comes with some conditions we may find hard to fulfil, primarily the notion that computers and minds are both machines that follow rules. It is at this point we have to stand back and realise the point at which strictly applying the computational metaphor starts to run into difficulty. The concept that is important here is the notion of *formality* – a computer is a 'formal' system as it operates according to a set of representations that it compares according to the form they take. If you ask a computer to make a comparison between two things it will conduct a process that essentially checks off each part of the pattern with the corresponding part from the other pattern. Essentially it is seeing whether the form of the symbols matches those contained in the other representation. This reliance on a formal system means that the computer is only making comparisons based on the overt physical representations presented to it and not on what the symbol means. If we enter a series of binary digits into a computer such as 0000010101 it will perform a specific action, and if we enter 0000010111 it will perform another one. The important aspect is that the computer has no actual understanding of the meaning attached to these two symbols. This is what Fodor termed the *formality condition* and it contrasts clearly with what we know about humans. We have thoughts and feelings about certain things, particularly when it comes to aspects from the real world. We are not functioning in terms of formality when we choose a pair of shoes over another pair because they make us feel good about ourselves – if we were using formality we would be choosing them based solely on a comparison between size, shape and function. Searle (1980) was one of the researchers who argued that no amount of computer programming, irrespective of its complexity, could help us understand how humans create what it termed intentionality, or the feelings and thoughts we associate with real world concepts.

Cognitive Processes

The next section aims to give the reader a very broad overview of some of the key concepts that we will be exploring when we talk about cognitive processes in cyberspace. The emphasis here is on trying to present the key elements that will guide later discussions in the following chapters. It is hard to introduce one cognitive process in isolation, so much of this section presents the cross-overs where they potentially exist.

Human Attention

Whenever I ask my students an essay question on attention, I will usually get the following quote firmly implanted somewhere in the first paragraph of the text:

> [Attention] is the taking possession of the mind, in clear and vivid form, of one out of what seems several simultaneously possible objects or trains of thought ... It implies withdrawal from some things in order to deal effectively with others. (James, 1890: 403)

This quote is taken from the work of William James, an individual who has a special place in the history of cognitive psychology, being one of the first to begin to theorise about the underlying processes that make up the paradigm. James's quote points to the fundamental purpose of attention, that being a mechanism that allows us to focus on one clear element or task. Similarly, we also need something that helps us reject unwanted or irrelevant information that may otherwise interfere with the task we are currently doing, or conversely take away valuable cognitive resources from something we should be doing to something that doesn't. Attention is the mechanism that is proposed to fulfil all these requirements, but there are key limitations to how far it can be stretched.

The concept of human attention in the context of Information Processing is extensive, with the literature stretching back to the foundations of cognitive psychology in the early 1950s. Attention is seen as the mechanism that is used by individuals to select and focus on important stimuli in the context of other irrelevant information. At one time it was thought that attention was the same as consciousness, so in order to process a piece of information the individual had to be *aware* of it. It is more widely accepted that some processing of information could still take place without us directly being aware of it, which gave rise to the notion of pre-conscious or subliminal processing. The scope of this report places these aspects outside of its parameters, but the reader should be aware that such processes can take place and that individuals do not necessarily have to 'see' everything conscious for them to have an effect on behaviour.

For the most part researchers agree that attention is linked directly to a finite resource, meaning that we only have a limited capacity to select and attend to information from our current environment (Broadbent, 1957; Hahn et al., 2008).

24

Attention acts in one of two key ways. Primarily, it can act as a filter that determines what aspect of the environment will be attended to by the individual. Second, it can act as a management system placing constraints on which task can be performed at any one time (Wickens, 1981; Wickens and Carswell, 2006) The literature from cognitive psychology makes a variety of distinctions in relation to attention – for instance it can be automatic or controlled, and it can be selective or divided attention.

Selective Attention

Selective attention is pretty much what it says on the tin – essentially you select an appropriate thing or piece of stimulus from the plethora of other things you have going on within your immediate environment. This will mean that all of the available resources can be devoted directly to that current task or stimulus. When we are trying to achieve a specific goal, it is important for us to be able to focus directly on those stimuli that relate specifically to the goal we have in hand, whilst also being able to block out irrelevant information that might distract use (Lavie et al., 2004).

Divided Attention

The notion of divided attention will become even more important when we move on to discuss aspects of multitasking (Chapter 6) and task switching (Chapter 7). Divided attention makes reference to the action of doing two or more things at any one time, and requires the individual to 'split' their attention effectively between these two tasks. Divided attention means that the individual has to carefully allocate resources between the different sets of stimuli that might be the current focus(es) of the tasks in hand. The important part here is that we cannot process all of the available information at the same time, or in parallel, so there are associated costs for dividing attention (Pashler, 2000).

FOCUS BOX: DIVIDED ATTENTION IN THE REAL WORLD

The growth of the mobile phone, and more recently the smartphone, is something that has been the focus of many researchers, particularly in the context of road traffic safety. Many researchers have noted that using a mobile phone, irrespective of whether the driver is using a hands-free device or holding the phone in their hand, can cause significant disruption in driving performance (Bianchi and Phillips, 2005; Drews et al., 2009; Strayer and Drews, 2006, 2007; Strayer et al., 2004). In the research

(Continued)

(Continued)

conducted by Strayer et al. (2004) participants were asked to engage in driving under divided attention conditions using a simulator. One group was asked to have a conversation on a mobile phone whilst another group simply completed the driving task. Right after the driving session participants were asked whether they had seen one of two objects during the activity as well presenting a rating for these in relation to road safety. In the mobile phone-using group there were fewer objects remembered, demonstrating that as their attention had been divided there were fewer resources available to encode this critical information.

Research has noted that in some instances the degree of similarity between the two tasks being completed can influence the level of disruption. Performance is generally better where the two tasks are dissimilar in terms of the underlying systems they require; for example, reading and listening to music usually causes less disruption than trying to speak out loud and rehearse a telephone number at the same time. Wickens (1984) noted that task interference is at its highest when:

- both tasks share the need for the same modality (e.g. visual, auditory);
- there is a need to use the same processing stage (e.g. at the point of input, the requirement for internal processing or output);
- they rely heavily on the same memory codes (verbal or visual);
- the response required is very similar (such as driving and trying to dial a mobile phone).

A very early example of the type of research that explored performance for divided attention is an experiment by McLeod (1977). In this experiment participants were asked to perform a tracking task, for which they had to keep a small dot (which would move randomly) positioned on a cross presented on a computer screen using a mouse controller. Participants were also asked to identify when a target tone was presented in their headphones in one of two ways. They either spoke the word 'now' when they heard the tone, or they raised the hand they were not using on the tracking task. It was noted that performance on the tracking task was significantly worse when there was a high response similarity, such as when both tasks required the use of motor function (e.g. raising the hand and tracking the dot on the screen).

Automatic versus Controlled Processing

When we first learn to do something, particularly when that thing involves a procedural skill such as riding a bike, it can be very hard to do. We are often faced with an uphill struggle to improve both our skill and level of co-ordination. Balance, direction and visual scanning all have to be accomplished in parallel if we want to be able to ride a bike. My own experience of riding my first bike without stabilising wheels was recounted to me recently by my parents, and of which I have a vague recollection of ending up in a neighbour's bush. Fast forward several years later, and I regularly complete rides of more than 60 miles (for fun!). Part of the process for learning a skill is the degree to which it can become automated, and for which we have very little conscious control over. This can be both a positive process and a negative one. For instance, allowing a regularly occurring skill to be taken over automatically allows the individual capacity to be able to do other things, such as being able to chat to a fellow biker, look at the trees or avoid potholes! Automated processes can occur very fast and interfere very little with other cognitive activities and belong to the non-declarative, procedural memories highlighted in Figure 2.2 (Shiffrin and Schneider, 1984).

Attention and Memory

The link between attention and memory is one that is fundamental to human cognition. The implications for not paying attention are pretty clear – if you aren't paying attention to something, then it won't be perceived. Consequently, if a piece of information is not perceived then in turn it will not lay down a residual trace within memory, essentially never to be recalled again. The two concepts are intertwined in various sections of this book, and there are some core aspects to the terminology and the structure of memory that will guide the reader through this discussion.

The notion of memory in the context of cognitive psychology has been divided into two hypothetical constructs, these being short-term and long-term memory. All of these structures have their own specific set of limitations and processes associated with them; short-term memory (STM) is a time and capacity limited storage area that is capable of holding approximately seven to nine pieces of information at any one time (Miller, 1956). If information is not continually repeated or rehearsed, then it faces the risk of being lost through a process of decay. Other processes, such as interference from other information set down in previous memories or attempts to recall older information being impaired by the presence of new information, can also affect the material stored in STM.

Working Memory

In more recent years the notion of STM has been conceptualised in terms of a 'working' memory (WM) (Baddeley and Hitch, 1974). The framework for WM highlights that STM is not just a simple area for retaining information. It includes a variety of specific processes and further sub-stores that allow the individuals to analyse information before it is either lost or transferred into the more permanent long-term memory (LTM) store.

The working memory model (see Figure 2.1) broadly comprises four key components, each of which assumes a different role in the context of memory. For example, the central executive is the part of working memory that governs what we pay attention to, as well as managing the other two 'slave systems' within the model. These two slaves systems each have specialised roles according to the type of material they can manipulate. For instance, the phonological loop is assumed to hold both verbal and acoustic information and includes an articulatory rehearsal mechanism where things we are trying to say are stored before we talk. On the other hand, the visual-spatial sketchpad assumes the role of maintaining and manipulating visuospatial representations, as well as perhaps also being able to store kinaesthic memories such as touch (Baddeley, 2000a, 2000b). The inclusion of the episodic buffer was something that came after the original model was presented by Baddeley and Hitch (1974) in an attempt to account for further findings from research. The episodic buffer serves to act as a limited capacity storage system that temporarily holds and integrates information from any number of sources. Control for this system is presumed to be the responsibility of the central executive, and the episodic label makes reference to the notion that it can hold

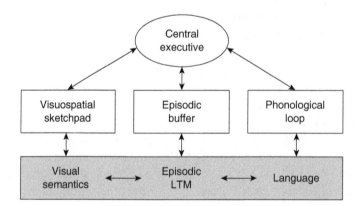

Figure 2.1 The Working Memory Model

Source: Baddeley (2000a)

'episodes' of our activities, and information can be integrated from across these episodes. The importance of this model in terms of the way in which we view a memory system that not only allows information to be stored but also acted on at the same time cannot be underestimated. As we will see later on, working memory presents a potential framework for explaining a variety of issues related directly to multitasking and interruptions alongside the notion that individual differences can also exist in the capacity of each of the subsystems.

Long-Term Memory

Long-term memory has been viewed as a more permanent storage system that has been further divided into two theoretical sub-stores in order to differentiate between the distinct types of memory. The overarching distinction is that between declarative and non-declarative memories, which refer to the level at which such information is available to conscious awareness. Declarative memories are those that can freely recall and report the result in terms of a concrete statement about that memory as long as relevant cues to those memories can trigger results in the memory being retrieved. In contrast, non-declarative memories are those that remain outside of conscious awareness but still exert an influence upon behaviour. An example of this type of memory could be a procedural memory, analogous to an instructional memory that tells the individual how to perform certain motor skills, such as walking and writing.

The focus in the context of the current discussion will be directly on declarative memories as these are the ones that most directly impact on day-to-day online lives. Research has highlighted a finer-grained sub-division according to

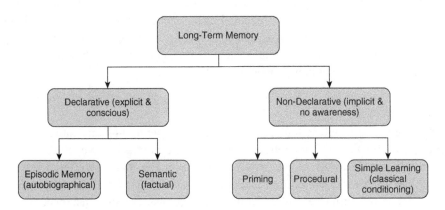

Figure 2.2 The Structure of Long-Term Memory

Source: Squire et al. (1993)

the memories contained in declarative memory: these are semantic memory and episodic memory. Perhaps the most important type for discussion here is that of semantic memory, or memory for meaning. *Semantic memory* is information directly related to real-world factual information (Tulving, 1972). If an individual is asked to report what colour the sky is, or what their pet is called, then they would be accessing semantic memory in order to find the relevant answer. *Episodic memory* is information relating to events or 'episodes' in an individual's life, and is an autobiographical history of activities up to the present (Tulving, 1972). Taking the example above, if an individual was then asked the name of their first pet, this would require access to episodic memory.

Learning

There are a wide variety of theories related to the way in which humans learn information, including those that are based on aspects of operant and classical conditioning. These theories, although relevant to the field of learning, remain out of the scope of the current discussion where the focus will be more directly on those based in cognitive psychology. In the context of the cognitive approach to learning, the process of learning involves the transfer of new information into either existing mental structures or the creation of new ones (Anderson, 1995). These mental structures are referred to as *schema*, and are essentially the building blocks of our knowledge. Each schema represents a mental rulebook or script that contains all the specific knowledge we have about a particular topic. So, for example, our schema for 'how to make cheese on toast' would include all we know about that topic, from the type of cheese, how it melts, how to use an oven or a grill, what temperature setting works best and so forth. Accordingly, cognitive psychologists have also noted that anything that serves to impact on the processing of information so that it is prevented from entering these schemata will have a negative impact on learning. If new information is disrupted whilst it is being encoded into these abstract mental structures it can be lost or distorted, therefore leading to weaker retention (Anderson, 1995).

Learning and Cognitive Load

The research on factors that can influence how we as humans integrate and interpret information from complex visual environments (such as the Internet) highlights three forms of cognitive load. Cognitive load (Sweller, 1994) is often used to describe a burden that is being placed upon the individual when they are committing resources to a particular task. In this instance, in the context of talking about learning, Sweller (1994) assigned cognitive load to three categories:

1   *Intrinsic load*: This is the load that comes from how hard the task is, something that is an inherent factor related to the material itself. Intrinsic load is usually a direct reflection of the level of difficulty that is associated with the material or information that is being learned. For instance, for most of us doing the calculation of '2 + 2' would have a lower intrinsic load than a more complex algebraic calculation. Intrinsic cognitive load can also be linked directly to the number of 'elements' or things we have to do whilst learning that thing, with the higher number of elements increasing cognitive load.

2   *Extraneous load*: This is the load that comes from the thing that is delivering the information that has to be learned, and is often the result of the design of that system. For instance, when we are presented with both auditory and visual information together, extraneous cognitive load is low as this allows us the chance to spread information capture across multiple modalities rather than one single stream of information. This means we have less chance of missing something in contrast to something that is being presented through just visual or auditory information alone.

3   *Germane cognitive load*: This is the effort we have to exert as a direct result of the learning process itself. So this would include the integration of new information into existing schema or the creation of new ones to help hold that information. As we learn more on a specific topic the germane load for the task actually reduces because the cost of adding new material to the existing set of information is reduced, meaning the task in hand becomes automated as the schema grows in size. This has the knock-on effect of also reducing intrinsic cognitive load as we have more knowledge to devote to the topic (although algebra never seems to get any easier!). As resources taken up by intrinsic load are reduced, we are freed up to do other things that might be related (or unrelated) to the task in hand. An example of this is reading. When we start out learning to read, it is hard and we have a high level of intrinsic load, which may be matched by high extraneous load (most of the time we learn reading by looking at words) – germane load is also high as we are adding new information to basic schema. As we progress, we become more competent, thus giving us the chance to both read and listen to music, or read and watch TV.

Researchers have noted that extraneous cognitive load can also be created when information is presented in an inappropriate way (too much information on a PowerPoint slide for example!). Similarly it can also come from a requirement to perform a series of tasks or actions that are completely irrelevant to the task that is being learned (Ayres and Sweller, 2005). This process is pretty easily demonstrated, particularly where we have a situation in which the individual is being presented with visual information from two very different spatial locations. This requires the individual to divide their attention between two points whilst also trying to integrate this information.

Human Decision-Making

Research on aspects of decision-making in the context of information processing has distinguished a variety of mechanisms individuals use in order to reach a decision. When individuals perform a search on the Internet they have to make a variety of decisions based not only on the information they have received, but also on the information they have already obtained. There is also a conscious comparison between these two aspects, and a decision as to whether or not the new information meets the current goals and objective has to be made (Dinet et al., 2012; Maglio and Barrett, 1997). The decision process individual human users go through differs from the very systematic way in which a search engine will determine which results to include in the response to a query; here the decisions are based on a logical series of processes that conform to the notion of an *algorithm*. An algorithm is bounded to mathematical principles of logic, and for all intents and purposes will provide a clear answer if the rule is applied correctly. In contrast, the user will have to make an individual decision about what information to select from the returned search, and indeed which of the links presented to follow. If users were to implement an algorithmic approach to analysing each of the available links, there would be two clear disadvantages to such a process. The average search for information on a given topic may return an excessive amount of information, some of which may be completely irrelevant to the current task in hand. In order to provide a systematic approach the searcher would have to process all the available information to make a logically informed decision about what information to keep and what to ignore. Such a process is time-consuming and more importantly a drain on cognitive resources; often individuals need to gain information through online searches quickly and efficiently (e.g. the time of the next train, weather information, current new information). Therefore humans, in terms of information processing and decision-making, do not process all the available information in a systematic and logical manner, but instead rely on a series of support mechanisms that aid decisions in uncertainty, and where there is an abundance of information to process. These mechanisms, or – as they are commonly referred to in the literature on decision-making – '*heuristics*', are learned 'rules-of-thumb' that allow individuals the luxury of a close approximation to a correct decision but without the associated cost of having to go through all the available information (Tversky and Kahneman, 1974).

Simon (1957) was one of the earliest researchers to suggest the notion of the human information processor working in the context of a 'bounded rationality' when it came to making decisions. This concept suggested that humans are capable of making accurate decisions but these are limited (or bounded) by the amount of information they have available at that current time, as well as the restrictions placed on limited cognitive resources. From the IP perspective, any decision-making activity is seen as being one that is mentally draining in order for an accurate decision to be made (Payne and Bettman, 2004; Wirth et al., 2007). If choices have to be made from a wide number of potential alternatives then the individual has to use a number of strategies that require complex processing. The end result is the most accurate decision based on the available information, but this comes at a cost in terms of the amount of time and resources that have been expended (Wirth et al., 2007). Gigerenzer (2004) suggested that the use of these more effortful decision-making strategies are no more likely to present a better end solution than those that are less time-consuming and more cognitively efficient. In this context the simpler strategies are seen to *satisfy* (Simon, 1957) the need to make a decision based upon the available information an individual has to hand in the most convenient time frame. Here individuals are making an unconscious acceptance that the results obtained through these heuristic processes are less than perfect but will do for their individual needs.

Summary

The material presented here will form the basis for our wider discussions throughout the rest of the book. I will be introducing more specific detail for the relevant topics in relation to cybercognition as we progress, but as it stands this chapter should stand you in good stead for understanding some of the wider concepts being introduced later. The important elements to remember are that human beings, when we talk about cognition, have a set of finite resources at their disposal. The information processing system that is used to conceptualise human cognition makes a clear statement about this, and where these limited resources run low or run out we start to encounter reductions in performance accuracy and efficiency (Eysenck et al., 2007). The second point to make is that humans don't like to spend a lot of time thinking about things – if there is a short cut to a solution, then we will take it, as long as it gets us close enough to the intended goal or solution. This isn't being lazy, but is rather a process via which we conserve our cognitive resources by relying heavily on past experience to govern our future decisions, particularly in instances where we haven't encountered a particular problem before.

In the context of our current focus, the use and manipulation of cognition in cyberspace, there are some obvious benefits for the use of digital technology. When we are talking about cognitive resources, some researchers believe that these may hold the key to expanding what we already have, hence removing these limitations (Prensky, 2009). There is also evidence that we are developing and using a variety of heuristic-based strategies when it comes to searching for information on the Internet (Lau and Coiera, 2007; White and Iivonen, 1999) as well as making decisions for what information is credible (Fogg et al., 2001).

3

THE POPULATION(S) OF CYBERSPACE

Learning Aims and Objectives

- To introduce the theoretical divide that exists between the generations according to their digital skills and cognitive abilities;
- to explore the evidence base for such a position;
- to highlight the current issues with such a distinction.

Overview

The aim of the previous chapter was to establish the basics of cyberspace along-side a further exploration of the psychology that sits behind these experiences. In this chapter the aim is to produce a current snapshot of the who, how and what of Internet use. A number of researchers have continually suggested that cyberspace is inhabited by two distinct groups based on their level of skill and engagement with digital technology. One of the first authors to write about this, Prensky (2001), suggested that this categorical distinction can in turn be related to differences in the way individuals are thinking and processing information. It is proposed that the newer generations occupying the Internet think in a fundamentally different way from the generations preceding them. Prensky used the label 'digital natives' to describe those individuals who have never known a world without digital tech-nology. Other authors have used labels such as the 'Clickerati' (Harel, 2002), 'Net Generation' (Tapscott, 1998) and 'Screenagers' (Rushkoff, 2006) to describe this same digitally embedded group of individuals. According to the work by Prensky there is a capacity for younger people to 'think and process information funda-mentally differently from their predecessors (2001: 1). This trend is evident in the myriad statistics that surround the use of the Internet and other digitally connected devices. For instance, 9 per cent of US teenagers aged between 13 and 17 reported that they were going online daily, with 24 per cent of these individuals reporting being online 'almost constantly' (Lenhart et al., 2015). Furthermore, 75 per cent of those questioned had access to a smartphone, with just 12 per cent having no mobile phone of any type. Statistical trends aside, the anecdotal evidence relates a current moral panic associated with the younger generation and their use of technology. For instance Choudhury and McKinney (2013) noted the rise in a belief that the young lack empathy and are passive, intellectually shallow and uncritical. It is also suggested that due to the rise in the use of digital technology this younger generation is also becoming desensitised to a variety of stimuli, expressing symptoms that are bordering on those observed in the context of individuals diagnosed with attention deficit disorder (ADD) (e.g. Chan and Rabinowitz, 2006; Gentile et al., 2012; Yoo et al., 2004). So it appears that the concerns of educators and parents map onto the findings from research when it relates to issues with the growing digital generation and their exuberant use of the technology. However, as with everything related to research, this isn't as clear-cut as it first seems.

Immigration Crisis Hits Cyberspace: Digital Migrants and Digital Immigrants

In the context of Prensky's work the digital generation possesses a unique capacity: they are fluent in the language of cyberspace. Helsper and Eynon (2010) defined the current generation of teenagers born after 1990 as belonging to the second generation of digital natives. First-generation digital natives are viewed as those who were born between 1983 and 1990. In accordance with these distinctions, those who belong to these digitally native generations have the capacity to use technology in a way that is blended into their everyday lives without paying much conscious thought to the actual use of that technology. They don't need to learn how to use a smartphone, send an email or post an image to Instagram as for this age group it is all very much second nature. Rather than seeing technology as a burden or a barrier, this generation see it as a tool via which a whole host of activities can be engaged in. In stark contrast to this technologically experienced group there sits another group, labelled as the 'digital immigrants'. This group is proposed to be older to and have witnessed the development of technology, hence have known a time pre-Internet. From this perspective this group is said to have migrated into cyberspace rather than being born into it. Now this is not to say that digital immigrants are a collection of technological luddites who have poor digital literacy and think that the word 'spam' can just refer to tinned meat. It has been noted that those who occupy this digital immigrant group are often more affluent, and therefore can afford to be early adopters of the newest and shiniest digital gadgets. Even though this caveat is accepted, it is still the case that the digital immigrants, whilst having the capacity to adapt to and learn the new culture that is cyberspace, still retain the same values and ways that belong to the 'old country', the land before digital technology. These little differences mean that the digital immigrants might be more likely to pick a phone up and make a call rather than thinking about sending a text via Whatsapp; they might look for a number of a local business in the telephone directory rather than checking the information on Google or Yell.com. For this generation, using technology comes as second nature, and therefore it is important to bear such differences in mind when exploring the impact of this technology on human cognition.

Can Culture Affect the Way in Which We Think?

There is some research precedence for Prensky's claim that the culture in which we are imbedded can drive the way in which we think. For example, research by Nisbett et al. (2001) noted that those from East Asian cultures have a tendency to think more holistically, and pay attention to the whole of something rather than the individual parts of that thing or system. They also use little in the way of formal logic, placing a heavier reliance on aspects of dialectic reasoning (debate between two opposing groups or people). In contrast, Westerners are more ana- lytically biased and pay attention to details or component parts, and use rules (including some aspects of formal logic) to understand the behaviour of the thing that they are examining. So the suggestion by Prensky that culture can have an important impact on thought processes does have some resonance in the literature. Cyberspace is, as we have explored in the first chapter, a digital environment that has its own set of rules and social norms. As such, cyberspace presents itself as a unique culture with such rules and social norms changing quickly, much quicker than in the context of the offline world. The culture an individual is embedded in does not just impact on *what* they are thinking about, but more importantly the *way* in which they actually think. If the proposition of a digital divide is actually a reality, then there is the possibility that those engaged in cyberspace may indeed think differently compared with their digital immigrant counterparts.

Losing the Capacity to Reflect?

According to Prensky those in the digitally native generation have lost one very important ability, that being the capacity to *reflect*. To take a step back for a moment, let's think about the ability we are gifted in the process of reflection. It is a process that will bug you, usually when you are going over the things that you could have done rather than what was actually done. The ability to reflect is an inherently important skill for humans as it also allows us to see how we can improve in the future. If we lack the capacity for reflection, then there is the possibility that we could be stuck in an ever-repeating cycle of the same mistakes over and over again (think *Groundhog Day* but without the humour of Bill Murray and the glorious romantic overtones!).

Prensky proposes that in the high-volume, high-speed culture of cyberspace individuals are finding less and less time to pause for objective reflection on what they have done. This does have some connections with other work that has been conducted on aspects of impulsivity, which will be discussed later on in Chapters 6 and 7. The predominant argument is that for those individuals engaged in digital technology, the displacement of other activities that may teach reflective processes serves to make this process a spiral of anti-reflection. The knock-on effect is that those who occupy the digital native generation are more prone to making the same mistakes, and these are repeated over and over again. The key premise for Prensky is that there is a mismatch, particularly in the context of education, between those who are in a position of instructing and those who are to be instructed. The two cultures are inherently engrained in their own environments and mechanisms of thinking, and as such there is a danger that neither will be able to understand the other.

How Much Evidence Is There for the Digital Divide?

Some of the suggestions made by Prensky, however, have been met with disagreement by other researchers. According to Bennett et al. (2008) there is no direct evidence to support Prensky's claim that digital natives process and use information in a different manner from those in the digital immigrant group. As this appears as one of the most frequently repeated distinctions in the context of the digital native and digital immigrant debate it has been assumed that there would be substantial empirical evidence to support this claim. However, Bennett et al. (2008) noted a complete dearth of actual research upon which these assertions could be based. It would appear that much of the earlier work by Prensky and Tapscott is based on conjecture and anecdotal evidence. Indeed the authors would appear to suggest that most of the people who have cited these differences between the two generations have done so without actually exploring the empirical evidence for such differences (Bennett et al., 2008). Hence, the suggestion that there are these generational differences resulting in associated differences in cognitive processes has given rise to research-based Chinese whispers.

Bennett et al. (2008) focused upon mapping the complex interactions that the younger generations are having with digital technology in an attempt to identify whether such differences do actually exist. The argument that is consistently touted by those forwarding the digital native/digital immigrant dichotomy is that younger generations have spent more time engaged in the use of digital technology, and therefore become 'fluent in the digital language of computers, video games and the Internet' (Prensky, 2005: 8). Bennett et al. (2008) noted that as engagement in digital environments was so immersive, those in the younger digital native generation often do not recognise technology as such, but rather see it as a tool. So from this perspective, as alluded to at the start of this chapter, those who are digitally native have the tendency to use technology as the thing they do something with or with which they achieve an action, rather than exploring the complete functionality of that device.

Of the research that was reviewed by Bennett et al. (2008) there was evidence that a large proportion of the younger population was adept with technology use, relying heavily on it for information gathering and activities involving some form of communication. It was also noted that a significant portion of this population does not have the advanced levels of skills and understanding that would be expected if the notion of the digital native is to be accepted. Bennett et al. (2008) further noted that the generalised claims about skills and understanding of technology for the digital natives only focuses on those who are technically adept. This, as a consequence, fails to recognise a potential underclass of individuals who may be completely disengaged from technology, or find themselves challenged when attempting to engage in the digital environment. Bennett et al.'s (2008) research noted that there may be as much variability in the skills and abilities that exist *within* the digital native generation as there is *between* the digital native and digital immigrant divide.

Another skill that is often presented as being a fundamental cornerstone of the digital native population is their capacity to multitask at a level far in advance of their digital immigrant peers. Brown (2000: 13) suggested that 'todays kids are always "multiprocessing" – they do several things simultaneously – listen to music, talk on the cell phone, and use the computer, all at the same time'. What writers such as Prensky have suggested is that digital natives are given certain *cognitive affordances*, which makes them better accustomed to learning at high speed. This is matched to a capacity for taking information from a widely distributed set of sources whilst simultaneously being able to make interconnections between associated items. Add to this a belief that this group also has an advanced capacity for processing visually dynamic information, and we have the perfect online information processor (Prensky, 2001). This latter element is supposedly linked to the digital native's experience in visually rich environments presented by webpages and social networking sites. Brown (2000) further suggested such enhanced skills lead digital natives to have a preference for more discovery-based learning. This process allows them to explore information and actively test their ideas in real time, which in turn also serves to create more knowledge through experience. This is seen as a stark contrast to individuals being passive receptors of information being presented to them (Bennett et al., 2008).

As has been reiterated several times in this section, there is a serious lack of any consistent empirical research upon which these assertions can be founded. The notion of multitasking will be discussed later in Chapter 6, and is not a skill that solely resides in the context of the current digital native generation. From a historical perspective it was not too long ago that parents argued with children who were supposedly engaged in homework but also had both the radio and television on in the same room. The literature on the digital skill divide also presents the notion that multitasking is a 'good' skill. This position may actually be erroneous, especially when we explore this in the context of divided attention and task completion. Evidence suggests that higher levels of multitasking can lead to a greater degree of distractibility alongside a loss of focus, potentially leading to cognitive overload and reduced efficiency (David et al., 2013; Pashler, 2000; Rosen, 2008; Wood et al., 2012).

Are We Failing to See the Finer Detail?

The generalisation about an entire generation and the way in which a group of individuals learns fails to acknowledge the wealth of information from cognitive psychology that notes differences in cognitive processes with age groups (Bennett et al., 2008). This aspect of human cognition is well demonstrated in research by Cowan et al. (1999), who noted that the storage capacity of short-term memory actually increases with age. In order to put this into context, the capacity of short-term memory is critically important when we need to maintain information for limited periods of time, and crucially it has a fast decay rate. The larger the capacity of short-term memory, the more information an individual can retain from their environment. This in turn allows us to manipulate larger quantities of information without the need to return to the source of that information repeatedly. The argument presented by researchers such as Bennett et al. (2008) is that these aspects of individual differences are being lost when the broad label of 'digital native' is applied to an entire developing generation. The issue is that the application of such a label would make the assumption that all of those included in this category have the same (or similar) level of capacity for certain cognitive functions irrespective of their age group (Bennett et al., 2008).

A further assertion that accompanies the digital native debate is that they are given special status in the context of their learning style, something that also comes under the scrutiny of Bennett et al. (2008). They raise the valid point that to assume all individuals within an entire generation share the same learning style is as problematic as the issue of cognitive capacity raised previously.

Research has already noted that there can be differences in learning styles across cultures (Joy and Kolb, 2009), so Prensky's suggestion that this could be the case for digital natives isn't a big leap of faith. However, other research has also noted that learning styles are dynamic in nature and can change over a short period of time (Mitchell et al., 2015), meaning that they might not be as stable as Prensky originally proposed. They are also unique in nature and often fail to be applicable to a full class of individuals, an issue that is particularly salient when they are being applied to an entire generation (Bennett et al., 2008). Learning styles are also adaptable in nature and can change according to both the task environment and the needs of the current situation. For example, Biggs (2003) noted that individuals have the flexibility to adopt a particular process based on what has worked well before in that particular situation. This work again highlights the issue of applying a 'one size fits all' metric that is being used to view an entire population. The key point is that to do so, particularly when applying these to an entire generation, fails to recognise each of these individual differences.

Helsper and Enyon (2010) further questioned the evidence for the distinction between these two generational classes. Previous research does agree that there are distinct differences between age groups according to the amount of digital technology that is being consumed, with the younger age groups occupying a high-use group (Cheong, 2008; Dutton and Helsper, 2007). There is another deeper issue here, and that is that there are also significant differences according to the way in which the younger generation is using this technology and also how effective they are in its use (Helsper and Enyon, 2010). For instance, research presented by DiMaggio and Hargittai (2001) suggests that the focus should not be on those who have access to technology and use it, but rather on the growing inequality in being able to use it. This is a fascinating perspective and suggests that even though individuals may have the necessary tools to engage in the digital environment they may lack the essential skills to enable them to use these effectively. This digital divide within the same generation may also be an issue with access to the technology as well, where not having access to digital technology also prevents an individual from engaging in the same experience their peers are having (Helsper and Enyon, 2010). Helsper and Enyon (2010) place emphasis on the need to understand that there is greater complexity and diversity at play in terms of technology uptake, use and skill set of new digital technology than the digital migrant versus digital native labels afford. They also suggest that it is important to further understanding the extent to which differences in technology use and the impact of this on changes in cognition are based directly on generational aspects, or more so on the consumption of digital technology. In terms of the original distinctions made by Prensky and Tapscott, the former viewed the importance of age as the determiner of the digital divide whereas the latter emphasised exposure and experience with technology. Others, such as Oblinger and Oblinger (2005), note that neither age nor experience can be used effectively to define the inclusion in the net generation.

Helsper and Enyon (2010) aimed to explore the digital immigrant and native discussion to see whether being a digital native could accurately be determined by the age of the individual. There are several key issues that the authors discuss that mainly relate to how both 'experience with technology' and also 'breadth of use' can influence the application of the digital native label. For instance, you could be a teenager who belongs to the digital native population (according to age) but may not have *experience* in using technology in terms of length of time. Similarly, you could be an older individual who has not grown up as a digital native, but may have many hours, experience of using this type of technology. In the same regard the concept of *breadth of use* explores how much the Internet is an integrated part of the individual's daily life, and is independent of both age and experience with it.

The information on generation differences presented above does support some aspects of the digital native debate, in so far as those who belong to first- and second-generation digital native groups are more likely to be using a wider variety of technology but are also more likely to be Internet users. Helsper and Enyon (2010) noted that the largest drop in Internet use is in the over 55 age category, which would imply the majority of those who are parents or educators of the digital natives are not frequent users of the Internet. The youngest digital natives (those in the second generation) are those living in households with the widest variety of digital technology at their disposal. They demonstrate a preference to use the Internet as their primary access point in order to facilitate a wider number of activities in comparison with individuals from other age groups. This group also presented a higher self-reported propensity for multitasking and relied on the Internet when exploring information for use in the context of scholarly activities such as homework or coursework.

Helsper and Enyon (2010) also noted a key difference in the type of activities each age group is using the Internet and digital technology for. For example, those in the first and second digital generation were the least likely to manage their finances online. It could be argued that this aspect should not come as a surprise as most teenagers don't really have a great deal of financial information to manage online. However, this group were also less likely to use the Internet as a mechanism for engaging in civic participation, such as voting, campaigns or support groups. This could perhaps fit into the suggestion that this age group is limited according to their capacity to empathise as well as the greater sense of apathy, but this may also just mean this group would rather do things offline in person rather than using the Internet for such activities. They are, however, more likely to use the Internet for entertainment purposes, including aspects of social networking and managing their diaries/calendars, demonstrating an emphasis on the social functions of the technology – teenagers like to keep in touch and they like to be entertained by the Internet. In the context of learning, the younger digital natives widely used the Internet as a mechanism for fact checking (such as finding definitions for words) as well as looking for jobs or training. The aspects of social and entertainment use dropped sharply for those who were neither first- nor second-generation digital natives; in other applications where money is needed, such as shopping, financial investment or travel, the first-generation digital natives were more likely to be engaged in this than the second generation for some obvious reasons – for example, they have money to spend.

So in contrast to the suggestion by Prensky, it is apparent that generation alone cannot adequately define someone as being a digital native. In some respects the findings presented by Helsper and Enyon (2010) do support some aspects of Prensky's claim. Younger individuals are more likely to be immersed in the digital environment and they do have a greater range of information and communications technology in their households. They are also more likely to exhibit higher levels of self-efficacy when using technology and digital media, as well as multitask-ing more and using the Internet for fact checking and formal learning activities. The extent to which such activities represent a shift in the underlying cognitive processes being conducted between the generations is still a matter of conjec-ture and remains an area highlighted for further research. In contrast to Prenksy's claim, it is noted that generation alone was not the only significant variable when exploring activities engaged in on the Internet – aspects of gender, education, experience and breadth of use also played a significant role in defining aspects of digital nativeness. Immersion in the digital environment (the number of activities the individual carries out online) is the most important variable in predicting the likelihood that the individual belongs to the classification of 'digital native'.

Helsper and Eynon concluded their research by demonstrating the issue of adopting a generational dichotomy when exploring the notion of digital natives and digital immigrants. They accept that whilst there were some differences in the way in which each generation used the Internet, there were also a large num-ber of similarities. Many of the differences were noted to be due to the level of experience the individual had with digital technology and the Internet rather than a generation distinction. They also suggest that Internet use and the associated labels of digital native and digital immigrant could be more adequately measured on a slide scale or continuum rather than a simple 'in-or-out' dichotomy (see van Dijk, 2005; Warschauer, 2002 for further detailed dicussion of this). Facer and Furlong (2001: 467) noted that young people are not a 'homogenous generation of digital children' as Prensky would have us believe. The take-home message when we are exploring this proposed digital divide is that one doesn't really exist, and it is a myth that has been perpetrated by educators, the media and in some instances researchers who have failed to explore the empirical basis behind such claims. Yes, young people do use the Internet more, but this does not mean this has resulted in a significant change in their capacity to process information, either in terms of breadth or speed. This similarly does not mean there is an immeasurable gulf between people of different ages when it comes to the use of digital technology; to use the vernacular presented by Prensky, it would appear that many in the older generation can still be fluent in the language of cyberspace, more so based on their level of experience rather than their age.

Adolescence and the Nature of Neuroplasticity

Neuroplasticity is a concept taken from neuropsychology that suggests both the brain and the nervous system in humans is in a constant state of flux. The reason for this is so that it can accept new information, perhaps in the form of a key skill or piece of factual information. This process then creates an underlying structural change in the brain, as it is seen as being directly linked to stimulation from the immediate environment (Trojan and Pokorný, 1999). Neuroplasticity also affords individuals the capacity to recover from impairments in cognitive function due to brain damage or age-related decline. In such instances there is evidence to suggest that the lost or impaired elements are subsumed by other regions of the brain or recovered via training (Rabipour and Raz, 2012). One of the key theoretical possibilities often posed in research exploring the digital migrant debate is the potential for an environment rich with digital technology to begin to influence structural changes within the brain (e.g. Carr, 2010; Small and Vorgan, 2008). On the surface this whole argument would appear to have some good support from research, and would appear to be a rational approach to two key concerns. Choudhury and McKinney (2013) noted these as being associated with the rise of abnormal social behaviour evident in the current adolescent population as well as the growing rise in potential addiction to digital media and digital technology. However, to counter this claim, Choudhury and McKinney (2013) noted that in terms of empirical evidence to support the link between the use and potential abuse of digital technology and changes in the adolescent brain, very little actually exists.

Crucially, much of the research that focuses on the impact digital technology is having upon the changing nature of developing brains is flawed in one key respect. All too often, research is conducted that explores behavioural aspects of elements such as multitasking during a period of development (see Choudhury and McKinney, 2013, for a more detailed discussion of this issue). The evidence from such studies is then used to argue that the use of such technology, alongside the neuroplasticity of the brain, is having a residual impact on cognition in the developing population. However, researchers often fail to recognise or discuss the notion that development itself can give rise to a variety of structural changes that could in turn provide an additional confounding variable to such data. For example, Choudhury and McKinney (2013) noted research which further suggested that the period of adolescence could be viewed in terms of a period of both risk and vulnerability. Research has proposed that this period is one of risk for the development of a variety of mental illnesses and problematic behaviours (Dahl, 2011; Op de Macks et al., 2016). Dahl (2011) noted that during the period of adolescence there are very large changes in areas of the prefrontal cortex, an area noted for being responsible for decision-making and planning. There is also a potential development lag between those elements of the 'control' cognition and those that are seen as being more 'emotive' elements. Burnett et al. (2011) referred to a network of brain regions that relate directly to aspects of social cognition, a term that included processes such as face processing and the capacity to empathise with others. This area, termed the 'social brain' (Burnett et al., 2011: 1654), is proposed to undergo a critical period of development during adolescence as demonstrated in magnetic resonance imaging (MRI) studies that have compared both adult and adolescent populations. On the 'control' side Ernst and Fudge (2009) noted that adolescence is a period of developmental transition that is, as Dahl (2011) noted, a time in which individuals increase their level of risky behaviours. The underlying reason for such a rise is directly associated with the ongoing changes in the neural circuitry of the brain, hence demonstrating the important influence of neuroplasticity.

So there is all this upheaval going on in the adolescent brain, and then we add in a group of researchers who are attempting to try to identify how digital technology is affecting cognitive processes. The key issue should be apparent: during a period of developmental turmoil, a period in which teenagers are going out, experimenting with a variety of 'risky behaviours' (we won't dwell on this – I am not your parents so I am not going to do the disapproving look!) and having some issues with restricting our impulses to act, researchers are proposing to be able to pick out which of these cognitive capacities can be attributed directly to being engaged in digital technology. As you can see, this is a theoretical and methodological nightmare, and something that isn't easily resolved via one or two small-scale behavioural studies that are conducted during this developmental period. The idea that the teenage brain is still undergoing a period of change and therefore is highly susceptible to new stimuli is used by two sides of the digital technology argument. On one side it is good, as it provides a new mechanism to engage the younger generation in aspects of teaching and learning and could be used to change the structure of the brain via repetitive training. On the other side, subjecting the brain to higher levels of stimulation from digital technology has negative connotations, leading to changes in brain development that mean that teenagers are turning into an army of digital zombies. Whilst the use of neuro-plasticity as a basis for exploring strands of this debate would appear to be fairly logical, the actual empirical basis upon which this argument is based is weak (Choudhury and McKinney, 2013). Using the notion of neuroplasticity as a per-vasive mechanism for explaining underlying changes in cognition would appear to be one possible route, but at the present time much more research is needed.

Prensky's Reprise: Digital Wisdom

It became apparent that, for most researchers, the notion of a digital divide con-ceptualised in terms of generations wasn't actually practical. As we have seen above, there are a variety of issues with making a number of key assumptions in terms of the cognitive skills attached to an entire population. Prensky himself finally admitted that the dichotomy of digital natives and digital immigrants wasn't perhaps the best way to view the key differences between those who embrace digital technology and those who do not. Prensky (2009) noted that these labels, although proving useful for conceptualising the difference in the uptake of digital technology and the associated differences in cognitive function aligned with this, offer limited scope for further exploration and are becoming less relevant. Instead he presents another concept, the notion of 'digital wisdom', which has two key components attached to it. We can gain digital wisdom by harnessing digital tech-nology to access cognitive resources beyond our current innate limitations, but also use the same technology to enhance what we already have.

At the core of Prensky's argument is that digital technology presents a capacity for human cognition to be enhanced via a number of key routes. This digitally enhanced individual, or as Prensky calls them 'homo sapiens digital', will possess a capacity for 'wisdom' that is wider than the view we currently have. How will this come about? Well, according to Prensky the digital environment presents us with a variety of new experiences and a broader range of resources that will enhance what we already know. More importantly the notion of digital wisdom is a concept that goes beyond (and negates) the need to have a digital divide based on generations. The level of digital wisdom the individual has relates directly to the level at which the individual accepts the process of digital enhancement and the way in which they use such enhancements to engage in aspects of cognition such as decision-making or memory.

The state of the art human being, according to Prensky, is currently limited by the processing capacity of the brain and hence we are at risk of missing out on a variety of opportunities. For example, Prensky suggests that we are only able to make decisions based on a small amount of total information available. We are also fallible in terms of our capacity to remember information; we aren't rational and we only experience our world in terms of our key senses, beyond which we have no additional capacity for perception. Fundamentally, Prensky states that these issues stem from either a lack of available data and information or our inability to be able to conduct more complex analyses on greater amounts of data. The saving grace for the homo sapiens digital is that the enhancements offered by the digital environment may overcome some of these limitations.

So how does the digital environment enhance our current capacity to think and reason beyond what we already currently do? Prensky offers a series of mechanisms via which digital wisdom can be attained, as follows.

Enhancement through Access to Data

As discussed in Chapter 2, the capacity for the human mind to remember information is limited, not only based on our ability to recall information but also in terms of storage. This process protects our brains and cognitive systems from being overloaded by irrelevant information, but also means that we might lack the capacity to analyse critical problems effectively as we don't have all the relevant information (Prensky, 2009). But according to Prensky, digital technology presents the solution to this problem with its capacity to gather, store and analyse vast rafts of data effectively and efficiently.

Enhancing Our Capacity to Conduct Deeper Analysis

Prensky (2009) presents the work of Anderson (2008), who has proposed that there is a new and emerging type of scientific analysis based on the vast volumes of data that are being collected and stored by search engines such as Google. In this respect, it would appear that investigators now no longer have to rely on experientially-driven educated guesses, the generation of hypotheses and the testing of these hypotheses through experimentation. This process is now replaced with a capacity for the individual to mine data for patterns that can in turn reveal the effects researchers are looking for (Prensky, 2009). As the data represents the sum of current knowledge in a given area, conclusions can be drawn without the need for further experimentation. In this regard Prensky suggests that this process actively reverses the traditionally accepted approach to human–computer interaction. Rather than the machine being used for just data collection and processing of information, it now becomes part of the iterative process in which it generates factual information and potential relationships. This means that the human mind no longer has the burden of creating a plethora of possibilities for which the data could conform; rather the data achieves this already without directly knowing the actual question set.

Enhancing Our Insight into Others

When we are communicating with people, whether this be online or offline, we are at a critical disadvantage in as much as we cannot see inside the mind of that other person. Therefore we are capable of misunderstanding the intended message or may be at risk of being susceptible to any number of devious or underhanded strategies (Prensky, 2009). Digital technology now presents us with an enhanced ability to go beyond what people say and perhaps explore what people are thinking through the use of computer-linked functional imaging (Mitchell et al., 2008, as cited in Prensky, 2009).

Enhancing Our Capacity to Engage with Alternative Perspectives

Prensky (2009) claims that our unenhanced senses as they currently stand mean that we often miss the finer details in the world around us. This may be due to such occurrences being infinitely small and outside our field of vision, or so large that the scope of such an occurrence is incomprehensible. The realm of possibilities offered by our digital enhancement means that we could soon be able to explore these multiple perspectives as well as having the added benefit of being able to pick up on things that would be traditionally outside of our normal sphere of perception.

Key issues

Prensky's suggestions are interesting and some of the points legitimately supported – yes, we have lots of data that are being collected online and yes, there are new ways in which to explore the functioning of the human mind. However, much of the information he presents is again conjectural, and falls foul of the same criticisms levied at the digital native/digital immigrant conceptualisation. There is limited empirical evidence at present upon which to base the notion of digital wisdom, and without further work in the area much of these suggestions are purely conjectural.

Summary

In this chapter we have explored the notion that cyberspace is currently inhabited by two different generations, determined by their access to and immersion in digital technology. As we have seen, the concept forwarded by writers such as Prensky has served to guide a whole plethora of further ideas related to the enhancing processing power that has been gifted to the digital natives within cyberspace. Endowed with a capacity to think faster, multitask at a speed that is outside of the capacity of their distant digital immigrant relatives, the digital natives present a challenge in terms of how to best understand the way in which they not only think but also learn. However, as many commentators and researchers have later noted, this concept of digital dualism within cyberspace is based on little empirical evidence. Arguments for augmented cognitive skills based on a developing neural network that is subjected to digital technology have been negated. Similarly other research has noted that if such a trend did exist, all those who are labelled as digital natives should possess a similar level of technical aptitude and capacity to engage with cyberspace. Just a sweeping generalisation has also been shown not to be evident, with many of those inhabiting the digital native population still not having access to the relevant skills enabling them to get online.

4

ATTRACTING ATTENTION IN THE DIGITAL ENVIRONMENT

Learning Aims and Objectives

- To introduce and define exogenous and endogenous drivers in attention and contextualise these for the online digital environment;

- to critically explore mechanisms that are used online with the aim of attracting end-user attention;

- to explore research that highlights we may not be seeing everything in the online digital environment.

Overview

[A] civilization advances by extending the number of operations we can perform without thinking about them. (Whitehead, 1911)

A wealth of information creates a poverty of attention and a need to allocate that attention efficiently among the overabundance of information sources that might consume it. (Simon, 1971: 40–41)

In this chapter I want to introduce some key mechanisms that influence the way in which we pay attention in the online environment. In order to attempt to put some type of parameters on the information in the chapter, the main focus will be directly on visually presented elements that we encounter in the context of the Internet. I shall leave aspects of wider digital technology and their impact on cognition until we explore interruptions in Chapter 7.

Much of the work on grabbing the attention online has been done, unsurprisingly, in relation to web-based advertising. To put this into context, in 2009 Internet advertising generated approximately $22.7 billion in the United States, increasing to $59.6 billion in 2015 (PricewaterhouseCoopers, 2016), so it is a pretty big business. Web-based adverts tend to employ a variety of mechanisms that are aimed at grabbing our attention and generating further revenue. However, there has to be a balance, as some of the cunning tricks and techniques that are employed by online advertisers can backfire, and end users often report being annoyed by intrusive adverts or giving negative feedback to websites that employ such techniques (Goldstein et al., 2013)

The task of grabbing an individual's attention in the online environment presents a series of challenges for web designers and advertisers alike, particularly when we explore such a task in the context of human cognition. As we have already explored in Chapter 2, humans have limited resources when it comes to attention, so their capacity to explore additional information is restricted by such limitations. Second, the Internet contains a vast amount of information, with conservative estimates suggesting that if you tried to print the entire Internet (including the Dark Web) it would equate to 305.5 billion pages (imagine that printing bill!; see www.washingtonpost.com/news/the-intersect/wp/2015/05/18/if-you-could-print-out-the-whole-internet-how-many-pages-would-it-be/). As you can see, it isn't an easy task to grab our attention to things on the Internet, particularly when we might be developing strategies based on experience to actively avoid such mechanisms (Bruner and Kumar, 2000).

What Processes Underlie the Tools Used to Grab Our Attention Online?

Research into human attention has highlighted the importance of two key processes when we are looking at how we direct our attention. Both of these processes have a clear contextual importance for our discussions here in relation to digital technology. These two processes are *endogenous* and *exogenous*.

Endogenous (Internally)-Driven Attentional Processes

These are the processes that are being driven by personal preferences, goals, objectives or expectations (Rensink, 2008). For example if you are in a shop looking for a particular colour of clothing, then endogenous processing will direct you towards clothing of that colour, rather than you being drawn to a specific colour. This aspect of the selective attention is consciously driven by the individual and reflects the need to fulfil our current needs or wants. An important aspect associated with endogenously-driven attention is that it relies upon an intricate knowledge of objects or scenes. This capability is critical in the context of selective attention as we need to have a mechanism that allows us to decide what we need to attend to and what can be ignored as being irrelevant to our current task objectives (Rensink, 2008). For our current discussion, having an understanding of these aspects of attention has clear implications for the development of information processing in cyberspace. Individual differences in current processing objectives means that the same information presented to two different people could illicit two very different focuses of attention. In this regard the presentation and interpretation of information in the online digital domain might not seem as straightforward as the 'one-size-fits-all' approach that is often assumed. Differences in attentional deployment can be directly associated with the individuals' own predispositions as well as their level of knowledge or expertise in a particular domain (Rensink, 2008). This could be as simple as the distinction between those who engage in frequent Internet use and those who are infrequent users, with endogenous drivers meaning that these two groups may have a differential level of attentional deployment.

Exogenous (Externally)-Driven Attentional Processes

These are driven directly by the perceptual content of stimuli and over which the individual will have very little control. This attentional process is typically a rapid and involuntary response that serves to automatically focus mental resources towards the location of the stimuli (Navalpakkam and Itti, 2005; Rensink, 2008). Often such a process can override current task focus, usually reflective of an abrupt or novel event. An example of this could include attention being 'captured' by a brightly coloured image or a sudden pop-up advert whilst someone is browsing a webpage. This could also be an email notification or a text message alert from a smartphone (Kushlev et al., 2016). Researchers have also suggested that exogenous shifts of attention remain outside our conscious control of the individual, linked to an evolutionary response to a perceived threat (Roda, 2011).

How Do These Processes Fit into Our Digital World?

To put these processes into a more direct context aligned with our current focus, both have relevance to our interactions with cyberspace. If you think about it, both processes react in very different ways when faced with stimuli not only within the digital environment but also more widely in our every use of digital technology. An exogenous process means that we would be driven to pay attention to material based directly on their capacity to grab attention away from the current focus of attention. In contrast, endogenous processes are predispositions that the individual will already hold and that motivate and guide interactions with material online. Such processes exist prior to any move towards engaging with a particular website or choosing a particular function. As such, they provide the individual with a more directed approach to online activities and help prevent the end user from being distracted by other task-irrelevant information.

There have been some attempts to separate the influence of these two processes on attention but such attempts have met with a degree of difficulty, even in the context of highly controlled experimental studies (Bacon and Egeth, 1994; Burke et al., 2005; Folk and Remington, 1998). If we extrapolate these attentional processes onto web-based behaviour where the goals of the user can be even less well defined, further challenges are presented. For example, things that have a direct and relevant meaning to us drive us endogenously to pay attention. This aspect of *semantic* salience could be presented in an advert, attracting attention as it has a particular link or relevance to us based on our needs or individuals' own predispositions. An example of such a process was presented by Burke et al. (2005) who suggested that the inclusion of the word 'FREE' in the content of a banner advert could attract attention that advert if the individual was trying to save money. It will come as no surprise that a lot of work has focused on how the end user pays attention to online adverts, something that we will be exploring in more detail later on in this chapter.

So let's try to bring these processes back into the context of the focus for this book and explore how they could be experienced by individual users within cyberspace. Exogenous system messages such as email, message alerts and web-based information can all vary our current focus of attention, and will obviously also impact on how we engage with the current task (see Chapter 7 for a discussion of interruptions). System messages or program alerts serve to highlight task-relevant information and important control features through the exogenous orientation of attention.

In some situations exogenous stimuli can re-direct attention even if the signal itself is completely irrelevant to the current task. This movement of attention outside of the conscious control of the perceiver has been termed *attentional capture* (Roda, 2011; Yantis, 2000; Yantis and Jonides, 1984). Franconeri and Simons (2003) suggested that new objects, objects that move suddenly or approaching objects represent clear significance in terms of possible threats. These therefore attract the observer's attention away from the primary task. In contrast to this, any visual objects that are moving away from the observer or objects sharing a similar colour have less of a behavioural significance, and are therefore failing to draw significant levels of attention away from the primary task. Notionally certain facets of visually presented information, whether this be online or offline, can draw attention away from the primary task. There is a clear suggestion that certain aspects of stimulus *saliency* are more capable of drawing attention away from the primary task. In instances where the task is of critical importance any further knowledge that can help to identify factors that prevent the end-user from being able to perform such is of clear importance for further investigation.

The Impact of Perceptual *Saliency*

As previously mentioned, the relevance of something within our field of view can impact on our likelihood to attend to that thing, particularly when it has semantic relevance. Exogenous processes, for the most part, place the emphasis on the end user selecting to attend based directly upon the notion of its *perceptual saliency* (Roda, 2011). The notion of perceptual saliency has been conceptualised in a variety of ways, but for the present discussion it is best seen as how much a 'thing' serves to stand out from the background in which it is being presented. The notion of saliency for any type of stimulus can be determined via a variety of basic aspects including colour, size, shape and motion amongst just a few (Rensink, 2011; Roda, 2012). Importantly, attention to salient stimuli is something that can be learned, therefore lowering the threshold for which certain aspects of the environment can capture attention. An example presented by Roda (2011) suggested that an individual hearing their own name in a conversation could act as a salient stimulus, causing attention to be directed towards that particular point in space. Lavie and colleagues (2003) noted that the appearance of a famous face caused more significant levels of disruption in a concurrent task compared to a face that was unknown. Importantly for our present exploration, we want to see whether users can be distracted from their current task objectives if perceptually salient stimuli are presented.

The Impact of Motion and Animation on Attention

Early work exploring the impact of animation and motion on attention in computer-based information systems highlighted its usefulness in attracting users to specific areas of the screen (Cropper and Evans, 1968; Smith and Goodwin, 1971). Much of this work focused on the use of simple 'blink' animation on elements in the visual display in order to attract the attention of the end user towards important elements of the screen. However, these early studies showed that many individuals found the presence of moving or animated visual elements distracting, obtrusive, disruptive, and perceived levels of increased fatigue (Hong et al., 2004; McCormick, 1970; Stewart, 1976). Similarly, as Hong et al. (2004) rightly point out, much of these earlier results were heavily based on technology that is a far cry from the current digital technology we have today, hence presenting outdated findings.

For the most part the exploration of animation and its ability to attract attention has presented two clear perspectives. On the one hand, there is the primary suggestion that animation and motion, when used correctly, can attract attention exogenously towards a target object (Zhang, 2000). However, in contrast further research has noted that endogenous processes, such as goal-directedness, can counteract the presence of such stimuli (Tuten et al., 2000). Individuals could also intentionally create a series of task completion strategies that remain fluid. This is endogenously driven in the first instance, but allows the end user to make irrelevant but salient aspects of the display relevant to the task, hence increasing the distraction from such features (Burke et al., 2005).

Animation and motion are common components used in a variety of contexts on the Internet. The use of these mechanisms can alert the user to task-relevant information or be presented as a distraction from current task objectives in the form of online advertising. Little information on the effect this aspect of inter-action with websites has upon information-processing activities existed prior to work conducted by Zhang (2000). Zhang (2000) suggested that there were a variety of limitations in understanding of perceptual and cognitive processes in the online environment. In order to overcome this, it was proposed that existing theories on visual attention could be used to explore the disruptive effects of animation on information processing. The basic premise for these theories relate again to the notion of a set of limited resources for completing any task. Perceptually salient stimuli that are not task relevant will theoretically reduce the amount of resources devoted to the current task. The net result is reduced processing efficiency and an increase in the length of time it takes to complete the task in hand (Allport, 1989; Duncan, 1984; Treisman, 1991).

There are some problems with making the assumption that previous theories used to explain offline processes will also be effective in explaining experiences in the digital environment. In traditional visual perception experiments, participants are usually exposed to test stimuli for periods in the order of milliseconds. In contrast, the experience of being exposed to material in the online domain can last for a few seconds or extend into minutes at any one time. Zhang (2000) suggested that this difference in the amount of time subjected to particular stimuli could be responsible for a shift in the perceptual and attentional mechanisms governing their processing. A second point highlighted by Zhang (2000) is that there is a key difference in the environments under exploration. Those used in traditional visual perception studies are limited to the parameters under the control of the researcher, and lack the ecological validity of the web-based environment. Web-based environments, in contrast, contain a rich variety of information, much of which is seen as superfluous to the task in hand. Additionally, the interactions we have with it are constantly evolving based on the current objectives or goals.

In order to fill this perceived gap in our empirical understanding, Zhang presented experimental work that focused on animation that provided no further information to the user. Therefore it was seen as being 'non-primary' inasmuch as it did not add anything to aid the completion of the primary task. The findings from Zhang's

(2000) study demonstrated that animation had a clear detrimental impact on the information-seeking capability of the participants. This effect was found irrespective of the perceived difficulty of the task. A second finding, and one that has been consistently demonstrated in later research in this area, is that there is a direct link between task complexity and the effect of animation on performance. Zhang (2000) also found that as the task complexity increased, the disruptive effect of animation on performance decreased. This is a pattern that has been noted in further research, and is hypothesised to be related to the limited attentional resources individuals possess. Attentional resources are diverted away from the primary task so that the end user can interact with extraneous aspects of the web-based environment. The overall result is less attention being paid to the current focus of web-searching behaviour, which ultimately results in longer search times (Zhang, 2000).

A study conducted by Burke et al. (2005) explored the effect of animation on both attention and memory. The underlying notion in this context is that more cognitive resources are deployed in the processing of attention-grabbing material, hence they become more memorable at a later time. Bayles (2002) explored this by using two types of banner advert (those placed at the top edge of the webpage); one was animated, the other remained static. Participants were asked to complete a variety of tasks requiring them to use key features of the websites, after which they were asked to complete a surprise recall task. In this they were asked to re-create the layout and contents of the previously viewed webpages from memory. The findings from this research demonstrated no clear link between the type of banner advert used (animated vs. static) and the memorability of the information presented. It was also noted that a vast majority of participants failed to notice the presence of the banner adverts at all.

The Impact of Motion

Bartram et al. (2003) explored the role of motion in the attraction or distraction of attention of the end user. In the hectic environments of our desktop computers, our attention is often distributed across a variety of different windows, websites or indeed applications. Some information might be relevant to what we are doing, and other information may be completely irrelevant (you don't really need to know that your friend is eating asparagus when you are trying to analyse data, or do you?). According to Bartram et al. (2003) we need something that can help us keep up to date with changes in information that lie outside our current focus but that may have direct relevance to the task in hand (e.g. virus update information, latest news information). Examples of this type of information include reminder boxes, stock-ticker-type scrolling message feeds or system alert boxes (2003). According to the design of these system feeds, particularly in terms of website design, such information is usually located around the edges of the screen (Bartram et al., 2003; Czerwinski and Larson, 2002; Maglio and Campbell, 2000). In other instances the updated information may be located elsewhere in the visual display, and in the instances of things like email message alerts are often directly attached to objects in the display (Bartram et al., 2003; Mitchell et al., 1997; Sarter and Woods, 1995). The important aspect of this form of display is that it is effortful in nature, and requires a high level of cognitive processing for the user to be able to compare the currently displayed information to previous material and make an assessment according to whether there has been any change. According to Bartram et al. (2003), only a very small amount of information can be included in each visual domain, with most visual information relying heavily on aspects such as shape, colour, size and texture (Bartram et al., 2003; Ware, 2000). The authors point to the importance of motion in attracting observers to salient aspects of the web environment, highlighting key aspects of the system of critical importance without distracting valuable cognitive resources away from the task in hand.

Bartram et al. (2003) noted that when motion as a notification mechanism is used it is much better than more traditional static codes such as colour or shape when attracting the attention of users. This is more apparent when the notification location is presented at the edges of the screen. In their research they noted that the percentage of undetected targets went from 2 per cent to 25 per cent where the peripheral visual targets were manipulated on colour alone. In comparison, the failure to detect a target that was altered in terms of motion was less than 2 per cent, even when the target appeared at the very edges of the screen display. Bartram et al. (2003) noted that motion as a mechanism for perceptual saliency appears to be better remembered in contrast to colour and shape. This has the added benefit of allowing the user to accurately identify *where* and *what* has changed in the context of the current visual display. There are differences according to the type of animation and its capability to distract the user from their primary task, with travelling motions (those moving from one point to another across the screen) requiring more tracking and detection. Such motions are shown to be more distracting in comparison with those that are static in nature or anchored to one particular part of the screen (2003). Zooming motions (where the icon increases in size and then returns back to its original size after a short period of time) are also seen as distracting, but less so than the previous two forms already mentioned. This aspect of distraction by motion via attentional capture could be linked back to the work of Franconeri and Simons (2003; Franconeri et al., 2005), as this movement would have significant behavioural significance for users.

The Impact of Pop-Up Ads

Additional work by Diao and Sundar (2004) further explored the effects of pop-up advertisements on attention and memory. The authors make reference to the concept of the 'orienting reflex' (OR; see Sokolov, 1963) to provide a basic framework from which to explore the impact of these adverts on attention and information processing. The OR in its simplest form states that attention will be drawn (exogenously) to new stimuli that do not currently match an existing template in memory. The work by Diao and Sundar (2004) highlighted that the appearance of pop-up advertisements on webpages should elicit an OR. As they usually appear after the main webpage has loaded, the sudden change in the visual field from an unexpected event should lead to an exogenous shift in attention (Diao and Sundar, 2004; Jonides and Yantis, 1988; Yantis and Jonides, 1984, 1990).

The OR is an automatic process that has been highlighted as being responsible for the allocation of resources to each of these different sub-processes (Diao and Sundar, 2004). More specifically the OR will automatically shift attention towards a stimulus to *encode* that information, resulting in reduced resources being available for the two other stages. Diao and Sundar (2004) suggest that any message containing an OR should therefore lead to a reduction in key differences in the way that message is encoded in memory. In their research Diao and Sundar (2004) supported some aspects of this proposal, with pop-up ads eliciting an OR resulting in increased ad recall. There was no residual effect of animation in terms of eliciting an OR, highlighting that this mechanism is not always sufficient or necessary to attract the attention of end users. The authors also found that a static banner advert was recognised more often in contrast to the rare and abrupt appearance of the pop-up advert. They mediate this result by suggesting that this was due to the increased presence of the banner advert for lengthy periods of time, therefore receiving more attention over time.

McCoy et al. (2004) also explored the retention of information from websites and the amount of advertisements the website contained. They found that the material from the website was better retained when pop-up adverts were not used. They also found that pop-up adverts reduced the retention of both site and advertisement content more than standard online adverts, such as banner ads. However Cochrane (2006) demonstrated no significant difference between experienced and inexperienced users in the recall of pop-up adverts as indicated through low memory recall. Both groups were shown to have seen the pop-up adverts, but failed to retain much information contained within them. Participants were able to provide a partial report of the information contained within the pop-up adverts themselves, such as the price of the product, but were unable to provide a clear description of the product itself. It was also noted that participants picked out salient words such as 'diet', which fits into aspects of endogenous shifting based on individual predispositions. The finding that habitual users of the Internet have acquired no special skills in terms of their ability to 'block out' such adverts, is an interesting one and suggests that the power of the pop-up advert is more pervasive that we assume.

The Impact of Task Type on Exogenous Shifts in Attention

The notion that there are distinct differences in processes governing goal-driven and free-browsing activities has also been indicated in the context of this research (Burke et al., 2005; Tuten et al., 2000; Yesilada et al., 2008). Results from Burke et al. (2005) supported a number of findings from previous research. The authors demonstrated that the nature of the task directly influenced the level of distraction from banner adverts. Here again the pattern showed that the higher the level of perceived cognitive load for the task in hand, the lower the susceptibility to distraction from task-irrelevant animated adverts. Furthermore, the results showed that there was no significant difference between the static and animated banner adverts in terms of their disruptive effect on performance. In later research Pagendarm and Schaumberg (2006) highlighted a clear difference in the memorability of banner adverts according to the processing objectives of the individual users. Participants given clear tasks to complete whilst using the websites retained less information compared with those individuals who explored the website without clear aims. It would again appear that individuals who have no direct goal have the attentional resources spare to pursue extraneous material via exogenous processing. On the other hand, those who are goal directed activate a cognitive mechanism that suppresses the processing of web-based banner advertisements further (Pagendarm and Schaumberg, 2006).

In more recent research Simola et al. (2011) present an updated picture of advertising saliency on attention and task performance. They suggest that the previous research in the area suggests that web users are relying heavily on endogenously-based strategies to help them ignoring adverts in visual field (e.g. Dreze and Hussherr, 2003; Stenfors et al., 2003). The suggestion is that such strategies are capable of overriding the exogenous attentional processes from low-level salient stimuli. However, Simola et al. (2011) noted that the effects of animation on attention and performance are not so clear-cut. In some studies there is little or no impact of such stimuli on performance, indicating that individuals are able to deploy these exogenous-blocking strategies driven by top-down processes. However, in other research there are subjective reports stating that participants find such adverts distracting and are aware of them, but in fact rarely look at them or indeed remember them (Simola et al., 2011).

The research conducted by Simola et al. (2011) presents a variety of findings that suggest that the view of animation and online advertising linked into performance is not as straightforward as initially thought. In contrast to previous findings from studies of a similar nature, the researchers found that online adverts were not ignored as much as initially proposed during an online reading task. This was demonstrated irrespective of task type (either goal-directed or free-browsing), suggesting that adverts were being overtly attended to through endogenous processes rather than covertly through subconscious automatic processing. Interestingly the effects of animation on reading performance for web-based text showed that attentional capture was greatest when one advert towards the right of the text was animated and a banner advert above remained static. This condition elicited the greatest level of disruption in performance, even when compared with the condition where both adverts were animated. The suggestion made by the authors to explain this finding was that two adverts animated simultaneously share salience, essentially cancelling out the disruptive effect. Where one advert is animated, this becomes a unique event in a static display, hence attracting attention via exogenous processes.

In relation to advertisements with abrupt onsets (e.g. those that suddenly appear and then disappear), the findings from Simola et al.'s (2011) research showed that these too can attract attention exogenously but the effect is mediated by task type and advert location. It was shown that when users were engaged in a reading task they were able to ignore the sudden onset of adverts if they occurred in the periphery of the visual display and outside of the designated task area. However, if the sudden onset adverts were presented within the task area, they were less well ignored and affected text-reading performance. Simola et al. (2011) suggested individuals were actively engaging avoidance mechanisms when abrupt onset adverts always occurred in the same location. As the adverts were always presented in the same place, this pattern of appearance became highly predictable, thus allowing users to be pre-cued to their presence.

Interestingly, the research conducted by Simola et al. (2011) demonstrated that advertisements (web-based text) placed to the right of task-relevant material were more likely to be attended to and cause a reduction in reading performance. This pattern of results was linked to the processes of reading web-based text, with individuals reading from left to right. The individual's gaze has a tendency to immediately overlap towards the area to the right of the text, hence individuals are more likely to attend to material in this area of the screen. Adverts based above task-relevant information are less likely to be included in reading-contingent movement, and as the individual gets further down the body of text they are even less likely to pay attention to material in this area. However, earlier research presented by Cooke et al. (2008) noted that participants usually ignored information presented on the right-hand side of the screen as they expected it to contain task-irrelevant information such as adverts.

A final finding from Simola et al.'s (2011) research that supports a notion discussed throughout this section is that more attention is being allocated to extraneous material (such as adverts) when the task constraints are less stringent. In the instance of free-browsing, the capacity for attentional capture by abrupt onset adverts is greater than in goal-directed comprehension tasks. Here it is assumed that the current goal is exerting a greater top-down influence on the allocation of attention, allowing individuals to override the exogenous influence of them. In free-browsing no such overriding influence from endogenous processes exists, thus freeing up attentional resources to process irrelevant material such as web adverts. Simola et al. (2011) conclude by stating that the findings from their research support previous theoretical discussions from research into visual attention, indicating that some aspects of online behaviours can be mapped onto existing models.

In the context of online cognitive processes, the visual saliency of motion or animation appears to be good at attracting attention exogenously. For the web user the use of motion in order to gain attention or focus the individual towards key aspects of the visual display is an important metric in gauging how end users are deploying attention in complex visual environments such as the Internet. Clearly, given the evidence thus far, it appears that motion has the capability to interfere with concurrent tasks, even when they are deemed fairly simple in nature (Bartram et al., 2003). However, as the task complexity increases (e.g. browsing and reading online text) there is a reciprocal decrease in the amount of distraction and irritation elicited by motion. This could be directly linked to the limited resources individuals have at their disposal when conducting these complex tasks, with little or no spare capacity to deal with extraneous input that is not relevant to the task in hand.

Failures in Information Processing

As we can see from the research that has been conducted into web-based advertising, both position and perceptual saliency can have a dramatic impact on the attention we pay to them. It is interesting that we often make the assumption that the individual is capable of attending to most aspects of the visual environment, and that they actively block out information that is not relevant to them. We would also assume that anything that is novel or distinctive in the web-based environment should influence saliency of that stimulus and cause attention to be directed to it. There is, however, a body of research that suggests that individuals often fail to see something that appears right in front of their eyes, with such events often being very obvious to the casual observer (Jensen et al., 2011). Two key phenomena can be used in order to view certain aspects of interactions with web-based material, and have some obvious theoretical and practical implications. The primary phenomenon is that of *change blindness*, and is defined as the failure to detect clear and substantial changes in the visual display (Jensen et al., 2011). The second phenomenon is that of *inattentional blindness*, which is characterised as a failure to notice an unexpected but fully visible item when attention is diverted to another aspect of our visual environment.

As our web-based interactions are spatially limited visual experiences and are restricted by the confines of the screen, we would assume that we can see everything contained within it. As researchers such as Varakin et al. (2004) have suggested, this may be a possible *overestimation of breadth*, where we assume that we are capable of taking in *all* aspects of a visual display. What could these overestimations mean in the context of the digital environment?

Varakin et al. (2004) present an early discussion of how these failures in the attentional system could impact on the use of a variety of human–computer interfaces. In the broadest sense, the discussion is directed towards general interactions with any computer-based interface where users are confronted by confined displays, with some key aspects having direct relevance to the present focus of online information processing.

A key example of inattentional blindness in the context of web-based activity has been discussed briefly in the previous section looking at animation and attention. In an original study by Benway (1999), research explored the failure of users to attend to an important aspect of the webpage containing critical pieces of task-relevant information. Employees were being encouraged to sign up to a training course via a brightly designed banner placed at the top of the screen. In follow-up interviews it appeared that the employees were successfully navigating to the webpage that contained the banner with the link to the relevant sign-up page for the training course, but were failing to actually read it. Benway (1999) later replicated this phenomenon in an empirical study, defining it as banner blindness. This is operationalised as the inattention to a prominent advert or banner containing task-relevant information. As discussed previously, such a trend is not isolated and has been documented by other researchers (Burke et al., 2005; Gorman et al., 2005; Owens et al., 2011; Simola et al., 2011).

Varakin et al. (2004) further highlight the impact of change blindness in the design of e-reading-based software. Participants in this study were asked to trial software that allowed them to browse current news stories, with the key task being to gather pieces of information located within target articles. Participants were then asked a series of questions based on the information they had been presented with, as well as a question related to any unexpected changes that had occurred during their navigation through the information. Despite large changes in the visual display only 50 per cent of participants taking part in the study noticed these changes taking place. Here is evidence that even in the confined space of simple e-reading software users can still miss important and distinct changes in the visual display. As in the case of banner blindness, individuals are missing perceptually and semantically salient pieces of information, and as such these are not reaching awareness.

Owens et al. (2011) took this notion of banner blindness one step further, and rather than looking at animated graphical information they looked at participants'

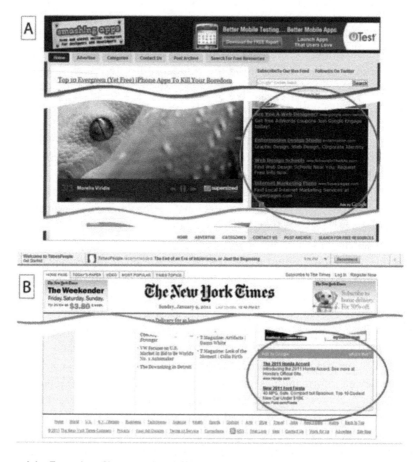

Figure 4.1   Examples of banner adverts (A) and text-based ads (B)

Source: Owens et al. (2011)

capacity to ignore web-based text adverts (see Figure 4.1). Participants were asked to find task-relevant information located on screen that could be placed in the main body of the text, at the top of the page or located in a side panel. Participants were then rated in terms of their success at finding the relevant information; 83 per cent found it when it was contained within the main body of the text, 52 per cent when it was located at the top of the page and 36.8 per cent when it was located in the side panel. The findings would seem to suggest that individuals adopt strategies to actively ignore text-based advertising, which is something that has been noted with other types of advertising information. This could perhaps be a moot point as many advertising companies have diverted their attention from text-based advertising to more laborious mechanisms for capturing attention online.

Similar findings have also been found for change blindness in a military context, which does have some relevance to our current discussion. Durlach (2004) explored the susceptibility of individuals whilst using a military-based command and control system. The system provided a series of real-time updates related to current mission objects, details of enemy location and that of friendly forces. Results demonstrated support for earlier research conducted by Durlach and Chen (2003) showing that participants were less likely to notice a change in a series of task-critical icons presented on screen whilst another task window was closed and opened. Participants were 50 per cent less likely to notice the change in the position of an on-screen icon when this occurred at the same time as a concurrent task window closing and reopening. Such findings have also been found by DiVita et al. (2004). If we think about how most people use the Internet, it is pretty clear that very few people use web-browsing windows in isolation, and often move between any number of concurrent screens (Ophir et al., 2009). It could be very easy to miss significant changes in any of these windows during the process of minimising and maximising them, and is something that has received little or no empirical research focus.

Steffner and Schenkman (2012) did present an exploration of change blindness in the context of viewing webpage information, one of the very few of its type. In this study the researchers explored the impact individual aspects of the change and the complexity of the task environment had on the detection of change. The study included four distinct kinds of manipulation according to the size of the change, the complexity and location of the change, and whether the change occurred to a person or an inanimate object or aspect of the webpage. The researchers highlighted a series of hypotheses based on previous research in the change blindness literature, indicating that larger changes, changes in simple objects, changes on the left of the screen and changes made directly to a person would all be easier to detect in the context of viewing a webpage.

The results from the research by Steffner and Schenkman (2012) presented some interesting findings. In contrast to what had been previously assumed, changes occurring to a person on a webpage were less easily noticed than those made to a non-person. The research also failed to highlight any significant difference in participants' abilities to detect change according to the manipulation of complexity. It was noted that one of the limitations to the presented study was perhaps the distinction of complexity, and that aspects of the visual environment contributing to the notion of perceptual 'clutter' may have had a limited impact on the detection of change.

Participants also found objects located on the left-hand side of the screen more difficult to detect as opposed to those located on the right. This could be related to work discussed elsewhere in this chapter by Simola et al. (2011), who found that material placed on the right-hand side of a webpage was more likely to interfere with text comprehension. This was seen as being indicative of this area benefiting from a more direct focus of attention than that of the left.

This research presents the first real empirical evidence that aspects of change blindness can and do have an impact on individual information processing for online content, but is obviously limited to one basic study. There is also no further discussion of the impact visual complexity has upon the process of change blindness, and how far visual clutter must go in order to induce such an effect. There is also a respective dearth of any such empirical basis for research exploring such effects for inattentional blindness, which should also be of importance.

Summary

In this chapter we have explored the capacity for our attention to be captured and directed elsewhere in the visual display. It would appear that, based on the evidence, some mechanisms can be used to attract our attention but there are a few key conditions that meter their performance. For instance, it appears that task type matters – when we have specific goals to fulfil whilst surfing the Internet, such as trying to find some information, we are less likely to fall foul of distracting animations. In contrast, when we are browsing for fun, the lure of the animated ad appears to be not so easily resisted. Similarly, it would appear that individuals surfing the web have adopted strategies that actively block attention to specific areas of a webpage that hold irrelevant information, or which usually present advert-based information. This is even more pertinent when we look at aspects such as 'banner blindness', which demonstrate that even though the information could have particular salience for the end user, we actively ignore information located at the top of the webpage. This occurs even when the information is animated, showing the resilience of the attention system to such presentation methods.

5

DIGITAL GAMING, BRAIN TRAINING AND COGNITION

Learning Aims and Objectives

- To introduce the idea that human cognition can be improved or enhanced through the use of digital video games;
- to define the key terms and concepts;
- to explore the evidence for and against the claims associated with cognitive improvements;
- to introduce the concept of brain training or 'cognitive training';
- to explore the evidence presented both for and against the benefits of such programs.

Overview

One element of the digital environment that has garnered a great deal of attention over recent decades is the impact of video gaming on a variety of cognitive and social skills. The much-maligned debate about the impact of violent video games is not one that will be the focus of discussion here, and there are plenty of other reviews that would do a far better job of this than I can (e.g. Griffiths, 1999). The accumulated research that focuses on the impact for cognitive skills is very broad in its scope, and the results are far from clear cut. Nonetheless many researchers have presented evidence that supports the notion that key cognitive skills can be enhanced when engaging in video game play.

To place this into context, a survey questioning 1102 individuals aged between 12 and 17 found that at least 97 per cent play some form of digital video game (Lenhart et al., 2008). Other researchers have noted that at least 60 per cent of individuals aged between 8 and 18 played video games on at least a daily basis (Rideout et al., 2010). There have been a variety of attempts to explore how digital gaming can enhance certain skills, with research suggesting the development of problem-solving skills (Adachi and Willoughby, 2013; Prensky, 2012), spatial skills (Dorval and Pépin, 1986; Feng et al., 2007; Green and Bavelier, 2003) and persistence (Shute et al., 2015; Ventura et al., 2013). However, these findings aren't so clear cut, and some researchers have noted that there are a variety of methodological issues associated with some of these findings (Boot et al., 2008) as well as a lack of detailed empirical support (Shute et al., 2015).

Serious Games: These Are Not Video Games!

You might come across some reference to 'serious gaming' when exploring the impact of gaming on improvements in performance and skill. For the most part these aspects will fall out of the scope of the current discussion, but do warrant some consideration, as there is a cross-over here with our present exploration.

Serious gaming is a more recent development in the context of training and builds upon the use of computer-based training applications. In traditional training applications there is a recognised system of knowledge delivery (on the behalf of the instructor) followed by learning and testing of retention (on the behalf of the trainee). As noted by Greitzer et al. (2007), such a system presents no real opportunity for the trainee to actually engage and utilise the material that is being presented to them. These traditional training systems usually allow the trainee the capacity to access knowledge-testing phases such as quizzes or multiple-choice questions for numerous attempts. Similarly the materials on which such test questions have been based are freely available for the trainees to review over and over again. Therefore such mechanisms fail to fully engage the individual in a state of active learning, which in turn aims to ensure that learners are exploring the functional elements of the material as opposed to a simple knowledge acquisition process.

Serious gaming has been championed as a mechanism to overcome this shortfall in traditional forms of training (Greitzer et al., 2007). Zyda (2005: 26) goes on to define the notion of serious games by linking it directly to the key application areas for such systems: 'Serious game: a mental contest, played with a computer in accordance with specific rules, that uses entertainment to further government or corporate training, education, health, public policy, and strategic communication objectives.'

Serious games have also been used in the context of both investigation and advertisement (Breuer and Bente, 2010; Muntean, 2011; Susi et al., 2007). Serious games have a goal of adapting elements of gaming to engage the individual beyond the basic aspect of 'playfulness'. However, serious games are designed with a specific task or purpose in mind and therefore have little direct application outside of that given environment.

Although serious games can be used to advance aspects of behavioural change, there are some specific disadvantages to such an approach. Primarily the cost of designing, piloting and implementing such systems can be a block to their implementation, especially when the potential user base is small and specialised. Second, as they are usually designed with a specific purpose in mind, the cross-applicability to other areas is limited, making them even less cost effective if further exploitation is a goal. In terms of engagement, serious gaming usually employs game-related dynamics and game environments that could potentially deter those individuals who have no interest in video gaming. There is also some discussion of how effective serious games are in terms of their intended aims and goals, with some indicating that an objective examination of their effectiveness is immensely problematic (Bellotti et al., 2013)

Defining the Concept of Video Games

According to Prensky (2001), video games typically consist of six key elements which combine to engage the player. These elements include aspects such as

Table 5.1 Categories of video games

---

1. Sport Simulations: This type is self-explanatory. These games simulate sports such as golf, ice hockey, athletics, etc. (e.g. *World Wide Soccer '97, NHL Powerplay '97*, etc.).
2. Racers: This type could be considered a type of sport simulation in that it simulates motor sports like Formula 1 racing (e.g. *Human Grand Prix, Speedster, Monoracer*, etc.).
3. Adventures: This type uses fantasy settings in which the player can escape to other worlds and take on new identities (e.g. *Atlantis, Star Trek Generations, Overboard*, etc.).
4. Puzzlers: This type is self-explanatory. These games are 'brainteasers' that often require active thinking (e.g. *Tetris, Baku Baku Animal*, etc.).
5. Weird Games: These games are not weird as such except they do not fit into any other category. They would be better termed miscellaneous (e.g. *Sim City 2000, Populous 3*, etc.).
6. Platformers: These games involve running and jumping along and onto platforms (e.g. *Mario 64, Sonic*, etc.).
7. Platform Blasters: These games are platformers but also involve blasting everything that comes into sight (e.g. *Robocop 2, Virtua Cop*, etc.).
8. Beat 'Em Ups: These games involve physical violence such as punching, kicking, etc. (e.g. *Street Fighter 3, Tekken 2, Mortal Kombat*, etc.).
9. Shoot 'Em Ups: These games involve shooting and killing using various weapons (e.g. *Blast Corps, Mech Warrior, Turok Dinosaur Hunter*, etc.).

Source: Griffiths (1999)

rules, goals/objectives, outcomes and feedback, conflict/competition, interaction and representation or story. Griffiths (1999) presented a review of the literature on video gaming and aggression, and within it highlighted nine distinct categories into which video games can be placed. These categories are presented in Table 5.1 above. Importantly, only the categories puzzlers and weird games are seen to include elements that are directly linked to aspects of education (Griffiths, 1999), although the research literature reviewed below notes the impact of games from wider categories on other cognitive skills.

Eichenbaum et al. (2014) noted that one particular type of video game, that of action video games (or 'shoot 'em ups' to use Griffiths' terminology), has been associated with a wide range of proposed benefits. These games are typified by fast-paced action and a heavy reliance on attention to keep track of many items moving simultaneously. Such games have been notably linked to improvements in aspects of low-level attentional processes as well as aspects of higher-level cognitive functions. The first part of this chapter will focus directly on these types of action video games (AVGs) and explore how they have been proposed to improve aspects of cognition. In the latter part of the chapter I will explore the rise of brain training, which, although it has some links to aspects of video game play, is more specifically designed with the aims of enhancing targeted cognitive skills as well as overall cognitive functioning.

How Do You Examine the Impact of Video Games on Cognition?

Studies exploring the impact of AVGs on perceptual and cognitive processes usually conform to one of two experimental paradigms. In the first type, researchers will assign participants to groups based on their level of previous expertise with AVGs, this being either novice or expert (Eichenbaum et al., 2014). Researchers will then explore whether there are any specific differences according to a variety of aspects of cognition (e.g. object tracking or a test of visual spatial memory). However, there is an issue with experiments of this type when it comes to making a causative link between the increased accuracy or speed noted in AVG players and their use of AVGs. It could be that those who play such games already have a pre-existing difference in these abilities, hence they are more likely to seek out the challenges that are presented by action video gaming (Eichenbaum et al., 2014). In order to overcome this methodological shortcoming researchers may instead implement the second type of experimental design. In this option they will search for a sample of participants who have no previous experience of playing AVGs. These participants are then asked to complete a battery of cognitive and perceptual tasks to establish a base-rate measure (Boot et al., 2008). Then participants are engaged in a period of practice where they play AVGs for a period of up to 21 hours, after which they are asked to complete the same tasks that they did in the initial stages of the research. The premise of such experiments is to establish whether practice on AVGs can produce a difference in the skills that have been measured. This performance is contrasted with a similar group of participants who have not engaged in the same practice on AVGs, but who have been typically using something from the non-action video-game genre (something riveting like Solitaire or Minesweeper!). Eichenbaum et al. do point out that in most instances the non-action video game is matched for level of interest, engagement and fun, but lacks the slash/hack/shoot aspect that is integrated into so many AVGs.

The Early Days of Research: Video Games for Training and Research

In the very early days of video gaming, research focused more directly on basic elements such as improvements in reaction times. For instance Clark et al. (1987) demonstrated that a period of seven weeks of game play significantly improved the reaction times of elderly adults (57–83 years old) in comparison with a control group that did not play video games. A few years later a special issue of the academic journal *Acta Psychologica* was entirely devoted to the exploration of a video game named Space Fortress. Space Fortress was a little different from those games that had traditionally appeared in video game arcades of the time, and perhaps would not have gained the same popularity as others such as Frogger, Pac Man or Donkey Kong. However, Space Fortress was important in one key respect – it had been designed by psychologists for the sole purpose of being a training and research tool (Mané and Donchin, 1989). The objectives behind the game play of Space Fortress were pretty simple in contrast to some of the more contemporary AVGs such as Call of Duty. The task for the player was to shoot missiles at a space fortress in order to destroy it (1989). In addition to this the player must dodge missiles that are being fired by the space fortress as well as avoiding damage to their ship from mines that have been scattered around the playing area.

Researchers used the game in a variety of settings, noting that there was an enhancement in some skills that were not directly linked to video gaming. For example, Frederiksen and White (1989) noted that young adults who played Space Fortress performed significantly better than a control group in a test of physics exploring how acceleration affects the motion of objects. In research by Gopher et al. (1994), Space Fortress was used to explore the transfer of skills in Israeli Airforce cadets. The researchers who implemented this noted that those cadets who played the game as part of their training significantly outperformed a group who had no experience of the game on tests of flight performance. This again demonstrated that the skills acquired through playing the game actually transferred over into complex visuo-motor skills that were relevant for flight control (Boot et al., 2008; Gopher et al., 1994). Researchers have suggested that this skill cross-over is related directly to the concurrent cognitive demands of the task with the addition of a requirement to engage in fine motor controls. Later research by Stern et al. (2013) showed that engaging older adults (mean age of 65) in the use of Space Fortress for a period of 36 one-hour sessions showed an improvement in a measure of executive control function.

Enhancement in Visual Perception

It has been noted that there have been improvements in contrast sensitivity which Eichenbaum et al. (2014) define as the 'ability to detect small incremental changes in shades of grey (p. 56). Li et al. (2009) also noted a significant capacity for AVG players to outperform non-video game (NVG) players in the ability to detect minute changes in shades of grey. These researchers then went on to demonstrate it was actually engaging in AVG play that produced these differences in this perceptual capacity. Green and Bavelier (2007) also noted the superior performance of AVG players on tests of 'crowded acuity' or the capacity to pick out individual targets within a display containing a high number of distractors. Eichenbaum et al. (2014) noted that this has an interesting link to the process of reading as we rarely look at the individual letters but rather the word or sentences. Such a suggestion links well to research that has demonstrated an improvement in reading speed without any residual loss of accuracy in children suffering from dyslexia (Franceschini et al., 2013). Work by Appelbaum et al. (2013) noted that AVG players displayed an improved sensitivity to visual stimulus, meaning that they were are able to 'take in' more visual information in contrast with their NVG player counterparts. However, there was no specific difference in the amount of information that could be retained between NVG players and AVGs, demonstrating that experience only impacts on the initial detection of information.

Improvements in Selective Visual Attention

Beyond the proposed improvements in aspects of low-level perceptual abilities, AVGs have also been demonstrated to improve aspects of visual selective attention. This is an essential cognitive capacity that allows the individual to isolate key elements from within their current visual environment and to select these for further processing. In this instance AVG players demonstrate a superior capacity to be able to identify critical elements within such displays whilst also being able to filter out and ignore those elements that are not relevant to the current task (Feng et al., 2007; Green and Bavelier, 2003, 2006b; Spence and Feng, 2010).

A great deal of the work exploring the impact playing video games has had upon aspects of human cognition has focused directly on cognitive skills such as perception and attention. This includes work by Green and Bavelier (2006a), who explored the differences between video gamers and non-video gamers and differences in visuospatial attention. Their work showed that those in the video gaming group showed improved performance in the capacity to pick out the appearance of target objects that fell outside of the central focus of attention. They also noted that video game players adapted this level of focus according to the level of perceptual load (or the amount of items they viewed within the display). In cases where there were few items and perceptual load was low, video game players were more able to attend to the peripheral aspects of the display. This would appear to map onto game play, where a lull in the action would present a prospective moment to gather thoughts and to scan the environment for new potential threats. On the other hand, where perceptual load was deemed to be high and multiple targets were presented on the screen the focus remained central. This would appear to again mimic the action of most video games in instances where attack from multiple enemies would engage the process of self-preservation, hence trying to eradicate the closest and most dangerous threats (Boot et al., 2008).

In other research that has used a paradigm from cognitive psychology termed the 'attentional blink' it has been shown that AVG playing improves the capacity of participants to keep track of items over a period of time. In the traditional attention blink paradigm participants are asked to watch a stream of visually presented items that are presented in black. One item, the target, is presented in white (the first target or T1), and in some trials this white target is closely followed by the appearance of a black 'X' (the second target or T2). Once the trial has ended participants are asked to indicate whether they have seen the black 'X', with the attentional blink phenomenon being the finding that in the majority of cases the participants will miss the appearance of such an object (Shapiro et al., 1997). Oei and Patterson (2013) conducted a number of cognitive tests exploring the link between enhancements in cognitive abilities and video gaming. They noted that for those who had been trained using the AVG, the attentional blink was completely eliminated, a phenomenon which has also been noted by others (e.g. Green and Bavelier, 2003).

The multiple object tracking task (MOT; see Sears and Pylyshyn, 2000) has also been widely used to explore the impact of action video gaming and visual selective attention. There are a number of variations to the MOT task, but the essential premise is that participants are shown a number of identical objects on the screen, of which a sub-set is highlighted as targets to be tracked. These targets are then moved around the screen alongside the other identical items in the visual display. After a period of time the random movement stops and participants are asked to identify the target items identified at the start of the trial. A variety of researchers have noted enhanced performance on the MOT task by those experienced in AVGs as well as improvements in performance after training (Green and Bavelier, 2003, 2006; Oei and Patterson, 2013). These improvements in the visual element of working memory have also been supported by research that has focused on children. Findings have demonstrated that children who frequently played AVGs had an increased capacity to keep track of target items on screen more accurately in comparison with those who had not engaged in AVG play (Eichenbaum et al., 2014; Trick et al., 2005).

Other researchers have, however, raised issues with the results from these studies, in particular the findings from the original study presented by Green and Bavelier (2003) as well as those presented by Feng et al. (2007). The findings from these studies concluded that video game players exhibited levels of temporal attention, spatial awareness and attentional capacity that were superior to those possessed by non-video game players. However, Murphy and Spence (2009) noted no such differences between those who played video games and those who did not, further suggesting more work was needed to be completed in the area in order to fully understand the impact gaming has on visual attention.

Improvements in Higher Order Cognitive Functioning

Boot et al. (2008) moved away from the previous narrow focus on the perceptual elements of engaging in video game play. Instead their work looked directly at what are commonly viewed as being higher-level cognitive functions or those which relate to executive functioning. In their study they manipulated the type of game the individuals were playing and then tested them on aspects of performance for a number of cognitive abilities including memory and reasoning. Participants played either a fast-paced first-person shooter/combat game (Medal of Honour), a puzzle game (Tetris) or a strategy/role-playing game (Rise of Nations). The researchers proposed that the first-person shooter would present the best mechanism for an improvement in both visual and spatial attention. On the other hand, the strategy game would aid in improving executive control as this has elements of planning involved within it, and finally the puzzle game would assist in improving spatial skills given the requirement to rotate shapes. The researchers asked participants to complete 20 hours of video game play, with cognitive and perceptual tests being implemented before the practice started, after 10 hours of practice and then after 21 hours. In their results Boot et al. (2008) noted that for many of the tasks tested there was some level of improvement in the practice groups in comparison with their pre-test scores, but in many of the tests they failed to reach a suitable level of statistical significance. In their comparison between expert and non-expert video gamers they did note that experts were better able to track objects that were moving at speed, could perform more accurately in a test of visual short-term memory, were able to switch between two different tasks quicker and make decisions about the match between rotated objects more quickly and accurately than non-experts. However, the level of practice that was given to participants on each of the three types of games failed to produce changes in performance that could match those of the expert gamers in the initial exploration.

One interesting aspect that was mentioned in the study by Boot et al. was the make-up of the sample for the longitudinal training groups. There was a high percentage of females in these groups, with a potential for such an issue to bias the results. For instance, differences in spatial cognition have been well recognised in the research literature (Geary et al., 2000). In the context of video gaming, earlier work by Feng et al. (2007) noted that females benefitted more than males when engaged in video gaming practice for improvements in tests of spatial cognition. In Feng et al.'s study both males and females were compared before and after ten hours of AVG practice. The findings demonstrated that females improved significantly more in detecting a target object within the display in comparison with males (55–72 per cent for females in comparison with 68–78 per cent for males). This research not only goes to demonstrate the impact video gaming can have upon underlying cognitive processing, but can also obliterate well-observed gender differences.

Aspects of problem solving have also been explored in the context of video gaming with some limited findings. For example, Steinkuehler and Duncan (2008) examined exchanges on the discussion forums related to the role-playing game World of Warcraft (WoW). They were looking for evidence of scientific thought, specifically related to theorising about elements related to in-game play. They found that there was something termed 'social knowledge construction'; the researchers present this as a process of collective development in understanding, usually through a mechanism of joint problem solving. They also found some evidence for aspects of system- and model-based reasoning, which requires an understanding of how certain processes interact and cause an impact on or change in other elements within that system. However, there were some residual methodological problems with the study, with one point being that there was no way of knowing whether this type of specific discussion was linked to the type of game being played or was common across all genres (it should be noted that WoW is more strategy-based, hence doesn't fit directly into the realm of AVGs). Also, it could be that those who are attracted to playing these types of games already have a higher level of scientific knowledge and awareness, rather than the development of such a skill being fostered through the playing of the game (Steinkuehler and Duncan, 2008).

Other findings have come from research that has used a mechanism of thinking out loud when participants are playing video games. In one study by Blumberg and colleagues (2008) participants were asked to tell the experimenter what they were thinking about whilst they were playing the well-known game Sonic the Hedgehog 2 (terribly addictive, very annoying!). They noted that those participants who engaged in more frequent video game play demonstrated a higher degree of insight (typified as novel approaches to in-game challenges) or more discussion about specific game strategies (such as what type of move is best used to kill off a certain type of enemy). However, other researchers such as Adachi and Willoughby (2013) have questioned the extent to which these problem-based skills could be extended out into wider problem-solving activities that are not specific to the game that is being played.

Sustained Attention, Impulsiveness and Vigilance

These aspects all link to the capacity of the individual to pay attention to elements for a longer period of time, and require aspects of visual working memory to be engaged whilst avoiding the urge to attend to distractions (Evenden, 1999; Logan et al., 1997; Wittmann and Paulus, 2008). Research exploring the impact of video games on the capacity for individuals to remain focused and on task has, however, presented some paradoxical results. As Gentile et al. (2012) noted, exploring the impact of AVGs on these elements requires individual differences to be taken into account before any real differences can be examined. However, they did find evidence to suggest that once these individual differences had been controlled for, those who played AVG demonstrated higher levels of impulsivity and had greater problems in terms of the capacity to focus attention. They also noted that this relationship goes both ways, inasmuch as individuals with issues related to attention and impulsivity will also have a proclivity to spend more time playing AVGs. Gentile et al. (2012) explored the reasons for the link between engaging in AVGs and associated problems with attention. It should be noted that although this work does not specifically mention aspects of Internet use, the association is hard not to make, with other work by Sun et al. (2009) noting similar findings.

The first possible explanation for the attraction to AVGs (as well as digital media in general) is one of excitement. Now let's be honest, being seated in front of any game that is not work is far more attractive when we are faced with the alternative. Indeed, as I am sitting here writing this book chapter, the lure of other more hedonistic endeavours is a far more appealing thought, but, fortunately for you, I have a great level of impulsivity control. However, the lure of the television, the Internet and AVGs is an obvious one when it is contrasted with the routine of work. There are flashy graphics, excitement, fun and attention-grabbing shiny things that make them a more plausible option compared with the joys of writing yet another report or essay. Many games use the notion of an 'orientating reflex' (Sokolov, 1963), something that was previously introduced back in Chapter 4. This exogenous shift means that we will turn and face the direction of something that grabs our attention, particularly in environments of low-level stimulation. The aspects that grab our attention also do something else: they act as an ongoing engagement mechanism, attracting more and more attention from the individual. The suggestion made in the excitement hypothesis is that for many, these features offer the individual a level of interest that sits outside of their normal everyday activities. If the individual is subjected to these exciting and attentionally enticing activities for a period of time, the individual's expectations for what is a normal level of stimulation will alter. When there is a greater discrepancy between the more interesting and stimulating activities and those that are more mundane and run-of-the-mill, the greater the chance that attentional difficulties will begin to arise (Gentile et al., 2012).

In contrast to these findings, other researchers have noted that AVG players have a greater level of resistance when it comes to preventing distraction from exogenous stimuli. Research presented by Cain et al. noted that when compared with NVG players, those who actively played AVGs could resist the attentional capture of task-irrelevant information in order to focus more directly on task-relevant, goal-orientated information. Such work is also supported by other work that demonstrates AVG players have a greater capacity for cognitive control, perhaps linked to the process of game play which requires focus on concurrent information in order to prevent the player from being attacked (Cain et al., 2012)

Brain Training: Does It Really Work?

There has been much hype over recent years about the use of digital technology, in particular the notion of brain-training games. There have been some high-profile cases in the media where companies have been fined considerable amounts of money for making a variety of claims that are not substantiated by the research. In 2016 Lumos Labs were fined $2 million (£1.4 million) for making claims that go far beyond the data. Lumos promoted a suite of 52 games, each one targeting specific cognitive skills. The company published a self-funded report that asserts that the entire suite of exercises is a 'gym' for the brain (Shute et al., 2015). The claims made suggest that the program can purportedly train specific areas of the brain, and if used for a period of 10–15 minutes three or four times per week it could help users maximise their potential in every aspect of their life. Now, apart from the fact that maximising potential appears to be a little bit vague, the company also claimed that the games could also alleviate the symptoms of more serious ailments such as dementia, stroke and brain injury (www.bbc.co.uk/news/technology-352417780).

In this section the aim is to explore the claims that have been made for brain training, and to identify the relevant research that has either found support for or debunked these claims completely.

What Is Brain Training?

The concept of braining training is more widely viewed as 'cognitive training' in the wider research literature. The theoretical perspective follows an analogy linked to learning and improving a particular skill. For example, when you start off doing something like playing darts, you might find it hard to hit the dartboard, but after a period of time you get better, your co-ordination will improve and you will become more proficient.

Brain training relies very heavily on concepts that are directly related to neuroplasticity, something that was introduced in Chapter 3 in relation to the digital immigrant/native debate. To be clear, neuroplasticity suggests that we can bring about changes in the underlying structure and therefore function in the brain as a response to stimulation from the environment (Rabipour and Raz, 2012; Shaw et al., 1994). The attractiveness of this argument means that cognitive training could span a variety of age groups, from the developing brain to one that is in cognitive decline due to old age. The latter is inherently attractive, particularly when the global population is getting older and the potential burden for age-related cognitive decline on already struggling health providers is of central concern for many (Rabipour and Raz, 2012). As we will see in the following section, brain training has been used extensively to explore how cognitive training could be useful in staving off age-related cognitive decline, with Rabipour and Raz (2012) presenting an overview of this research and its ultimate value. Their conclusion is that whilst brain training does improve specific elements of cognitive function, it does not appear to be effective at improving overall global cognitive functioning.

Transfer Effects

Something that does crop up frequently in the literature on brain training is the notion of transfer effects. The concept of transfer effects has been studied extensively over the past century or so (see Barnett and Ceci, 2002, for a very meticulous review of the research in this area) and refers to how training in one task can benefit or improve another. Transfer effects can be viewed according to how 'close' they are to the original trained skill and are classified in terms of their 'distance' from the skill that is the focus of current training. *Near* transfer in cognitive training speak makes reference to the way training impacts on similar types of skills to those being targeted. If we take an example from our daily lives, this might be an improvement in our hand-to-eye co-ordination as a result of training to play tennis. The key here is that an improvement is noted on a similar but not identical skill or task. In contrast, *far* transfer refers to a residual improvement in skills that are outside the current focus of the training, such as finding an improvement in mental arithmetic as a result of training to play tennis.

As we will discuss, the actual evidence for transfer effects is something of a mixed bag, with some researchers finding evidence for this, whilst others have found no such trends. There are a variety of issues that muddy the interpretation of key findings, including aspects of methodological inconsistencies as well as the issues with a clear definition of both transfer effects (Barnett and Ceci, 2002).

Evidence for the Benefits?

Brain Training and Its Benefits on the Developing Mind

Miller and Robertson (2010) presented a comparison between three distinct conditions in an attempt to explore the claims that brain training could improve cognitive functioning. In their research they used the popular program *Dr Kawashima's Brain Training* which was available on the Nintendo DS Lite system. The program itself contained a variety of puzzles that targeted mental calculations and memory retention. However, as Miller and Robertson (2010) noted, there is no evidence from empirical studies examining the objective benefits of such a program. They also included another educational intervention, termed 'Brain Gym', which posits that aspects of physical movement facilitate a process of neurological reorganisation. This in turn supposedly promotes 'whole brain learning' (Miller and Robertson, 2011; see also Dennison and Dennison, 1994). Brain Gym has gained wide acceptance in an educational context, and according to Miller and Robertson (2011) remains popular in classrooms as a mechanism for enhancing the learning process.

Miller and Robertson's (2011) study set out to explore which of these two interventions could potentially improve the mental computation skills of children aged 10–11. One group of participants used the brain-training program installed in the Nintendo system, whilst another group engaged in activities from the Brain Gym website. There was also a no-treatment control condition group that essentially did nothing other than their regular daily schoolwork. The results noted a significant difference between pre- and post-test scores on mental arithmetic for both the brain-training group and the no-intervention group. This would appear to indicate that doing nothing is just as effective as doing something, but when we take a look at the actual level of changes there is a key difference. For the brain-training group, participants showed an improvement that was almost double that in the control condition. This effect was also paired with a similar improvement in time to complete a maths test, with those using the game console to train showing a significant reduction compared with the other two groups. The researchers do, however, note a degree of caution when interpreting these results, given the small sample size of the study and the lack of controls employed related to the expertise of the individual delivering the Brain Gym sessions.

Jaeggi et al. (2011) explored the impact of cognitive training on transfer effects into other areas of cognitive functioning, specifically that of fluid intelligence. Fluid intelligence is often seen as the capacity to engage in aspects of abstract reasoning as well as being able to understand and solve less well-defined problems (Cattell, 1963). As noted by Jaeggi et al. (2011), fluid intelligence is also important in many other respects, predominantly because it can act as a predictor for both educational and professional success (Deary et al., 2007; Rohde and Thompson, 2007; Spinath et al., 2006). The study by Jaeggi et al. (2011) focused on school children aged 8–9 and demonstrated that brain training did work, but there were some moderators. First, the participants only showed beneficial transfer effects to measures of fluid intelligence if they had demonstrated a high training gain in the original working memory task. They also noted that group differences in terms of the benefits of training appeared over time, and in the first three weeks of training no consistent changes were noted. These differences were also persistent, and lasted for at least a three-month period after training had ceased. Such results are supported by earlier findings from Karbach and Kray (2009), who noted that in task-switching training, participants improved on aspects of fluid intelligence alongside aspects of verbal and spatial working memory. However, more recent work by Xin et al. (2014) noted no such improvement in a measure of fluid intelligence for a group of participants aged 60–82, showing how disparate the findings from the research literature in this area can be.

Impact on the Developing Mind: Using Brain Training to Stave Off Cognitive Decline

As I introduced earlier, part of the push towards the development and use of brain-training activities has been directly related to a potential way of helping stave off cognitive decline, which comes about as a result of old age. Researchers have explored using video games in an attempt to improve the cognitive skills of older adults with some surprising successes (Basak et al., 2008; Clark et al., 1987; Dustman et al., 1992). For example, Anguera et al. (2013) explored an aspect of cognitive control in older adults, a mechanism that allows us to undertake goal-directed behaviours in complex environments. In their study, participants were asked to play a driving game in which one group had to perform a multitasking activity (keeping track of the car on the road as well as reporting back about information on the screen). For those participants in this multitasking mode, it was found that the residual costs associated with multitasking (in terms of the interference associated with doing both tasks at once) were significantly reduced for those aged 60–85). These gains were also noted for a period of six months after the initial training, with further findings from brain-imaging data showing that the age-related deficits in neural stimulation for cognitive control were reversed through multitasking training. They also found further transfer effects for aspects of enhanced sustained attention and working memory, aspects that were not directly trained for in the original task.

Additional research by Nouchi et al. (2012, 2013) also demonstrated that the use of a specific brain-training program could also improve executive functioning and processing speed. Two groups of participants were asked to play either *Brain Age*, another creation from the mind of Ryuta Kawashima marketed by Nintendo, or *Tetris*. They engaged in playing the game for 15 mins for five days per week over a period of four weeks and were assessed on four key cognitive measures comprising global cognitive status (which included memory for space/time, memory and attention as well as language and visuospatial skills), executive functioning, attention and processing speed. Both groups demonstrated a significant improvement in overall game performance from the first time they played the game up until the end of the training period. For the *Brain Age* group, significant changes were noted in the scores for executive functioning and processing speed, but no such differences were noted for measures of global cognitive status and measures of attention when compared to the *Tetris* group. These findings suggest significant transfer effects for near cognitive skills related to the areas being trained within the game itself.

Brain Training: When Doesn't It Work?

Just to throw a fly in the otherwise untainted ointment of brain training, there have been some dissenting voices from the world of research. Buitenweg et al. (2012) conducted an extensive review of the literature related to brain training and the senior population and made a variety of broad conclusions. They noted that the results from across the studies they reviewed presented little consistency, and the evidence for transfer effects was limited. Other researchers such as Dahlin and colleagues (2008) noted that transfer effects in the context of working memory training were either small or non-existent.

In one of the largest studies of its kind, Owen et al. (2010) found no consistent evidence for transfer effects from brain training into other skills in a sample of 52,617 participants aged 18–60. Participants engaged in a process of training over a six-week period that included a variety of tasks aimed at improving reasoning, memory, planning and attention. Although the researchers did find a significant improvement in the task on which participants were trained, these effects failed to carry over into untrained tasks even though they shared related cognitive processes. In order to quantify the level of transfer effects elicited, they suggested a partial improvement in memory equivalent to remembering an extra 300th of a digit. Based on their calculations, they suggested it would take an additional four years of training to show an improvement where participants could remember one whole extra digit. The control group actually presented an improvement in memory retention even without any training, demonstrating the issues related to brain training (Owen et al., 2010).

Shute et al. (2015) compared the use of a well-known video game (*Portal 2*) and the software suite provided by Lumos Labs (Luminosity). *Portal 2*, for those who haven't experienced the joy of playing it (and trust me, if you start, be prepared to lose part of your life!), is a first-person puzzle game. The player has to solve a series of puzzles using a variety of tools including a 'portal gun' that can create a portal between two distant points through which the player can travel or transfer objects.

Shute et al. (2015) presented an interesting set of findings from that counter some of the claims made by those who extoll the virtues of brain-training programs. In their study, participants engaged in either an eight-hour period of playing *Portal 2* or the activities presented by Luminosity. They found a significant improvement in three key skills – problem solving, spatial skills and persistence – but for those participants who had been playing *Portal 2* and not those engaged in the activities presented by Luminosity.

Summary

In this chapter I have aimed to introduce a very broad review of the research that has been conducted into the impact video games and aspects of brain training have on human cognition. As I hope you can see, the findings from research present something of a mixed bag when it comes to making any conclusive statements. One of the key issues that needs resolution if we are to be able to make more direct links between video gaming and subsequent enhancements in cognition is the disparity in methodology between studies (Boot et al., 2011). However, research has noted that those who play video games, or who undergo a period of training on them, can experience benefits in cognitive skills such as sustained attention, spatial awareness and attentional control to name but a few.

Research has also presented a focus on the potential for video games to be used specifically as a training mechanism to facilitate the improvement of cognitive skills. This focus, stemming from the area of brain training, has presented a number of attractive potential benefits. These relate directly to enhancing cognitive skills in younger children and adults as well as providing a cost-effective mechanism for reversing aspects of age-related cognitive decline in the elderly. However, as attractive as brain training appears, there are the same issues with this type of training as there are for the use of video gaming on more general aspects of cognition. Some researchers have noted that brain training can provide an effective mechanism for training specific cognitive skills as well as presenting far transfer effects in untrained cognitive skills. However, others have noted no such benefits in the context of transfer effects, again demonstrating the importance of more research in this area.

6

MULTITASKING

Learning Objectives

- To define the concept of multitasking in the context of the digital environment;
- to explore the theoretical underpinnings of multitasking from an information processing perspective;
- to highlight the impact multitasking can have on task performance;
- to explore the concept of media multitasking and examine how this can impact on performance;
- to examine the literature on smartphone and mobile phone use whilst performing other tasks to highlight the clear safety issues of such activities.

Overview

I would like to beg for the reader's indulgence here and in doing so ask you to ponder the following quotes:

> [T]he ability to multitask is considered to be a desirable job skill by many employers, which is not surprising given that, on average, workers shift between tasks every three minutes. (Monk et al., 2008: 299)

> We are moving from a world where computing power was scarce to a place where it now is almost limitless, and where the true scarce commodity is increasingly human attention. (Satya Nadella, CEO Microsoft, 10 July 2014 (http://news.microsoft.com/ceo/bold-ambition/))

So that's it – even if you have never multitasked in your life, you'd better get used to it. There is a certain inevitability about the quote from Monk et al. (2008), which would indicate that in today's high-paced, digitally enhanced work environment the skill of multitasking is something that, if you haven't got it, you'd better get it, and soon. However, there is ample research that has explored the impact of individuals trying to do more than two things at once, and the results aren't really that great. For example, the research on divided attention examines our ability to attend to two things at once, with the key findings demonstrating that there are subsequent trade-offs in terms of performance and accuracy (Chun, 2011; Koch et al., 2010; Rosen, 2011; Wood and Cowan, 1995). The literature from psychology gets a little confused when we start to talk about multitasking as a concrete topic. Technically, multitasking doesn't really exist; it is a misnomer that is usually perpetrated by recruitment consultants and those who like to think they are good at doing two things at once. What most people would call multitasking is actually more accurately viewed as task switching. We are often presented with the illusion of multitasking as we are switching between tasks at such speed it appears that we are actually doing these things concurrently. Task switching can also be apparent when we get interrupted whilst we are focused on a primary task, something that we will look at in more detail later on.

Irrespective of how we conceptualise it, the term 'multitasking' has entered into everyday language and is used to describe a skill that is viewed as being good, but the consequences of engaging in such behaviour are far from positive (Becker et al., 2013). The term 'polychronicity' in this context refers to an individual's preference to engage in multitasking as opposed to performing one task at any one time (Slocombe and Bluedorn, 1999). The notion of polychronicity is not a cognitively-based skill, but more a trait-based preference for shifting attention between ongoing tasks (Poposki and Oswald, 2009). However, research from Sanbonmatsu et al. (2013) would suggest that individuals have a massive disconnect between their perceived ability to multitask and their actual ability. Findings from their research showed that scores on a measure of multitasking were negatively correlated to self-reported multitasking activity. Similarly this measure was also negatively correlated to self-reported incidences of using a mobile phone whilst driving. So in essence it would appear that those who are least able to multitask are indeed those who are engaging in it more. Multitasking is presented as a mechanism through which individuals are able to achieve more in a shorter space of time, but what this chapter will do is explore the reality behind these anecdotal claims.

The Origins of Multitasking

The actual term 'multitasking' has been adopted from computer science and originally made reference to the capacity for computers to complete a number of key operations simultaneously (Rosen, 2008). In contrast to computers, humans do not possess the hard-wired logic that allows such complex processes to be undertaken in the same space and time, and multitasking has taken on a variety of different connotations. According to Rosen (2008), the term multitasking has evolved (or, if you prefer to use the original term presented by Rosen, 'hijacked') to describe 'the human attempt to do simultaneously as many things as possible, as quickly as possible, preferably marshalling the power of as many technologies as possible' (p. 105). Other researchers, such as Delbridge (2000), have described the concept of multitasking as the attempt to perform multiple goals in the same general time period by 'engaging in frequent switches between individual tasks" (p. 3). Yet others, such as Adler and Benbunan-Fich (2012), have noted that multitasking occurs when the individual is seen to shift their attention in order to perform several independent but concurrent computer-related tasks. It should be noted that these researchers place a direct emphasis on the use of computer technology in the process of multitasking, something that will become even more apparent as we move on through this chapter. Benbunan-Fich et al. (2011) noted that there are two key principles that should be adhered to when attempting to define an activity as multitasking. These are as follows:

- There must be some aspect of *task independence*, so that each of the tasks being conducted is self-contained and there is no cross-over in terms of the cognitive processes being used to conduct them.

- There is also an element of *performance concurrency*; this means that the two tasks are carried out in the same time frame, and there is some temporal overlap within a specific time period.

What is apparent from the definitions presented by Rosen and Delbridge is the repetition of the word 'attempt'. This resonates well with previous research from cognitive psychology which indicates that doing more than one task at the same time is something that isn't guaranteed to produce the best results. The other key aspect that strikes you when you are reading these definitions is the heady mix of technology within the melee of concurrent cognitive processes. Rosen (2008) presents a short but incisive discussion that essentially debunks the notion that multitasking is actually a possible cognitive process, and there is a great deal of evidence that suggests that this is true. Even James (1890) presented an exploration of multitasking, and viewed it in terms of a *child-like* inability to focus attention on one key task. Perhaps James had the fortune to view the future where the young and old alike are engaging in two tasks at any one time, usually accompanied by social networking apps, digital media and our beloved shiny smartphones.

Rather than multitasking being a state of two cognitive tasks engaged in at the same time, Dzubak (2007) argued that multitasking is more likely to be a *sequence* (hence something that occurs in serial rather than parallel order) of processes that occur in rapid succession. This would also mean that multitasking is essentially task switching, a process that enables the individual to select information for attention, process that information and then encode it ready to be stored and then acted upon. For writers such as Delbridge (2000), the notion of 'task switching' is linked to attention switching – there must be a process through which attention is re-focused from the current task to the secondary, switched-to task. We will come to aspects of task switching when we explore the notion of interruptions in Chapter 7, but for now it is important for the reader to understand the cross-over between these two concepts.

Previous Research

As indicated at the start of this chapter, there is ample evidence from the literature in cognitive psychology that discusses the capacity for humans to perform more than one task at once. The conclusion from most researchers is that there is little capacity for two competing cognitive tasks to be conducted at the same time without there being some residual impact on performance (e.g. see Broadbent, 1957; Kahneman, 1973; Pashler et al., 2001). Such a suggestion links into the concept that attention is a limited resource and has a finite quality attached to it. This therefore means that the individual cannot attend to an unlimited amount of information simultaneously, and that by dividing resources between tasks, poorer performance will be evident. An example of this has been provided in work by Rubinstein et al. (2001), who noted that where individuals do engage in multitasking, the tasks take longer to complete and are usually accompanied by more errors in contrast to when they are focusing on a single task.

How Do We Organise Multiple Tasks?

When we explore the research into the concept of multitasking there has been some attempt to understand how this process fits into the way in which we accomplish tasks. Bluedorn et al. (1992) presented an exploration of how multiple tasks are organised in the context of three distinct temporal mechanisms. These essentially look at how timing comes into the process of conducting more than one thing at once, and are presented as follows:

- *Sequential processing*: Each task starts after the previous one has been finished. In this context there is no concurrency between tasks. In this instance this process is far removed from the notion of multitasking as the individual isn't conducting multiple tasks in the same time frame.

- *Parallel processing*: All the things we are doing are attended to at the same time, hence there is the highest level of task overlap or *concurrency*.

The reality of this process is actually something of a near impossibility, but we can gain the illusion of doing two things at the same time. Similarly, attention is very hard to divide across multiple tasks unless there are key differences in the type of attention being used (such as writing and listening to music at the same time). However, as we will see when we look at media multitasking later on, even this has its own set of issues.

- *Interleaving*: During the performance of a current task attention is reallocated through either voluntary or involuntary actions to another task. There is the potential for the primary task to be resumed, but the actual process of resuming the original task will actually have costs attached to it. This mechanism is the one that is more akin to task switching and can be linked to two key reasons for suspending the original task:

  o *An external disruption*: Here there is something within our immediate environment that requires our urgent attention, therefore the current goal is displaced (e.g. getting a text message from a friend who has some 'urgent' gossip whilst you are writing an essay?!).

  o *An internal decision to stop*: This may be due to an obstacle that currently prevents the completion of the current goal or task. It might be related to a lack of specific information or resources (you can't make that cake if you suddenly realise you haven't got any eggs!). The goal will become suspended and another goal will become the focus of attention (going to buy some eggs) until the obstacle is removed. These are often termed 'self-imposed interruptions' and are something that we will be exploring later on in Chapter 7 (Adler and Benbunan-Fich, 2012).

Theories for Multitasking

Limited Resource Capacity Models

As I have stressed throughout the first few chapters of this book, a variety of researchers have highlighted the notion that our cognitive resources are limited, directly associated with the limited capacity of human processing (Lang, 2000). When we have a number of tasks that have processing requirements that exceed the available resources we have, we usually see some form of decrement in performance. This could be in the form of errors or a longer time taken to perform the tasks. If you think about this in the context of your finances – if you only have £50 to spend on a pair of trousers and some decent shoes (for decent, don't go mad, this isn't a night out on the town, this is an emergency purchase!), and the shoes cost £30 and the trousers cost £40, you are essentially stuffed – so this is mostly a big decrement in performance.

Multiple Resource Theories

The limited capacity theory would suggest that there is just one common pool of resources available for us to use when conducting a task (so in the case of the previous example, this would be our wallet or purse containing some money). In contrast, the multiple resource theory proposed by researchers such as Wickens (2002) suggests that we have a set of specialised resources that subsume specific functions related to cognition and perception. The theory holds that when we have two tasks that require the involvement of the same resources, competition will occur, thus resulting in a similar decrement in performance (2002). For example, this could be multitasking on two activities that require an individual to pay attention to two visual tasks at the same time – obviously, as these two tasks share the same requirement for visual attention, there will be some issues related to performance. Individuals are often wise to this process, and for the most part will choose to multitask in a way that actually minimises disruption. For example, work by Carrier et al. (2009) would indicate that people are more likely to text or surf the Internet whilst listening to music, meaning there is less chance for competition between resources. However, as we will see in the context of media multitasking later, this isn't always a guaranteed strategy.

The Unified Theory of Multitasking

There has been some attempt to move towards a theoretical conceptualisation that focuses directly on multitasking. The Unified Theory of Multitasking Continuum (Salvucci et al., 2009) is an amalgamation of a number of other theoretical positions. The theory itself views multitasking on a continuum (see Figure 6.1) where processes are viewed in the context of the time frame in which they occur. At the one end we have actions or tasks that are taking place within a matter of seconds, for instance the capacity to drive and talk at the same time. This requires an element of simultaneous processing where there is less control over switching between tasks as well as less time. In contrast, sequential multitasking could also perhaps be seen more as task switching, in which there is more direct control over the processes that are taking place and indeed more time between the switches.

The first component of the Unified Theory of Multitasking is the ACT-R Cognitive architecture proposed by Anderson et al. (2004). The main purpose of Anderson's model was to be able to explore the processes involved in cognition on a practical or functional level. The model contains a number of individual modules each with their own respective purpose. The first one of these is the *declarative memory module* that contains information related to factual knowledge, including aspects such as episodic memory or instructions related to the current task. There is also a *goal module*, which contains information about the current goal for the

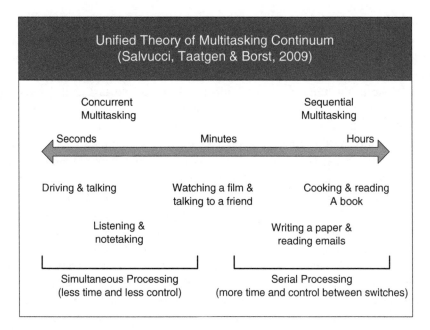

Figure 6.1   Unified Theory of Multitasking Continuum

Source: Salvucci et al. (2009)

system as well as being able to keep track of the progress towards that particular goal. The *problem representation module* holds representations of the environment that are incomplete, but which are essential for successful completion of the current task. This could be a sub-total for a mental arithmetic problem or perhaps notes related to an essay or a report that is being written. The final component, the *procedural module*, is the overall controlling component that connects all of the other modules together. According to Salvucci et al. (2009) the ACT-R model is important in one key respect when it comes to multitasking as it allows the capacity for each of these modules to act in parallel. However, more importantly each of the modules can only be used in one single task at any one time.

The second component to this theory of multitasking is that of the threaded cognition theory presented by Salvucci and Taatgen (2008). Essentially each task is seen as being a thread of activity that can be interleaved through the modules which make up the ACT-R model. Threaded cognition allows for multiple tasks to be performed, but different tasks will compete for different resources (or modules); the point at which these tasks compete for the same module resources is the point at which interference is noted. This perspective shares some commonality with the multiple resource theory we have discussed above. The way this is presented in the threaded cognition framework is that in the instance where two tasks require the same module, one task or thread will be forced to wait its turn for the required module to be released. Accordingly this waiting period will cause a residual delay in task completion and produce an increase in the time it takes to finish off the current task and resume the previous one; this is referred to as the resumption lag (Salvucci et al., 2009).

The final element introduced by Salvucci et al. (2009) in the context of a theory towards multitasking is that on the memory for goal theory (Altmann and Trafton, 2002, 2004; Trafton et al., 2003). Where we are attempting to multitask, the new task goal must appear within our attentional system at a higher level of activation in comparison with the older tasks. After this point, the memory trace for the old task will fade. The consequences of this process mean that once the interrupting task is completed, the original task will take longer to resume. This is due to the process of 'reactivating' the memory trace of the older task that was interrupted, which means reviving the relevant instructions for the task, the goals as well as the current level of progress towards those goals. In the context of our present discussion, memory for goal theory would highlight the existence of key threads that exist according to each of the tasks the individual is undertaking. In the situation where one task is presented at the same time as another, the older thread is weakened and becomes faded, hence it will need more time to resume later on.

For now the essential point to take away from this theory is that multitasking as a process isn't as clear cut as doing more than one thing at any one time. As we can see from this basic introduction, even the process of conceptualising the cognitive skills that underlie the process requires the amalgamation of more than one specific theory. It would appear that, at least from the information processing perspective, multitasking can and will result in a decrement in performance some-where along the line, and as we will see in the next section, such incidences have also been presented in the research literature.

Multitasking in the Digital Age: Media Multitasking

Right, now we have got the boring theory out of the way, let us turn our atten-tion to the actual research that has been conducted looking at multitasking in the context of digital media and technology. There is a surprising amount of research that covers this topic, with one of the most popular topics being that of media multitasking. To put this in a nutshell, the notion of media multitasking (or MMT) is the practice of engaging in more than one form of media at any given time (Ralph et al., 2013). This should start to sound familiar to lots of people, particularly those of us who like to surf the web ... whilst listening to music on our iPads … with the TV on … whilst we send a text … when we are doing work. The picture painted is all too familiar, but one that researchers have noted could have serious implications for our capacity to perform simple tasks.

Let us begin with some kind of sense check to put this type of work into context. Rideout et al. (2010) noted that those aged 8–18 have significantly increased the amount of time they spend using more than one medium at any given time. Approximately a quarter of the participants questioned in their study (29 per cent) said that they engaged in using two or more types of media concurrently. Furthermore, the using of digital media in multitasking was also apparent, with 48 per cent of young people saying that they multitask either 'some of the time' or 'most of the time' when playing video games, 46 per cent when using a computer and 73 per cent when listening to music. The researchers also noted that those who fell into the heavy media-use group (more than 16 hours per day) were more likely to be getting into trouble to express feelings of sadness or unhappiness, or were bored. Similarly, 47 per cent of all the heavy media users in the survey said they usually got poorer grades in comparison with the moderate or light users group. The research presented on media multitasking has attempted to present some clear mechanisms for why high levels of MMT could lead to residual decrements in academic attainment. The focus on multitasking and education is something that we will be returning to in Chapter 8 so I won't dwell on it more here, but safe to say that the results aren't very promising.

In an original piece of work, Ophir et al. (2009) made the suggestion that those who were frequently engaged in MMT possessed a different approach to processing information in comparison with those who engage in MMT on a less frequent basis. According to these researchers, the process of consuming multiple streams of media at one time creates a cognitive bias in high MMT individuals, which means that they are taking in all information at any one time rather than just the relevant information they need. In this regard they suggest those in the higher-level MMT band are typified as follows:

- They have a poorer capacity to ignore information that is irrelevant to the tasks they are doing.

- They are less likely to ignore information that is contained within memory that is also not relevant to the current task.

- They are also less effective at preventing the activation of information related to previously completed tasks. Such suggestion is at odds with the previous theories discussed above that would see successful task switching (which involves the completion of one task to take up another one) as being critical to any multitasking behaviour.

The theoretical reasons as to why those who engage in high levels of MMT are more prone to distraction were also the focus of some discussion in the work by Ophir et al. (2009). They make two key suggestions:

- High MMT individuals are more easily distracted by multiple streams of media. This would suggest that they have a stimulus-driven (exogenous) attentional bias, meaning they are constantly on the lookout for new information within their immediate environment – irrespective of its relevance to the current task. According to Ophir et al. (2009) it would appear that those in the high MMT group actually sacrifice focus on one specific task in order to allow other pieces of information into their attentional field.

- Low MMT individuals are much better at directing their attention towards task-relevant information. This would suggest they are better at focusing attention using a top-down (endogenous) process allowing them to focus more easily on a single task.

There has been some work conducted into the concept of MMT since this work by Ophir et al. (2009). For example Alzahabi and Becker (2013) noted that those who reported as being in the high MMT group were significantly better at switching between tasks in comparison with those in the low MMT group. They also found no significant differences in the ability to multitask between the high and low MMT groups. Additional work by Minear et al. (2013) noted that those in the high MMT group reported themselves as being more impulsive and performed less well on tests of fluid intelligence in comparison with those in the low MMT group. However, these researchers failed to find any support for the notion that high MMT individuals were worse in a multitasking situation and were unable to filter out irrelevant information.

Ralph et al. (2013) noted the disparity in such results, highlighting the fact that the relationship between MMT and laboratory-based tests are not as clear-cut as we would expect them to be. They presented their own set of findings, which focused specifically on media multitasking alongside the individuals' own interpretation of their attentional control in daily life. The study actually made a comparison between the frequency of participants, engagement in MMT alongside incidences of attentional lapses they had experienced during their daily lives. The findings from this study go some way in supporting the original work by Ophir et al. (2013) where the level at which individuals engaged in MMT was directly associated with their level of inattention in daily life. Those reporting higher levels of MMT also showed positive correlations with attentional failures in daily life, symptomatic of things like sudden lapses in concentration or a spontaneous capacity for mind wandering. They also found that there were no significant differences between MMT groups and subsequent memory failures, which was interpreted by the researchers as indicating that the issue is more directed towards an attentional component rather than on related to memory.

The results from Ralph et al. (2013) also noted that those with higher levels of MMT were associated with individuals actively withdrawing elements of attention and demonstrated limited awareness of real world events or those related to past experiences. They were also more likely to display a number of attentional failures that were linked directly to them doing other things whilst failing to focus on current tasks. Ralph et al. (2013) again suggested that such a finding might be more evidence that those who engage in higher levels of MMT are more easily distracted compared with those in the lower MMT groups. They presented a further notion that high MMT individuals possess a higher threshold of arousal in comparison with those from the low MMT group. This would mean that high MMT are actively seeking out additional forms of stimulation (in the shape of additional media) in order to satisfy this need.

We have to be careful when interpreting research such as this because the directionality of the results isn't entirely clear. For example, it could be that being subjected to higher levels of MMT is actually creating these underlying changes in attentional processes. However, it could also be argued that these results could be linked to individual differences and may highlight already established attentional problems. This could be the notion that certain individuals could have an actual need or addiction to seek out multiple streams of information (Ralph et al., 2013). Findings related to individual differences in relation to multitasking are the focus of the next section.

Individual Differences and Multitasking

Research has noted that some individuals do not show the expected decrement in performance whilst being engaged in multitasking (Rubinstein et al., 2001; Schumacher et al., 2001). The question remains as to why some people are more affected in the context of multitasking than others, and more importantly whether such elements can be trained so that an improvement in performance can be found. Many researchers have pointed towards underlying individual differences in cognitive processing that can coincidentally be linked to differences noted in multitasking performance (Brooking and Damos, 1991; Ishizaka et al., 2001). It should also be noted that gender differences and the capacity to multitask have also been debunked. For example, findings from Buser and Peter (2012) noted there was no significant difference in ability to multitask between men and women.

Elements of inhibitory control have been posited as one aspect of individual differences that may predict the individual's propensity for multitasking. Sanbonmatsu et al. (2013) noted that two key traits, namely sensation seeking and impulsivity (which is directly linked to aspects of attentional control), have been widely associated with multitasking behaviour. In their exploration of these factors, they noted previous work that suggested that those who are categorised as high sensation seekers are more likely to engage in multitasking as it presents a capacity for them to experience a wider variety of sensations (Roberti, 2004; Sanbonmatsu et al., 2013; Zuckerman and Kuhlman, 2000). Similarly they also noted that sensation seekers are less likely to see loss in a negative light, meaning that they are more likely to focus on the enjoyment aspect of multitasking irrespective of the negatives (Franken et al., 1992; Horvath and Zuckerman, 1993; Sanbonmatsu et al., 2013). The results from Sanbonmatsu et al. (2013) supported the notion that sensation seekers do indeed show a higher preference for multitasking, and were more likely to report MMT as well as using a mobile phone whilst driving.

In wider research, Cain and Mitroff (2011) have also noted that certain individuals will choose to pay attention to a broader area of their environment, therefore meaning that they are more prone to distraction as well as having the potential for engaging in a secondary task. This point was also picked out by Sanbomatsu et al. (2013), who suggested that those individuals who have a higher level of executive control are perhaps the ones who are most likely to be able to multitask but are less likely to do so. This comes through in the context of impulsivity, a dispositional trait that has come into focus when discussing aspects of attentional control. For example, Gentile et al. (2012) noted that those who played action video games (AVGs) demonstrated higher levels of impulsivity and had greater problems in their capacity to focus attention. They also noted that this relationship goes both ways, inasmuch as individuals with issues related to attention and impulsivity will also have a proclivity to spend more time playing AVGs. Sanbonmatsu et al. (2013) also noted that those individuals with a higher level of impulsivity also present an inability to focus directly on the current task, often preferring to take on multiple tasks. Their findings would again support the link between impulsivity, attentional control and an inability to plan effectively, with each of these elements being positively correlated to higher levels of self-reported multitasking. It would appear that the preference to engage in multitasking is directly linked to an inability to focus attention on one specific task in favour of a broader attentional capture.

Can There Be Supertaskers?

Watson and Strayer (2010) present an interesting theoretical possibility that there might be a small proportion of the population who are bestowed with special capacities when it comes to completing complex multitasking activities. For these individuals, they suggest that they do not experience the detrimental effects associated with completing two tasks in a similar time frame. They rely on existing evidence from the literature on those individuals who display memory that falls outside the normal capacity limits (Price and Davis, 2008). Based on their work, they found that 2.5 per cent out of 200 participants exhibited the capacity to supertask, or more specifically be able to complete a simulated driving task whilst using a mobile phone without residual decrements in performance or attention. However, they do suggest there may be associated trade-offs in terms of other processing abilities, such as these individuals demonstrating a poorer capacity to plan or remember things. They also suggest that the reason for the limited proliferation of supertaskers throughout the human population is to do with selection. At present, the skill of supertasking is something that has become more specifically an advantage in the modern digital age, hence it is only just being realised in the current generation. According to Watson and Strayer (2010), such a skill will become more prevalent in future generations as the need to multitask becomes more and more important and evolutionarily beneficial.

When Multitasking Isn't So Good

For many of us, the use of multitasking skills is usually confined to times when the actual consequences may result in minor errors that would not have a significant impact on us. However, there is one area of research related to multitasking that does have significant implications for safety, and that is the use of mobile phones whilst conducting another activity. Much of these findings relate directly to the use of mobile phones whilst driving, but other researchers have demonstrated that even whilst we are walking, using a mobile phone can have a significant impact on our capacity to pay attention. Studies have noted that talking on a mobile phone can actually increase the risk of crashing by a factor of 4, which is why legislation has moved to prevent people from doing it (Strayer et al., 2011).

As we explored earlier, the capacity to perform two tasks at the same time will depend entirely on the extent to which a secondary activity shares similar demands to that of the primary task. Previous research exploring the use of hand-held devices focused directly on the physical interference that was caused as a result of holding the device and driving at the same time (Strayer et al., 2011; Young and Regan, 2007). As technology has changed with the proliferation of hands-free devices and consequent changes in legislation about the use of such devices whilst driving, the actual handling of the mobile phone has decreased (though not been abolished), but research has still noted a significant threat from cognitive distractions. A number of researchers have noted that there is no significant difference in terms of safety between using a hands-free mobile-phone system and a handheld phone whilst driving, although most of these focus more on talking rather than texting (Strayer et al., 2004, 2011; Young and Regan, 2007).

In a series of experiments, Strayer and colleagues (Strayer and Drews, 2007; Strayer and Johnston, 2001; Strayer et al., 2003) demonstrated that using a mobile phone could actually produce aspects of inattentional blindness. Just to recap, inattentional blindness is the notion that individuals fail to see novel or distinctive objects or elements within their immediate visual environment whilst engaged in a secondary, cognitively demanding task (Jensen et al., 2011). Strayer and Drews (2007) asked their participants to complete a simulated driving task whilst they were having a conversation on a mobile phone. Interestingly they noted that even though participants were looking directly at objects within the driving environment, they failed to commit these elements to memory if they were talking on a mobile phone. If the capacity to multitask successfully relies directly on the extent to which both tasks are competing for the same resources, Strayer and Drews (2007) suggested that there shouldn't really be any direct impact of talking on a mobile phone whilst driving. According to them, the auditory/verbal/vocal elements of the mobile phone conversation shouldn't cross over with the visual/spatial/physical aspects of the driving task. However, there is a degree of interference noted, which makes the models related to multitasking based around different pots of resources appear a little redundant.

So what about other activities in our daily life, such as walking and talking on a mobile phone? Surely we don't miss really novel things whilst we are walking around if we are on our phones? Well, the short answer to this is actually yes, we can miss out on things within our immediate environment that we would assume should be perfectly visible. Hyman et al. (2010) presented some novel findings that highlight this suggestion pretty well. In their experiment, they compared participants according to their behaviour, for example if they were walking and talking on a mobile phone, if they were listening to music on an MP3 player, if they were walking in a pair or if they were just walking along. Their initial findings showed that those who were engaged in conversations on mobile phones took longer to walk across a predetermined route than those who were listening to music and those walking alone. They also noted that mobile phone users were more likely to change direction as well as weave, which could potentially be linked to aspects of decreased spatial attention. In the second part of the study, the researchers introduced a novel stimulus: that of a unicycling clown. Now for most of us, we would surely be able to recount the amount of times we have walked around a city and encountered a unicycling clown, wouldn't we? Well, for those of us who like to talk and walk at the same time, be prepared for a shock – you'd have probably missed the clown! Those who were classified as using a mobile phone whilst walking were the group least likely to report seeing the presence of the unicycling clown. Only 25 per cent of those participants questioned in the study who were walking and on their mobile phones noted the presence of the unicycling clown. To put this into context, over 61 per cent of people using the MP3 whilst walking reported seeing the clown, along with 71 per cent of people walking in pairs. What becomes apparent from this research is that even for a very concrete and well-practised skill such as walking, the deficit in attention when accompanied by the use of a mobile phone is tangible.

Incidences of injuries to pedestrians who are either walking whilst talking on their mobile phone or texting are becoming more commonplace (Nasar and Troyer, 2013; Nasar et al., 2008; Schwebel et al., 2012; Stavrinos et al., 2009). For instance, the study by Stavrinos et al. (2009) explored the simulated road crossing of children aged 10–11. In one condition, the children crossed the road whilst being simultaneously engaged in a mobile phone conversation with a person who was part of the research team. In the other conditions the children crossed the road without any specific distractions other than those that usually accompany a typical road-based environment. The findings from their study demonstrated a significant impairment in the children's awareness to their surroundings whilst being on a mobile phone. The children who were distracted paid less attention to traffic, reducing the amount of time between them crossing the road and the approach of another vehicle; they experienced more incidences of collisions or very close calls with oncoming traffic and had a longer delay in starting to cross the street. The research also examined whether the children's previous experience of using mobile phones served to mitigate this safety risk. The results showed that there was no significant difference between those who had used a mobile phone previously and those who had not (Stavrinos et al., 2009).

Later work by Schwebel et al. (2012) expanded this work and explored the differences in distraction for participants who were randomly assigned to three different conditions. Participants aged 17–45 were asked to cross a road in an interactive simulation that portrayed a typical pedestrian street environment. The condition to which the participants were assigned included conducting a mobile phone conversation whilst crossing, texting and listening to music. Their performance was compared with a control group who crossed the road undistracted. The results demonstrated that those in the music and texting conditions were more likely to be 'hit' by a virtual vehicle compared with the participants in the other groups. They also noted that those in the texting group experienced more virtual hits than those who were having a conversation on their mobile, a result that contrasts with the work of Starvrinos et al. (2009) discussed above. It could be that texting – which involves not only the motor co-ordination to type a response, but also the facility to read and formulate a reply (which means converting a verbal code into a symbolic one) – is more cognitively demanding and therefore more distracting in comparison to simply having a conversation on the phone. Schwebel et al. (2012) do, however, note that this is the first piece of research to produce such a finding and express the view that the aim should be to replicate these findings before we jump to massive conclusions.

The Rise of the 'Zombie Smartphone User': A World-Wide Epidemic

The issue of people using their smartphones has become such an problem that a variety of initiatives have been implemented around the world in an attempt to curb injuries and accidents related to their use. The problem has reached such serious levels in places like Japan that they have even invented their own term for it, that of 'Aruki Sumaho', or 'smartphone walking' (www.bbc.co.uk/news/blogs-news-from-elsewhere-23666695). In 2013 a news article by Renee Loth (www.bostonglobe.com/opinion/columns/2013/07/12/distracted-texting-rises-pedestrian-deaths/GGNWwpjuVDM6aEPf08PuoI/story.html) it was reported that the town of Fort Lee in New Jersey had implemented a new law that made walking whilst texting illegal, with pedestrians caught doing so risking a fine.

Figure 6.2 An example of the signs designed by Swedish designers Jacob Sempler and Emil Tiismann warning drivers that there might be distracted pedestrians about

Source: Photo: Jacob Sempler

Figure 6.3 A stark yet humorous warning to would-be Facebookers that they may be putting their lives at risk whilst texting

Source: Robert Galbraith/REUTERS (taken from http://www.wsj.com/articles/texting-while-walking-isnt-funny-anymore-1455734501)

Figure 6.4 In certain parts of the world pathway segregation has been implemented to stem the rise of collisions between distracted smartphone users and other walkers and cyclists

Source: Reuters (www.wsj.com/articles/texting-while-walking-isnt-funny-anymore-1455734501)

In the city of Stockholm designers have gone to the extreme measure of designing road signs warning car drivers of the potential threat of zombie-like pedestrians who might be walking around aimlessly trying to post images of their breakfast on Twitter. These signs (see Figure 6.2), designed by Swedish designers Jacob Sempler and Emil Tiismann (http://jacobandemil.com/#/new-page-1/) highlight two things: people are texting whilst walking, and they are doing it so much that motorists are being made aware of the fact!

Other designers have taken a bit more of a humorous, tongue-in-cheek approach to the issues of the zombie smartphone user, choosing to make them think more about the actions they are performing. The image in Figure 6.3 is taken from the town of Hayward in California, and makes the point of telling pedestrians that updating their social media probably isn't worth doing whilst crossing the road!

And finally we have the image in Figure 6.4 from the popular tourist destination in Chongqing, China. The rise of the zombified smartphone user was becoming so much of an issue that they actually created a specific walkway for those who were using their smartphones whilst walking!

Summary

The notion of multitasking as a ubiquitous skill that everyone possesses and everyone is really good at doesn't really come across in the research literature we have explored above. For the most part the take-home message is that yes, we might think we are able to do two things at once and yes, we might think we are really good at it … but in actual fact we aren't. Researchers have noted that the actual truth is that those who think they are good at multitasking are potentially those who aren't. Conversely, those who have the capacity to be able to multitask may be those who choose not to!

Is the use of digital technology impacting upon our capacity to multitask? Well at the moment, the research just isn't there to be able to draw this type of conclusion. According to the work of Watson and Strayer (2010), there is a possibility that our experiences with digital technology are driving a sort of evolutionary selection towards the notion of 'supertasker' who will be armed with the capacity to do several complex activities at the same time. However, such a suggestion is a long way off in terms of the development of humankind and its underlying cognitive processes. The reality of today is that we attempt to multitask on a daily basis, and digital technology is influencing the frequency of such activity. Both work and home environments present a plethora of opportunities for us to engage (and indulge) in multiple tasks at any one time. Sending a text whilst watching a video online, tweeting whilst walking, trying to send an email whilst on the phone to a colleague – all of these things are multitasking, and all present an opportunity for our cognitive resources to be stretched beyond their limits. The consequences of multitasking can span from the humorous (watch out for people walking into things whilst texting – this is one of my favoured pastimes!) or the downright dangerous. What underlies this issue is the well-established fact that our cognitive systems are ill equipped to be able to do multiple tasks in what appears to be the same time frame. Rather than making the word multitasking a common term and a process we should all be striving for, perhaps we need to take a step back, establish the reality and start to refocus on the things and tasks that are most important.

7

TASK SWITCHING AND DIGITAL TECHNOLOGY

THE IMPACT OF INTERRUPTIONS

Learning Aims and Objectives

- To define the concept of interruption in the context of digital technology;

- to highlight the cost that interruptions can have upon the individual's capacity to focus and complete tasks in their daily lives;

- to review research looking at the impact that notifications from both smartphones and email can have upon human cognition;

- to explore the ways in which disruption from emails can be mediated and managed;

- to examine more recent research focusing on 'self-initiated' interruptions and examine how they fit into the digital environment.

Overview

> **QUESTION BOX**
>
> Take a few moments and think about how often you get interrupted in your daily life – then think about where these interruptions come from and how they relate direct to digital technology. Were you interrupted by a message notification, a friend request from Facebook, an email or even a phone call?

Let us just take stock of our daily lives and think about the common events and working practices that we engage in during such a typical day. You could, for example, be sitting at your computer happily writing an essay, reading a journal article, writing a best-selling book or report when you suddenly get an email alert that links to an email from a colleague asking you if you have a particular document you filed away several years ago. So you go off in search of this document, perhaps looking through a list of archived PDF files or scanning your bookshelves and shifting through draws in order to find it. Whilst doing this task, you get a text message from a friend asking you if you have the contact details of another friend as they have managed to accidently flush their phone down the toilet (apparently a common occurrence these days!) and they urgently need to speak to them. Whilst sending these contact details through you get an update from your eBay application telling you that joebloggslikescutekittens1948 has placed a bid on your retro-style solar-powered torch – and then you remember you need to get back to the thing that you were originally doing about two hours ago.

If any of this scenario appears to be familiar then that is probably because many of us are now being interrupted frequently, and much of these interruptions originate from the presence and use of digital technology. According to some researchers individuals can be interrupted as often as once every 12 minutes during their working day (Jin and Dabbish, 2009). The constant presence of digital technology in both our work and social lives means that interruptions can become an all too common occurrence. For the most part, the cost of being interrupted would appear to be pretty trivial, and perhaps would mean that what we are currently doing might get delayed for a few minutes. Research exploring the impact of interruptions on productivity serves to quantify the true cost of these incidences, and demonstrate that they can have wider-reaching consequences.

In this chapter I want to begin to explore the current findings from research that has focused on the impact of interruptions from a number of sources closely aligned with digital technology. There is a degree of cross-over between the aspects of multitasking introduced in the previous chapter and being interrupted. In the context of our discussions, multitasking is viewed for the most part as a process that the individual has some conscious awareness of and control over, whereas interruptions are usually motivated by sources external to us. These interruptions direct attention away from the primary task in which we are engaged, whereas multitasking switches our attention between two consecutive tasks. Interruptions will usually mean that the primary task is suspended (perhaps indefinitely) whilst we go off and deal with the interrupting alert and the task that has been associated with it. This will in turn lead to a longer time away from the primary task, and rather than two things being attempted in parallel (as is the case with multitasking), we tend to press the 'pause' button on one task whilst doing another.

In order to start this discussion off, it is important to present some clear outlines on how researchers have defined the notion of an interruption and how these compare to other occurrences such as distractions.

How are Interruptions Defined?

The process of defining an interruption against the backdrop of other effects such as distractions can prove challenging. Van Solingen et al. (1998) presented the notion that an interruption can be conceptualised as 'any distraction that makes an [individual] stop his planned activity to respond to the interrupt's initiator'. So in the context of this definition the concept of a *distraction* has been presented as being part of the process of being interrupted. There is also a requirement for the individual to respond to the 'interrupt's initiator', meaning we have to reply or take an action towards the thing or person that has deemed it necessary to disrupt our daily working life, usually by emailing us images of cute cats. Coraggio (1990: 19) presented an earlier definition for an interruption as 'an externally generated, randomly occurring, discrete event that breaks continuity of cognitive factors on a primary task'. If we start to dissect this definition a little bit further there are a number of key principles that need some further expansion. First, for Coraggio the interruption can only be externally generated, a concept that up until recently many researchers would have generally agreed upon. However, there is mounting evidence that individuals can and do choose to perform what has been termed a 'self-interrupt', meaning they may choose to actually interrupt themselves whilst performing a task. Second, the interruption also has some form of randomness attached to it, and it is this element of randomness that is seen as being the key element in producing the greater levels of disruption (Adamczyk and Bailey, 2004). If the individual can predict when an interruption may come about, or if they occur at regular intervals, then the individual can take action in order to mitigate their effects, through either planning or dealing with all interruptions at one time.

The notion of 'discrete events' links directly to those attention-grabbing events we discussed in the context of exogenous processes. A discrete stimulus is usually an event that stands out as something that is novel or different within the environment in which it occurs. In the context of interruptions, this novel event will direct our attention away from the task that we are currently doing towards the source of the interruption.

The last element of Coraggio's definition is perhaps the most important element for our present discussion: the fact that the presence of an interruption can divert cognitive resources away from our current task. The action of the interruption will mean that our finite cognitive resources are redirected towards the task that is now related to the interruption. This will in turn lead to the possibility of an increased amount of time to complete the original task, as well as the chance that the original task may not be returned to at all.

Further work has attempted to dissect how interruptions and distractions differ, although they may appear to be one and the same thing at first glance. Speier et al. (2003) provided some useful clarification regarding the similarity and differences that exist between these two phenomena. Both interruptions and distractions share a common characteristic in that they can both occur whilst we are engaged in doing something else. However, they do differ in terms of how they are detected by our primary senses. In the context of distractions, these are detected by senses that sit outside those currently being used for the primary task. This in turn means that we can choose to ignore the disrupting stimulus (as it isn't directly relevant to the current task) or we can process the distraction at the same time as the primary task. If we do the latter, we can usually get away with doing so without incurring a great deal of impairment on the primary task as the two tasks do not share a common set of resources. Cohen (1980) noted that whilst distractions can have the capacity to divert our attention away from a current activity, they often don't require us to make a response. In contrast, an interruption will usually occupy the same sensory channel as the primary task, hence we find it a lot harder to ignore them (e.g. an email notification whilst we are writing a paper on the computer). This ultimately means that we are splitting cognitive resources between two tasks above what we have currently available, usually meaning that the interruption will be processed in favour of the primary task.

Work by Trafton et al. (2003) focused directly on mapping the critical events attached to an interruption. They detail these four key events as follows:

- *An interruption alert*: This is the 'thing' or event that makes the individual pay attention to the interruption itself. This could be a sound, a message alert, and usually has some element of urgency attached to it – this in turn will determine the speed and level of response by the individual.

- *Starting the interrupting task*: There is a point at which the individual will switch from their current (primary) task to that of the interrupting task. The process will involve a set of 'switching costs' which is the changeover in the mental processes associated with the primary task to those needed for the secondary (interrupting) task.

- *Ending the interrupting task*: This is the point at which the individual reaches a satisfactory conclusion for the interrupting task and engages in a process of extinguishing the associated memory traces for it.

- *Resumption of the primary task*: This is the point at which we now have to resume the task we left in order to deal with the interruption, which also means we have to remember where we left it, what we were doing, as well as the associated goals aligned with that task. This process of task re-engagement will also add additional time to its final completion.

There are two further concepts that are closely aligned with these stages that appear frequently in the literature on interruptions. In the first instance we have the 'interruption lag', which is conceived as the time between the alert and the start of the secondary (interrupting) task. Then we have the time between leaving the secondary task and the re-engagement of the original task; this is the period termed as the 'resumption lag'. All of this, as discussed before, adds additional time to the task we were originally doing (Trafton et al., 2003).

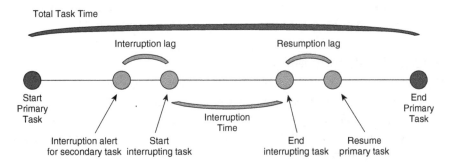

Figure 7.1 Timeline of an interruption (adapted from J. Gregory Trafton et al., 2003)

How Does the Context of the Interruption Affect Us?

Research from the area of human–computer interaction has noted that a variety of contextual elements related to the interruption that can influence the level of disruption caused by them. It is useful to explore this literature in order to provide a basis for our wider discussions throughout this chapter, particularly when the digital environment can present such a wide variety of backdrops for interruptions to take place.

Interruption relevance

A number of researchers have noted that an interruption which has direct relevance to the task in hand (new information related to current task or search parameters) is far less disruptive than an irrelevant one (Czerwinski et al, 2000; Kalyanaraman, et al., 2005; Roda, 2011). Users are continually searching for information that is directly relevant to the current task goals, with more relevant information leading to a more positive view of that particular website (Kalyanaraman and Sundar, 2006). In contrast, task-irrelevant interruptions have been shown to create feelings of frustration and irritation in users, which is proposed to stem from the perceived intrusiveness of task-irrelevant interference (Li et al., 2002).

Assessing the relevance of any information contained in an interruption is not necessarily an automated task that is governed by an unconscious attentional process. Individuals must first highlight the interruption and assess the relevance of the information contained within it to the current task. This processes is based on semantic information (factual information) that requires a lot more in terms of cognitive resources than a simple visual match does. Therefore the mere process of highlighting whether or not the interruption is relevant reduces the amount of cognitive resources we can devote to the primary task (Roda, 2011).

Nature of task complexity

The notion that task complexity has an interaction with the presence of an interruption has been documented in previous research. The concept of task complexity has been operationalised for research purposes as a function of the amount of specific information the individual has to deal with at any one time. In this regard any task that requires the use of multiple steps or requires a number of concurrent operations to be stored and later processed is seen as being typical of complex tasks (Coraggio, 1990). As such, these tasks require a great deal of cognitive resources to be available in order for them to be completed successfully and accurately. As one would expect from this regard, research has shown that interruptions are far more damaging to performance on complex tasks as a result of competition between the task and the interruption itself for access to limited resources.

Coraggio (1990) noted that interruptions in their broadest sense are far more disruptive when the individual subjected to them is engaged in a more complex and highly cognitively demanding task. Here Coraggio (1990) introduced the notion of task granularity, a term that is used to describe the overall structure of tasks; a highly granular task contains a variety of sub-tasks entrenched within it, with each task needing to be completed before the individual can move on to the next stage. A task of this nature could be analogous to an individual who is searching for information requires visiting multiple webpages, each aspect representing a 'grain' in the task process (Smith, 2010). Coraggio (1990) noted that performance was affected less by an interruption when it occurred during a stage in the task which moved them naturally from one task to another, particularly when they had just engaged in that task. Bailey and Iqbal (2008) further noted that the disruptions via interruptions serves to increase the length of time spent on tasks. This suggests a pattern of information processing where the individual who is close to completion of a task is holding a lot of information. It is at this point that multiple task 'grains' could be active, hence the individual becomes more susceptible to any form of interruption. This in turn would lead to a greater decrement in performance as more resources are diverted away to deal with the nature of the interruption.

Content of the Notification

Designers of information systems are constantly exploring the limits to the amount of information that can be contained in a notification. The consideration for such mechanisms is to ensure that the level of disruption users experience is kept to a minimum whilst ensuring the individual is orientated to relevant information (Roda, 2011). Roda (2011) goes on to highlight three key mechanisms for notification according to their content type, each one having specific ramifications for the level of disruption that the user experiences:

1 *Pure notification*: A simple icon or pointer that serves to highlight new information or the presence of a new task that needs to be completed. Common examples of pure notification mechanisms include animated or 'jumping' icons that alert the user to new system information or an appearing and fading modal window that tells users about newly available information (Roda, 2011). These types of notifications have low-level disruptive capacity on the individual and require the user to take action in order to deal with the interruption.

2 *Awareness mechanisms*: These types of notifications provide the user with the actual information without referring them to it in a secondary window or system. This could include the appearance of a tutorial-based dialog box indicating relevant options and help information to the user. According to Roda (2011), these types of notification have a medium level of disruption.

3 *Complete switch of context*: This is where a new window/new application is opened. In this instance the individual has no prior warning that a new task has to be completed. In this instance there is no annunciation signal and the end user is taken straight to the new task (McFarlane and Latorella, 2002). These types of notifications are the most cognitive demanding and jarring as they present a completely new task with little or no warning to the end user.

Timing of Interruption

Research into this area has suggested that the point at which an interruption occurs in the context of the task has a mediating effect on the level of disruption that occurs. A number of studies have found that an interruption occurring in the middle of a task is more likely to disrupt performance in contrast to one that appears towards the beginning of the task (Coraggio, 1990; Speier et al., 2003). Such a pattern is linked to aspects of cognitive load and the notion of granularity introduced earlier (Coraggio, 1990). Interruptions that occur early on in a task are easily mediated through the use of resources that have not already been deployed in the pursuance of completing the primary task. However, as the task progresses, more and more task-relevant resources are being taken up, so anything that diverts these away from the completion of that task will result in disruption. Czerwinski et al. (2000) asked participants to complete a web-based research task and found that this was less easily disrupted when the interruption occurred at the beginning of the task. Interruptions that occurred early on in the planning stages where a search strategy was being formed failed to significantly increase response times. In contrast, an interruption that occurred during more cognitively demanding aspects of the task, either during execution (actually completing the search) or evaluation (assessing the results of the search and highlighting the most relevant aspects) was far more disruptive (Czerwinski et al., 2000).

Why Are Interruptions So Important for Us to Understand?

I am sure many of you are sitting there thinking that being interrupted cannot be that bad, it is just part and parcel of our everyday lives – right? Well let's take this assumption to task and explore it in the context of the rise of digital technology. The impact of interruptions from external sources, in particular those being caused by computer-based technology, has been the focus of much research in the area of human–computer interaction (Adamczyk and Bailey, 2004; Cutrell et al., 2001; Czerwinski et al., 2004; McFarlane, 2002; Sykes, 2011). The take-home message from much of this research is pretty consistent in suggesting that interruptions to any ongoing task present a wide array of negative consequences (Eyrolle and Cellier, 2000). These negative effects can include an increase in the time it takes to complete the primary task (which has been interrupted), an increase in the individual's general feelings of annoyance and higher levels of anxiety, as well as an increased perception of task difficulty (Bailey et al., 2000). Other researchers have noted that individuals who have been frequently interrupted report feelings of distraction, stress and anxiety, all as a result of the impact digital distractions have within the workplace (Kushlev and Dunn, 2015; Mark et al., 2012). Workers who received random notifications whilst performing common workplace tasks expressed feelings of annoyance at constantly being interrupted and were more likely to demonstrate clear feelings of frustration. A consequence of these interruptions is that workers may also feel more pressure to complete tasks in a given time frame and therefore report a need to exert more effort on the primary task on which they were currently focused. These findings were presented in stark contrast to another group of workers who had no such interruptions and in turn did not experience any of the negative consequences (Adamczyk and Bailey, 2004). Additional work from Gupta et al. (2013; see also Gupta and Sharda, 2008) noted that workers can lose up to 5 per cent of their overall working day as a result of interruptions (which roughly equates to about 25 minutes in an 8-hour working day, or 11.75 days over the average working year!).

Interruptions and Smartphones: Everything Happens within the 'Push' Economy

Researchers have more recently started to explore the impact those shiny little devices we choose to covet so much can have on the way in which interruptions enter our daily lives. In contrast to interruptions and notifications that are presented through the medium of the desktop PC, those initiated by the smartphone are something a little bit different – but why? Well, it all comes down to the way in which messages are 'pushed' through to the individual (Basoglu et al., 2009). Researchers such as Bawden and Robinson (2008) and Schultze and Varden-Bosch (1998) noted the capacity for digital technology to 'push' notifications to the end user. These push notifications can be highly intrusive and appear totally at random throughout our daily working (and sleeping) lives. Many of these notifications also have another element attached to them, that of a sense of urgency in which to perform the action being requested by the notification. Many will ask for immediate response or action from the end user and are often presented irrespective of their relevance to the current task being completed (Basoglu et al., 2009).

The research by Basoglu et al. (2009) noted a number of key detrimental effects that interruption mediated by smartphones could have on the individual, including:

- a level of mental effort and attention that is hard for the individual to sustain;

- mental resources becoming strictly limited in order to deal with the interrupting task, meaning that if any additional processing requirements come along, they will be postponed or performed poorly;

- broken task flow: the concept of 'flow' is an important concept in the performance of any task and can be equated to the notion of being 'in the zone' – any interruption can severely impact on this aspect of flow, hence reducing the individual's performance on such a task;

- increased time spent engaged on the task: this goes without saying, as when we get interrupted we have to not only complete the interrupting task but also continue with the task we were originally doing. (Basoglu et al., 2009)

According to Sahami Shirazi et al. (2014), one of the key issues with smartphones is that they present a concentration of notifications that are presented through one unified system, rather than being delivered individually by different programs on a computer desktop. They can also come from a wider and broader set of programs, not just limited to elements such as email or instant messaging. For instance, notifications can come from applications linked directly to communication (such as SMS, email and Whatsapp), wider applications linked to e-commerce (such as eBay) and gaming notifications (clash of clans, etc.), and then there are the more generic system notifications (low battery, memory full, messages about software updates). Sahami Shirazi et al. (2014) noted that smartphone users will click on notifications presented on their devices in less than 30 seconds from the point at which they receive them, irrespective of where the notification has come from (e.g. if it is a message or a more generic system notification). The constant presence of the smartphone in nearly every aspect of our daily lives makes such notifications even more invasive, particularly when such devices are nearly always with the owner (Wiese et al., 2013). For example, 79 per cent of those questioned about their daily use of their smartphone said they had their phones on or near them for all but two hours of their working day (Levitas, 2013). In additional work produced by the PEW Internet Research Centre (Smith et al., 2015) it was noted that 57 per cent of respondents reported being distracted by their smartphone in the week preceding being questioned. However, as an additional point it should be noted that 79 per cent of those who responded also noted that their smartphone device had helped them be 'productive', presenting something of a paradox.

Research into interruptions mitigated by smartphone technologies is currently developing at pace, but at the moment there are a limited number of studies exploring such. Amongst some of those studies that have already been conducted, Leiva et al. (2012) explored the impact of interruptions on the actual use of mobile phone applications themselves. They noted that being interrupted whilst using a smartphone application is actually a rare occurrence accounting for approximately 10 per cent of their daily use. However, when individuals are interrupted whilst they are using smartphone applications there is some evidence to suggest this can be disruptive at the very least. The impact is usually manifest in terms of a time delay in the process of completing the primary task. The interruptions manifest whilst using a smartphone can either be from another smartphone application that could be presenting an alert or message or could be the occurrence of a phone call. The research noted that participants were actually very reluctant to switch between applications in order to transfer into the interrupting application, which may be surprising given the widespread assumption that individuals frequently switch between apps. The researchers suggested that this reluctance may be in part due to a fear of losing focus on their current task and the lack of any suitable mechanisms that would guide them back to the point at which they left their previous task (Leiva et al., 2012). Overall the researchers concluded that the cost of being interrupted whilst using a smartphone application can be particularly costly in terms of time, with a four-fold increase in the amount of time it takes to complete a primary task in comparison with a task that is not interrupted.

In other work, researchers have noted the potential for smartphone notifications to be creating symptoms akin to those seen in individuals who have been clinically diagnosed with attention deficit hyperactivity disorder (ADHD). ADHD has been characterised by a set of symptoms that include aspects of inattention, impulsivity and hyperactivity (Castellanos et al., 2006). To date, the root cause of ADHD has been linked to be both structural and neurochemical differences in the brain in those individuals suffering from the disorder in comparison with those not diagnosed (Castellanos et al., 2006). Although researchers such as Kushlev et al. (2016) are keen to stress that digital technology is not *creating* ADHD, they do suggest that random interruptions mitigated by smartphone devices could be producing ADHD-like symptoms in a clinically normal population. In their research, they noted that interruptions from smartphone devices increased two key underlying aspects of the disorder, namely inattention and hyperactivity, in a population that had been screened for ADHD. What also came out of the research by Kushlev et al. (2016) is that most individuals actively increased their susceptibility to these types of interruptions by keeping notifications on and by leaving their smartphones within easy reach. In terms of managing these issues, the authors of this study suggested that actively suppressing notifications could actually create more stress and anxiety. This could in turn increase the frequency of self-motivated interruptions as individuals search out their smartphones to check for messages and other alerts (Kushlev et al., 2016). This would follow a similar process to that of fear of missing out (FoMO) to be discussed in Chapter 11.

Is There a Difference in What Types of Notifications We Pay More Attention To?

A variety of research has explored how quickly we respond to mobile notifications as well as how a perceived level of importance can manipulate our speed for responding. Sahami Shirazi et al. (2014) noted that participants had a shorter response time to notifications they perceived as being personally important. It should be noted that even though this was a significant result, the authors of the study do state that the actual strength of the correlation was weak, indicating that the results are perhaps as not as robust as first assumed. Other results suggest that the user is less likely to block notifications that originate from communication-based applications, these being viewed as being of critical importance. This practice was also found for those applications who had a significant 'social' element attached to their usability, including elements such as calendars and social networking. In contrast, notifications that were generated directly by the system were seen as being of least importance and were the ones most likely to be switched off. End users in this study also noted that where there was a high volume of notifications, their perceived usefulness decreased and the level of annoyance increased as a result.

Other researchers have noted the tendency for individuals to choose what type of notifications we actually receive, which in turn influences how we pay attention to them. Chang and Tang (2015) noted that there are three key purposes associated with changing notification type from ringing to silent and vice versa:

1   to actively avoid unnecessary interruptions (we just want to be alone);

2   to avoid disrupting the environment the individual is in (we don't want other people to be disturbed by the message notification);

3   to still be able to notice important notifications – this is to make important and personally relevant notifications more obvious, especially when the individual might be expecting an important message or call.

The researchers noted that there was no significant difference according to their responsiveness to notifications. Even though the individual may be expecting a message and may attend to the notification (so they know it is there), it does not necessarily mean that they will respond to it immediately. This may appear at odds with other research presented by Sahami Shirazi et al. (2014).

What about These 'Self-Interruptions'?

As was mentioned in a previous section, the lure of digital technology may also be having a wider impact on the potential for individuals to automatically 'self-interrupt' their current activities. A great deal of work has focused on the impact interruptions via external factors can have, but according to other researchers the work examining potential internal factors is somewhat limited (Jin and Dabbish, 2009). A variety of previous research coming from a human–computer interaction background have noted that almost 50 per cent of task-switching activities were actually motivated by the individual themselves rather than being caused by an external source (Czerwinski et al., 2004; González and Mark, 2004; Jin and Dabbish, 2009; Mark et al., 2005). Other researchers have noted that individuals experience approximately 22 disruptions from external sources during the average working day; in contrast, individuals are seen to self-interrupt their workday around about 65 times per day (Wajcman and Rose, 2011). As you can see, the notion that digital technology is always the instigator behind interruptions to our daily working life may be a little bit erroneous.

Of particular interest, particularly from a productivity perspective, is the finding that those tasks that are self-interrupted are a lot less likely to be resumed in comparison with those that were initiated by an external force (Mark et al., 2005). This tendency for individuals to make a sudden decision to halt the primary task in favour of a secondary one has been more technically termed 'discretionary task interleaving' (Payne et al., 2007). These authors viewed this process as being a self-initiated switch away from a current primary task in favour of another prior to its completion. Although not firmly stated in the research literature in this area, it could be the case that digital technology is presenting the individual with a wider set of opportunities to engage in self-initiated shifts in favour of other, more attractive activities outside of their primary task focus.

Jin and Dabbish (2009) presented an interesting piece of research that aimed to detail the key reasons as to why people engage in self-interrupts whilst using computer technology, alongside the potential positives and negatives for them. These seven typologies for self-interruptions are presented in Table 7.1.

This research by Jin and Dabbish further noted that the use of self-interruptions such as inquiries, breaks and adjustments could facilitate performance on the primary task. These types of self-interruptions actually help the individual find valuable additional information, or change environmental work factors to enhance productivity.

In the context of the cyber-related activities, Dabbish et al. (2011) explored self-interruptions in the context of high-tech organisations. They examined over 900 hours of task-switching activities from 36 individuals, noting that in the

Table 7.1 The typology of self-interruptions on the computer

Self-Interruption Typology	Description	Potential Positives	Potential Negatives
Adjustment	The individual halts work on a primary task in an attempt to improve/change an element of the work environment. This could perhaps be finding a better working position, changing the location of the computer on the desk or altering the height of a chair.	The interruption could result in an increased level of productivity as a direct result of the improved comfort afforded by the adjustment that has been made.	If the individual decides to cease an activity to change one element of their work environment this could lead to an unexpected delay in the completion of the primary task. Additionally, where the adjustment takes more time than was initially expected this could lead to the individual abandoning the primary task completely. Similarly, if we fail to sufficiently improve our personal workspace, Jin and Dabbish suggested that this could in itself lead to feelings of frustration and stress.
Break	The individual initiates a temporary switch from their primary task to one that offers a more enjoyable or desirable experience as a direct consequence of experiencing frustration or boredom with the current primary task.	The interruption leads to the potential for a reduction in stress and fatigue whilst also increasing the level of mental stimulation the individual experiences – this could in turn result in a level of improved performance on the primary task, as well as introducing an improvement in the mood of the individual.	As with the previous type of self-interruption, this one also leads to a delay in the completion of the primary task. It could also lead to a level of procrastination where the individual fails to actually re-engage with the primary task and spends more time doing the more attractive task. There are also those switching costs attached to such a process where the individual has to re-engage with the original task after they have swapped over to the more stimulating task.

Self-Interruption Typology	Description	Potential Positives	Potential Negatives
Inquiry	The individual seeks out some additional information that adds support or context to the completion of the primary task.	This self-interruption would appear to have some obvious advantages as the individual gains additional information that helps them to complete their primary task, but this is only a positive when the additional information is relevant and easy to locate.	Engaging in the secondary information-gathering exercise leads the individual to delay the completion of the primary task. This can be further exacerbated when the required additional information is hard to find, and where this does happen re-engagement in the primary task might become increasingly difficult.
Recollection	During the execution of a primary task the individual remembers that they have another completely unrelated task to be done.	This process prevents the 'remembered' task from being lost or forgotten in the future, and can in turn create a sense of accomplishment for the individual.	Once the individual remembers one forgotten task there is the potential for the process to turn into a cascade, where the person continues to remember other forgotten tasks. This in turn means that it will be harder for the individual to re-engage and focus on the primary task they interrupted.
Routine	This is related to a process of ceasing the primary task in order to perform another by way of habit or as part of a learned sequence. This could, for example, be logging onto an email system before beginning the primary task in the morning, even though the email system has no relevance to the current task in hand.	This self-interruption presents a positive in terms of the automation of work flow based on both experience and expertise, meaning less cognitive resources have to be devoted towards more trivial activities.	As a consequence of engaging in other, non-essential activities outside of the primary task the individual diverts mental resources away from the main task. This could in turn have a detrimental impact on the completion of the primary task, especially when it is particularly taxing or cognitively demanding.

(Continued)

Table 7.1 (Continued)

Self-Interruption Typology	Description	Potential Positives	Potential Negatives
Trigger	Some form of stimulus serves to trigger a change to a new but related task.	This self-interruption can lead to the potential for new discovery and new information that may otherwise have not been found or developed. For example, this could be developing a new project idea after following up a piece of research that you have found during research for an essay.	The downside for this mechanism is that it could actually lead to further self-interruptions, meaning that the individual may find it increasingly hard to re-engage with the primary task.
Wait	The individual actively fills time with an additional task when there is an unexpected 'block' or delay in being able to perform the primary task – perhaps a lack of information that is time-dependent or maybe the dreaded 'technical failure' which means the Internet is unavailable for an eternity (five minutes is usually sufficient!).	An obvious positive for this type of self-interruption means that the individual isn't idle whilst they are waiting to resume the primary task, so in turn is serving to maximise their productivity.	There is again a significant period of delay in the resumption of the primary task whilst the individual is waiting for the block to be removed. This could be further exacerbated where the individual has grossly under-estimated the waiting time needed; in some cases, where this waiting time becomes excessive the individual may fail to resume the primary task.

Source: Jin and Dabbish (2009: 1083)

office-based environment there was a 64 per cent increase in the level of self-interruptions. Individuals were more likely to return to a central sphere of activity, or something that they had sole responsibility for, by implementing a self-interruption. They were also highly likely to use self-interruptions to return to a solitary mode of working, indicating they use these mechanisms to allow them to focus directly on their own work. A further interesting point was that when an individual experiences an external interruption in the preceding hours they significantly increase their chances of initiating a self-interruption in the subsequent hour. Rosen et al. (2011, 2013) also noted findings related to task switching and the impact on education, and these will be discussed in more detail in Chapter 8.

Interruptions from Email Use and Instant Messaging

Many researchers have noted the pervasiveness of email in our daily lives, not only from the perspective of work but also in our personal lives. Emails can distract the individual from the current task that they are engaged in with an additional requirement to process information that may not be related directly to the current task (Zelikovich, 2011). In a report by Ofcom 2016) it was noted that sending emails was the most common activity for adult Internet users to engage in, with 75 per cent of those questioned having done this in the preceding week. In early work by Jackson et al. (2001, 2002) they noted that it took an individual an average of 1 minute and 44 seconds to react to an email notification, with this being indicated by someone actually opening up the email. They further noted that 70 per cent of emails are reacted to within six seconds of them arriving; 85 per cent of emails are reacted to within two minutes of arriving. So it would appear that for the majority of the time, most individuals are reacting to email notifications almost instantaneously, irrespective of the task that they are currently engaged in. The research also noted that for the majority of individuals set their email clients to check for new emails within a five-minute cycle rather than individuals setting themselves a set time to check and deal with them in one period. Czerwinski et al. (2004) presented a surprising finding that only 3 per cent of those interruptions reported were due to an email message alert or reminder, with a staggering 40 per cent of interruptions being due to self-interruptions where individuals actually chose to cease their primary task in favour of checking their emails. In terms of the actual cost associated with email interruptions it was noted that it took an average of 64 seconds for the individual to re-engage in their original work task at the same speed prior to the interruption taking place (Jackson et al., 2002).

In more recent work (Marulanda-Carter and Jackson, 2012) the impact of email interruptions were explored within a work-based environment. As a secondary objective, they also explore the suggestion made by previous research that individuals may present a tendency to be addicted to email. For example, widely reported research from a study conducted by AOL (Gifford, 2008) noted that 17 per cent of respondents could not go one day without access to their email, and 23 per cent checked their emails first thing in the morning after waking. Hair et al. (2007) also noted that individuals would voluntarily and regularly change their current activity to check for new emails, as well as continue with this behaviour throughout the rest of the day. Marulanda-Carter and Jackson (2012) make the critical point that email presents perhaps one of the best reinforcement schedules for rewarding behaviours that are of variable interval level. For this schedule of reinforcement, the period of reward varies and isn't always guaranteed; sometimes we might get an email we really, really wanted (perhaps a message from a loved one or a payment refund), but this might be interjected by other messages that we really didn't want (e.g. a spam PPI message that has spelt your name wrong). Previous work has noted that 56 per cent of employees spent in excess of two hours in their email inbox (although it does not directly state what they were doing in there!) (Marulanda-Carter and Jackson, 2012)

The results from Marulanda-Carter and Jackson's work showed that the time cost for handling an interruption from an email was 116.5 seconds, noted to be in excess of the 90 seconds that was previously suggested by Jackson et al. (2002). In addition, the researchers noted that 15 per cent of those questioned were classified as being addicted to email as demonstrated through a number of behavioural markers. These markers included elements such as checking emails on an hourly basis and opening up email clients before doing anything else, essentially showing a preoccupation with checking emails above all other work-related activities.

The impact of interruptions presented by instant messaging (IM) systems was the focus of further work by Gupta et al. (2013). IM systems are widely used, and perhaps more commonly so in the US with 90 per cent of organisations based in the northern US using some form of IM (Gupta et al., 2013). The focus of the study was to examine how social dynamics within the organisation served to influence the level of disruption experienced by the employee when they were interrupted by an IM. The researchers suggested that the level of disruption and the speed at which the individual responds to the IM would be directly related to the position of the sender within the hierarchy of the organisation; the higher up the sender was in the organisation, the quicker the response.

The results from the study by Gupta et al. (2013) demonstrated that interruptions from IM produced a clear reduction in the overall quality of work being produced as well as increasing the perceived overall workload the individual was experiencing. They also noted that the position of the sender in relation to the receiver within the social network of the organisation also had a dramatic impact on the time it took to complete the primary task. When the message sender was from within the individual's peer group, the interruption experienced as a result of receiving the IM significantly increased the time taken to complete the primary task; in contrast, the total time to complete the primary task was significantly reduced when the message sender was seen as being more senior in the organisation. Gupta et al. (2013) suggested that there is an underlying heuristic element to this process that is activated when the individual sender of the IM is seen as being more senior, thus giving priority to completing the primary task whilst also being able to deal with the interruption. In the case of the IM coming from a peer, such a strategy appears not to be activated, which explains why it takes the individual longer to complete the primary task in the presence of the interruption. It should also be noted that the implementation of the heuristic strategy might also come at a cost, and the reduction in completion time for the primary task might also lead to errors creeping into the task as well.

How Can We Stop Ourselves Being Interrupted?

Researchers have suggested a variety of strategies in order to help individuals deal with interruptions from digital technology and email notifications. Marulanda-Carter et al. (2012) suggested the creation of 'email schedules' in order to mitigate the impact of being constantly interrupted by emails throughout the working day. One of these mechanisms would be to create a realistic routine for checking emails throughout the day, with the authors suggesting perhaps three times per day. They also make the suggestion that this should occur at specific times in the day (perhaps at 9 a.m., 1 p.m. and just before the end of the working day). Gupta et al. (2011) also made the suggestion that the best way to deal with emails is to respond either two or four times daily rather than in 45-minute cycles or on a continuous basis. Marulanda-Carter et al. (2012) also suggest that individuals seek to limit the amount of time they spend dealing with emails in any one session, with an upper limit of 30 minutes being proposed. Finally, the researchers noted the disruptive influence of emails could be further mitigated by creating a series of specific tasks that have to be completed during each of the scheduled time periods – so, for example, in the first session emails are simply read, with no further actions being taken. In the second session emails may be chosen and replied to, with the final session being reserved for the sending and filing of emails. The suggestions do present a logical approach to dealing with the interruptions presented by emails, but they do, however, rely upon the individual to self-impose these scheduling techniques. In addition, if the individual is applying such mechanisms by themselves, one person doing so in isolation could perhaps cause wider issues when others in the organisation are pushed to reply to emails in a time-critical manner. Research by Soucek and Moser (2010) noted a significant decrease in measures of email-related strain and work impairment after employees had engaged in a period of training. Such a strategy could be an effective approach for helping office workers deal with the daily information overload presented by endless email traffic. Consequently there is the potential for effective training sessions to provide useful strategies for reducing the overall cognitive load on the individual worker (Soucek and Moser, 2010).

Summary

As we have seen, the modern digital environment offers a plethora of mechanisms through which the individual can be interrupted. On the one hand, we have the ever-present smartphone devices that inhabit nearly every part of our waking day (and for some are present during their sleep as well). These devices are omnipresent, and the notifications that they spew forth appear at random, without warning, and place a great deal of pressure on us to respond. This process diverts our attention away from the current task we are focusing on, but also means that we may find it a lot harder to resume that primary task once we have dealt with the interruption.

Importantly it is becoming more apparent that it may not just be digital devices that are to blame for interruptions in our daily lives, and there is a bigger culprit at large – ourselves. The work presented on self-initiated interruptions, particularly for those engaged in computer-related activities, shows that there are a number of reasons why individuals will choose to self-interrupt. Some of these mechanisms can be beneficial to the individual, and may provide them with much needed information that will help them complete their primary task. However, other forms of self-interruption can lead the individual to become inherently sidetracked, perhaps engaged in a cascade of activities that lead them further and further away from their current primary task.

Email is viewed as a ubiquitous tool, not only in our work lives but also for personal communications. The potential for us to react and respond to emails almost instantaneously means that it offers another mechanism for us to be interrupted. Researchers have shown that being interrupted via email notifications cannot only impact on the time it takes to complete the primary task, but also influence our chances of actually re-engaging with that primary task in the first instance. A variety of methods have been suggested in order to mitigate the impact that interruptions via email have on our productivity, as well as aiming to reduce the potential for stress and information overload from such systems.

8

TECHNOLOGY AND EDUCATION

Key Learning Objectives

- To explore the impact digital technology can have upon learning and academic outcomes;

- to examine how the use of social networking sites can both enhance and also detract from the learning experience;

- to focus on the invasion of digital technology into learning contexts and how this may be impacting on learning;

- to discuss the possible implications of this research and what it could mean for teaching in the context of the digital age.

Overview

The literature surrounding the impact of newer forms of digital technology on aspects of education presents something of a mixed bag when it comes to making firm conclusions. Much of this research has been mapped onto the belief that those in the digital native generation are adopting different learning styles based on their use of technology. Similarly, there is a growing moral panic on the behalf of educators and parents alike that the use of digital technology is having a detrimental impact on the capacity for students to focus on their studies. This process is said to be having a knock-on effect on their capacity to retain key pieces of information, hence impacting on academic grades.

On the one hand we have researchers who are extolling the virtues of integrating technology within the learning environment so that students can be fully immersed in education. On the other, there is contradictory evidence that technology use in the classroom and lecture-based environments can have a detrimental impact on learning and education attainment. It should be noted that much of this research focuses on individuals aged 12–18 (Alloway et al., 2013). As highlighted previously, this developmental period is linked directly to a variety of structural changes in the brain that impact on aspects such as executive control and motivation (Choudhury and McKinney, 2013). Therefore making any clear links between the use of technology and its impact on learning during this period should be tentative at the most. The results may not be directly associated with the impact of technology and could most likely be confounded by these significant developmental changes.

Research has noted that student engagement can easily be impacted on by the use of social networking technology. For instance, Bliuc (2010) noted that the use of discussion boards was heavily associated with a process of answer finding, which in turn encouraged a surface reproduction of existing material rather than actually completing the task that has been set. This had the knock-on effect of limiting the level of deeper learning that also resulted in a lower final course grade. Distance learning conducted through the use of virtual learning environments has also come under scrutiny. Sapp and Simon (2005) noted that students enrolled in distance learning often failed to complete the course, and that where they did, they received lower overall grades in comparison to those who received the same course through face-to-face teaching. Furthermore, Weatherly et al. (2003) noted that students who were supplied with lecture slides via a learning management system (e.g. Blackboard) had lower exam results in comparison with a control group who took normal paper and pencil notes. The authors suggested that this could be also linked to a lack of engagement related to attendance issues, a point that could also be limitations in the transferral of tacit and implicit knowledge (e.g. Özdemir, 2008). Further research by Grabe and Christopherson (2005) explored the pattern of access for online notes and examination performance, presenting a contrast to the findings from Weatherly et al. (2003). They showed that students who frequently accessed notes online performed better in examinations, and students who attended classes were the most consistent in their use of such a facility. This suggests that those students who are achieving higher grades are using online notes as a supplementary resource rather than as a replacement for lecture attendance.

For the most part much of the research that has been conducted into the impact of newer forms of technology on learning can be grouped under two very broad headings. The first of these looks at the impact social networking use has upon academic performance, whilst the second directly explores the impact of technology such as smartphones, mobile phones and laptops on the retention of information. In this chapter we will be exploring the research that has been presented under both these categories to see the potential benefits and pitfalls of each.

The Changing Face of Education in the Light of New Technology

Kolikant (2010) presented a series of ideas based on original work by Wertsch (1998) that serves to provide a background for exploring how individuals from different generations engage with new tools. Such work is easily extended to the use of digital media and technology, and serves to highlight the current issues we are facing when introducing such into the realm of education. According to Wertsch, when we encounter a new tool there is a phase of exploration in which the individual tests its capacity, for example what it is and what it can be used for. As time progresses, both our understanding and use of this tool develops. In the context of the Internet and digital media the way in which we use these is constantly evolving. This process of evolution is driven by our understanding of how we can use technology, but also by how such practices are accepted as valid uses for such tools. For instance, Kolikant suggested that the Internet does not just present us with a mechanism for collecting data and information but can also fundamentally changes the actions of the user. More specifically, the Internet does not change just the way in which we learn, but also the values we attach to that learning process in terms of what is 'good' and what is 'bad' (Turkle and Papert, 1992). This process is best demonstrated through what Turkle and Papert (1992) termed 'bricolage', which has become a legitimate way of learning in the context of the net generation. Bricolage is a French word that essentially means 'do-it-yourself', and in the context of work is seen as taking things that are currently available to create a separate project or piece of work. Rather than learning being seen as a logical and systematic exploration of key facts and concepts, in turn leading to greater understanding and a wider synthesis of newer ideas, bricolage is seen more as 'tinkering'. This tinkering process involves a trial and error approach to problem solving, essentially akin to finding elements that will work (Kolikant, 2010) What does this mean for the process of learning? Well, essentially it means that individuals are less likely to establish the fundamental elements of knowledge and remember facts and information. Instead, people are remembering the tools, resources or mechanisms they are using to piece together answers to questions or complete tasks – so rather than recalling information, individuals may recall the website to go to in order to get this information (Sparrow et al., 2011).

Social Networking and Educational Attainment

In initial research presented by Kirschner and Karpinski (2010) the results they reported showed that non-Facebook users achieved a higher overall grade than those who did use Facebook. These results were interpreted as highlighting a capacity for those using Facebook to engage in higher levels of procrastination, in turn suffering from poorer time-management skills. The use of Facebook is essentially seen to facilitate the capacity for individuals to engage in an activity that isn't their primary task, hence leading to less time being devoted to academic study. There is a chance that this process could be intrinsically linked to individual differences in attentional control (Kirschner and Karpinski, 2010), a notion that further highlights the difficulty for researchers attempting to pinpoint the influence technology is having on learning. Junco and Cotten (2011, 2012) also noted that those students who spent more time using information or communication technologies such as Facebook or instant messaging whilst doing their homework reported lower overall Grade Point Average (or GPA).

In later research Alloway et al. (2013) an opposing view was presented, that the use of social networking sites (SNS) such as Facebook could actually be linked to improvements in key cognitive skills. They found that participants who reported using Facebook on a regular basis actually scored better on testing of working memory, verbal ability and spelling. The research however failed to note any significant difference for skills related to mathematics. The improvement in tests of verbal ability were best predicted by the frequency with which the individual was seen to be checking their friends' status updates. So why should this be the case? Well the researchers suggested that exploring and interacting with Facebook shares a variety of similarities to tasks associated with those used in a working memory experiments. For example, the individual is presented with a wide variety of both visual and verbal information that they are required to decode and manipulate. This manipulation is critical if the individual is to make sense of that environment and the information that is presented within it, and requires the integration of data from across both modalities. The individual may also be required to present an output (which may be a 'like' or a response to a post) or a need to store information for later use (Alloway et al., 2013). Such a process is representative of all the elements subsumed by working memory, where there is a need for integration of verbal and visual information using aspects of executive control. In terms of the improvement in verbal skills for high users of Facebook, Alloway et al. (2013) suggested the existence of a potential 'training effect'. This would come about as those individuals engaged in more frequent communication are developing and honing these core skills. Second, there could also be an element of self-efficacy and social comparison at work in the context of this study; as individuals are communicating with peers and those who they respect (so therefore they want to look good in front of them), they may wish to display a degree of competency at least on a level with their peers.

The use of SNS has also been linked to the concept of student engagement, this being defined as 'the quality and quantity of the physical and psychological energy that students invest', predominantly in their academic experience

(Astin, 1984: 528). Pascarella and Terenzini (2005) noted that increased levels of student engagement lead to a residual increase in academic performance. Those students who were more engaged in their educational activities had better grades and also displayed a higher degree of persistence towards the point of graduation. Additional research in this area noted a positive correlation for SNS use and the level of engagement presented by students in their academic work. Studies have also noted that those students who engaged in more-frequent SNS use were using them to facilitate their offline relationships rather than as a substitute for offline interactions (Jacobsen and Forste, 2011; Junco, 2011). Higher-frequency SNS users also engaged in daily interactions with individuals they knew offline, thereby creating stronger interpersonal connections (Junco and Cotten, 2011; Junco et al., 2011). This work is echoed by research conducted by Junco (2012a), who also noted that time spent on Facebook was positively correlated to students' engagement in extra-curricular activities outside of those being purely academic in nature. Junco (2012b), however, noted in addition that the time spent on Facebook served as a negative predictor for overall grades. This was in contrast to time spent checking the status updates of friends and sharing links, which was shown to be a positive predictor for overall final grades. The assertions made here is that more time spent on Facebook leads to less time for the student to engage in academic study. Frequency of checking and posting may be a brief, time-limited activity, which in turn could be linked to the earlier findings by Alloway et al. (2013) on practice effects.

Digital Technology, Multitasking and the Teaching Environment: A Force for Good?

Research into effective learning has previously noted that the efficient deployment of attention plays a critical role in the retention of material for later recall (Hidi, 1995; Posner and Rothbart, 2005; Reynolds, 1992; Wilson and Korn, 2007). When a situation arises where attention is diverted away from the main focus of the learning, then such information is at risk of not being remembered. The rise of the use of digital technology within educational contexts has been linked to aspects of inattention and distraction in students. Kessler (2002) noted that 73 per cent of college students (from a sample of 500) stated that they were unable to study without some form of technology, with a further 38 per cent also saying that they were unable to go at least ten minutes without checking their smartphone or tablet device for updates and messages.

As we have already noted in Chapter 6, the research on multitasking shows that people are inherently poor at attending to multiple inputs of information or doing two tasks at once (Pashler and Johnston, 1998). It is generally accepted that some form of performance deficit will occur when we are required to carry out two tasks at the same time (Pashler and Johnston, 1998; Pashler et al., 2001). In terms of the impact multitasking can have upon individuals in an educational context, the findings don't present a good picture for those who like to sit in lectures thinking about their dinner. For instance, Junco and Cotten (2011) noted that those students who used instant messaging whilst studying reported a detrimental impact on their capacity to focus on their work. Furthermore, Wood et al. (2012) explored the use of Facebook during lectures and noted that those students who used it during lectures had lower test scores on lecture material than those students who did not. Ravizza et al. (2014) also noted a significant impact on academic performance when the Internet was used in academic settings for non-academic purposes. Their research showed that those individuals who reported frequently using the Internet for activities such as being on Facebook whilst being engaged in classes reported lower exam scores.

Risko et al. (2013) presented a number of theoretical possibilities as to why multitasking has such a detrimental impact on learning:

- *The resource competition account*: Essentially we are gifted with a set of cognitive resources (think of these in terms of tools) that cannot be shared across different tasks. Therefore tasks must be completed *sequentially* rather than *simultaneously*. Imagine that you are trying to build a piece of flat-pack furniture and need to use a screwdriver, but your housemate/ friend/partner already has the screwdriver (and you only have one) – in order to complete the current task you have to wait for the screwdriver to become 'free'. This is the same process with resource competition, but with cognitive skills rather than screwdrivers. This means that if we are engaged in non-lecture-based activities whilst also trying to attend to the lecture, competition for the same resource will arise and there will be a residual cost.

- *The interleaving approach*: This is the capacity that is afforded to individuals that allows them to choose which tasks are completed based upon the perception of an optimal point of timing. It should be noted that even though interleaving may take place, there is no guarantee that this will automatically lead to successful task completion. Risko et al. (2013) further defined the notion of *efficient interleaving*, in which participants may be able to selectively attend to the most important parts of the lecture and then redirect attention elsewhere when they view the cost of not paying attention as being minimal. So, for example, we may pay attention in the lecture when the instructor is saying something about exams and the types of topics that might crop up. Once this material has been presented and the more 'boring' information about writing references in a report comes in, the individual may switch off and daydream about what they are having for dinner. What this means in real terms is that there will be a reduction in the amount of attention that is being paid to the lecture, but theoretically there should be no real impact on the loss of key points mentioned in the lecture.

- *The absorption account*: Risko et al. (2013) noted that individuals actually spend 40 per cent of their time during lectures engaged in mind wandering when they are not presented with a secondary task. This in turn would suggest that students are not devoting 100 per cent of their attentional resources to a task that essentially constitutes one task. In this case we could theoretically add to an existing task by taking up the 40 per cent currently being used for mind wandering with non-lecture-related activities (e.g. email or texting). This would mean that there would have to be a reduction in mind wandering (which is absorbed into the additional task) but there should be no additional cost (in terms of errors or loss of information).

- *The enhanced arousal account*: There is an opposing perspective that actually engaging in an additional activity may improve the retention of information. Previous work by Andrade (2009) noted that adding an irrelevant task for participants to do whilst they were performing a sustained attention task actually improved performance on it in comparison to performing the task by itself. The suggestion here is that adding the extra task increases the level of arousal in the individual to a level that is 'optimal', which thus results in a facilitation effect for the primary task. This premise has some basis in previous research, with findings noting that presenting task-irrelevant information can actually lead to an enhancement in performance in the primary task (Broadbent, 1971; Risko et al., 2013).

Risko et al. (2013) noted findings consistent with the resource competition account. Those participants who were based in a laptop access condition were asked to answer a number of emails or respond to updates on Facebook. Overall, these participants paid less attention to the lecture (hence this is competition for the resource of attention) and performed poorly in a test of lecture material. This key piece of research again reiterates the difficulty that is posed for those attempting to multitask in an education environment. There is a residual issue associated with the increased availability and use of digital technology at all levels of education. If differences do exist between individuals and their capacity to perform two tasks at once (e.g. Cain and Mitroff, 2011; Ophir et al., 2009) this could mean that employing digital technology as part of a learning environment may disadvantage some students.

Closely aligned to the research into multitasking are the findings linked to task switching and its impact on education. A variety of researchers have showed that the practice of task switching could have a direct impact on learning and retention of information. Marci (2012) compared two groups of participants according to their uptake of digital technology and their propensity to task switch. In the late adopters' group they switched between tasks approximately 17 times per hour in comparison with 27 times per hour for the early adopters. In research by Rosen et al. (2013) they found that for most students in their study, on-task behaviour was maintained for less than six minutes before switching to another task during a 15-minute observation period. This difficulty in sustained attention was related directly to distractions from technology, such as accessing Facebook or watching television. In terms of preferences for task switching, those individuals who were in a technology-rich environment and had more technology within their reach demonstrated a higher preference for task switching rather than focusing on one single task. Similarly, those who demonstrated a preference for task switching also exhibited shortened attention spans during their study periods, again highlighting the potential link between this aspect of cognition and learning. The researchers also noted an interesting trend for participants to have potentially pre-loaded their working environment with a plethora of technology so that they were able to engage in potentially distracting task-switching behaviours. This would indicate a clear intention to engage in task switching even before the actual study period has been entered into, which seems to hint towards a dispositional element for this type of behaviour. Once again it was noted that those who were checking SNS during their study period were also linked to a lower overall score on their final GPA.

Digital Technology and Learning

Kessler (2011) noted that in a sample of 500 students, 73 per cent were unable to study without some form of technology. In the same sample, 38 per cent reported not being able to go ten minutes without checking their smartphone for new messages and updates, while 64 per cent of the students in Lenhar's (2010) study admitted to texting in class, even in instances where mobile phones were actively banned in those environments. Rosen et al. (2011) also explored the impact of getting interrupted during a lecture in which participants were sent a number of text messages to which they had to respond. They found that those who received and interacted with text messages performed worse on a post-lecture test of content versus a control group who did not receive any messages. Wei et al. (2012) also

explored the impact of texting during lessons and found evidence of reduced attention in the classroom. From this initial exploration of research it would appear that
the use of mobile phones within the classroom again link to the capacity-based
discussion, and engaging in texting during a session could be impacting on the
individuals' capacity to listen effectively (Kuznekoff and Titsworth, 2013). As
we have seen in Chapter 6, mobile phones can have a key impact on other skilled
tasks, in particular that of driving, so the potential link to an impact in education
is not an extreme leap of faith.

Kuznekoff and Titsworth (2013) randomly assigned participants to three groups.
In the low distraction group, participants received a simulated text or SNS notification once every 60 seconds. In the high distraction group they received the same types
of notifications but had these once every 30 seconds. In quantitative terms, those in
the high distraction group viewed approximately 24 texts or posts and those in the
low distraction group viewed approximately 12. There was also a control group that
received no such text messages during the lecture. All this took place in the context
of a 12-minute lecture that explored a variety of key theoretical concepts from psychology. The results present quite a startling eye opener, particularly when we think
about how students are using digital technology in the context of their studies. The
control group scored the higher on a post-lecture multiple-choice test, followed by
the low distraction group and then the high distraction group. There was a significant
difference in terms of the scores between the control and the high distraction group,
and the researchers presented a critical discussion point. Once the scores were con-
verted into a percentage, the control group had an average score of 66 per cent, with
the high distraction group presenting an average score of 52 per cent. In the context
of most UK universities this is a difference in classification of a high 2:1 and a low
2:2. Food for thought for all those back-row text-senders who think they can attend a
session and while away their time sending messages to their friends!

Kuznekoff and Titsworth (2013) also noted another critical difference according
to the level of detail contained within the notes taken from the lecture and the level
of distraction presented to that group. Kuzenkoff and Titsworth highlight previous
research which showed that most students typically recall just 40 per cent of the
information that has been presented in a lecture, leaving a vast 60 per cent being
unaccounted for (Kiewra, 1984). For the experimental groups in Kuznekoff and
Titsworth's (2013) study, they found that whereas the control group recalled around
about 33 per cent of the detail contained within the lecture, the low distraction group
recalled 27 per cent and the high distraction group just 20 per cent.

There are some critical limitations for this research, however, with Kruashaar
and Novak (2010) presenting an argument that if the use of technology is linked
directly to the context of the course, this could actually be helpful to learning. This doesn't, however, get away from other extraneous texting that might

be going on, particularly when smartphones have become the ubiquitous tool of choice for most students in terms of social and educational communication. There are other key limitations here, and the research by Kuznekoff and Titsworth (2013) had a particularly small sample of just 47 participants who were split into three groups. Although they fulfilled the necessary requirements in terms of conducting the key statistical test, there is ample room for engaging in wider research with a larger sample size. Similarly, the use of simulated text messages that are not directly relevant to the participants' interest could have also had an impact on the level of engagement. Individuals may be more likely to view a text message and respond if they have a vested interest in that particular message. Finally, the lecture used only lasted for 12 minutes and contained a variety of complex ideas that were presented in a very short space of time. For most undergraduate students lectures typically last in the region of 50 minutes, and although they contain a variety of key theories or topics, these will be less condensed, which could in turn allow for better retention rates even when information has been missed through inattention.

Does Internet Use Impact on Academic Performance?

A variety of research has been presented in order to assess the impact that both use and abuse of the Internet can have on the individual's academic performance. Amongst some of the earlier research, the focus was very much on the impact excessive levels of Internet use had on academic attainment, with the general consensus being that the increased amount of time being spent online led individuals to suffer from sleep disturbances (Brenner, 1997; Cheung and Wong, 2011; Choi et al., 2009). Although the link is often not explicitly made, it has been suggested that these disturbances could in turn contribute to poor academic performance, with individuals experiencing fatigue and poor attentional focus during the school day (Hazelhurst et al., 2011). For example, Chou and Hsiao (2000) noted that those who were classified as Internet-addicted were more negatively impacted in their daily life routines, including sleep and classes. Early research by Kubey et al. (2001) also noted that those who were classified in a 'heavy recreational Internet use' group had impaired academic performance. This excessive Internet use was also linked to individuals staying up later, missing classes, as well as experiencing fatigue during the day. Impaired academic performance in this initial study was linked more directly with the use of synchronous mechanisms of communication such as chat rooms or IM rather than through the use of email. Later work by Chen and Peng (2008) explored the influence of students' Internet use on a variety of measures, including their interpersonal relationships, self-evaluation and academic performance. They found significant differences in academic achievement between those spending greater than 33 hours per week on the Internet (classified as heavy or excessive users of the Internet) and those who reported spending less time online. Those who fell into the 'non-heavy' Internet-use group reported better grades and expressed a better level of satisfaction with their learning compared with the heavy Internet-use group.

Some researchers have noted that much of the previous research exploring the impact of the Internet on academic attainment has been based on students' perceptions of academic attainment rather than actual academic grades (Englander et al., 2010). Englander et al. (2010) noted that previous research in the area had focused more on whether or not students 'believed' the use of the Internet had a positive or negative impact on their academic work. In order to counter this criticism, the research by Englander et al. (2010) noted a statistically significant relationship between the number of hours the student was spending online and their examination performance in an end of course test. Those individuals who reported spending more time on the Internet were more likely to receive lower grades, again suggesting there is a link between higher levels of Internet use and academic attainment. Work by Hazelhurst et al. (2011) highlighted the relationship between both Internet use and SNS use on academic performance quite succinctly. They classified individuals as either heavy or light users of the Internet as determined by the amount of data they were downloading over the period of the first half of the academic year. Those in the heavy users' group performed more poorly as measured through their average grades than those classified as light users. Moreover, those in the heavy-usage group were associated with higher failure rates, significantly more than those in the light Internet-use group. There was also a statistically significant difference according to the average mark of those classified as very heavy Internet users and very light users, with those in the first group having an average mark of 50.4 per cent and those in the latter group having an average mark of 54 per cent. Whilst such a difference may, on the face of it, appear to be a trivial 4 per cent, if this difference was on the edge of a degree banding it could mean the difference between a 2:2 and a 2:1.

Hazelhurst et al. (2011) also examined whether the time of day for browsing activities had a direct impact on academic performance. They noted that for those individuals choosing to browse in a typically asocial period (between the hours of 11 p.m. and 7 a.m.), academic performance was significantly impacted. Again, as hinted earlier, the potential link here is between individuals experiencing fatigue and poorer capacity to concentrate on study-related activities as a result of sleep disturbance.

Hypertext and Hypermedia

There is another aspect of the digital environment that can directly impact the way in which we experience information and in turn the way in which we learn. Much of the information that we experience on the web is usually presented on a variety of levels using a mixture of images and hypermedia. For the purposes of this discussion, I am using the term 'hypermedia' to refer to a webpage that consists of multiple types of visual and auditory stimulation.

Figure 8.1 An adequate example of hypertext taken from a Wikipedia page outlining what Hypertext is!

These types of environments place a number of requirements on the individual. They may require some level of interaction as well as the requirement to make a number of decisions based on the content that is contained within. As a learning environment, it has been noted that such environments may increase the cognitive load the user experiences in contrast to processing more traditional, linear forms of text.

Lee and Tedder (2003) examined the impact individual differences in working memory capacity could have upon the use of such hypermedia environments. The researchers proposed that if hypermedia environments place additional demands on our information processing capabilities, then differences in such capacity should be reflected in performance. For instance, those who have greater working memory capacity should (in theory) be less affected by the hypermedia environment as they are capable of distributing the load better, whereas those with lower capacity will have limited resources, therefore demonstrating more distractibility (Smart, 2010). Lee and Tedder (2003) split students into two groups according to their working memory capacity and asked them to navigate through a variety of web-based environments. Their results demonstrated that for those who fell into the low working memory capacity group, recall from a hypermedia environment akin to an actual website was lower than their capacity to recall information from standard linear text. This research is important as it actually demonstrates that our capacity to interact with online environments, such as those rich in media, is more specifically governed by our own inherent cognitive capacity. To put this simply, those of us who have lower working memory capacity are actually limiting the amount of information we are taking in from such environments, missing out on elements that those with higher working memory are experiencing.

It has also been noted that the use of hypertext can also impact on our ability to interact with and integrate new pieces of information from the digital environment. Hypertext is embedded in the vast majority of websites and gives users the opportunity to access new or associated information from within the body of text they are currently reading (DeStefano and LeFevre, 2007). However, as DeStefano and LeFevre (2007) and Smart (2010) pointed out, the flexibility that is afforded by the use of such a mechanism could be a source of increased cognitive load. Crucially, particularly in the context of our current discussion, it appears that being presented with and using hypertext presents a potential for processing that is seen as being more cognitively demanding as opposed to the reading of normal linear text (DeStefano and LeFevre, 2007).

DeStefano and LeFevre (2007) suggested that the use of hypertext-based environments engages an aspect of the cognitive system that has been termed 'dual-processing' (Baddeley and Logie, 1999). In its simplest form, dual-processing refers to the level at which performance becomes impaired on two tasks due to the number of cognitive resources they simultaneously share at the same time (DeStefano and LeFevre, 2007; Wickens, 2002). For the example of engaging in a hypertext environment, the individual is required to engage in spatial navigation (not only on the page but also between webpages), the comprehension of information as well as remembering their current position in webspace or text. In the instance where a concurrent task requires the user to manipulate or remember other complex spatial information, resources already deployed on interacting with the hypertext will have to be redirected. According to DeStefano and LeFevre (2007) this process would therefore result in a decrease in task performance, both on the concurrent task and the comprehension of hypertext.

DeStefano and LeFevre's (2007) research aimed to explore the suggestion that our capacity to successfully interact with hypertext is partly related to the number of structural links that are embedded within it. The researchers hypothesised that the level of disruption users experience when using such hypertext is increased as the number of links or possible pathways from a corresponding node also increases. The authors define a node in the context of hypertext as a specific decision point in the text, such as a highlighted link to another series of webpages. Here the individual has two choices: they either click on the node and follow it to another webpage or portal, or they don't click on it and remain on that page. According to DeStefano and LeFevre's (2007) work, an increase in cognitive load is directly related to the additional decision-making processes that have to be made as the number of nodes increases.

In an early exploration of the use of hypertext Zhu (1999) compared the learning performance of two groups of participants. In one group, the participants read material from a hypertext document containing 3–7 links per node, whilst the other group had hypertext that contained 8–12 links per node. In a later test of learning performance via the use of a multiple choice test and a fact-based summary, it was shown that for those who had learned in the 3–7 links per node performance was better than for those who were in the higher links per node group.

Antonenko and Niederhauser (2010) further explored the impact that processing hypertext had upon cognitive load alongside factors that could mediate such an issue. They introduced reading hypertext as an exploratory activity, which in turn requires an additional navigational element. According to the researchers, reading linear-based text is sequential in nature and we follow a set path when we read this type of information. In contrast, processing hypertext is viewed as a more fluid process in which individual paragraphs are presented as unique nodes of information. Accordingly, such a node of information is viewed as standalone, and there is no guarantee that information presented prior to it or afterwards has been accessed by the end user. Crucially, Antoneko and Niederhauser suggested that hypertext presents a unique online activity and places additional strains on cognitive processes that will, in turn, impact on cognitive load. Niederhauser et al. (2000) had already previously noted that extracting the meaning of information from a hypertext environment places a variety of additional demands on the end user. These additional demands are seen to involve aspects of both cognitive (decision-making processes linked to the integrating individual nodes of information) and metacognitive (highlighting navigational pathways to information, assessing which ones to follow vs. others). It is suggested that the presence of these dual information-processing tasks leads to a residual increase in cognitive load that provides the contrast with more linear-based reading (Antonenko and Niederhauser, 2010; Niederhauser et al., 2000; Shapiro and Niederhauser, 2004).

Antonenko and Niederhauser (2010) suggested some potential mechanisms that could be useful in mediating the impact of hypertext on cognitive load. These mechanisms (which the researchers termed 'leads') serve to reduce the conflict between attention directed towards reading and the additional load coming from navigating hypertext. Leads present the user with a brief snapshot of information that shows relevant information associated with the linked node but allows the end user the capacity to keep the current node of information visible (Antonenko and Niederhauser, 2010). This means that users are able to make an assessment of the suitability of the currently selected node in terms of its relevance to the current task objectives without having to navigate away from the current website. This is therefore seen to reduce the cognitive load by removing the meta-cognitive aspect of hypertext navigation (Antonenko and Niederhauser, 2010).

Antonenko and Niederhauser (2010) actually showed that in conditions where a lead to node information was presented there was a reduction in cognitive load. Participants also spent significantly more time reading material in the lead condition as opposed to conducting web-based navigation activities, thereby reducing the split in attention between the two reading and navigating. The evidence also showed that in tasks where a lead was used there was better overall retention of information in terms of domain (subject)-specific knowledge as well as structural details (how material is organised in terms of hierarchical structure).

Critical for the discussion here is the notion that hypertext and hypermedia are presented as using distinct and different cognitive processes to those used in processing traditional linear-based text (Antonenko and Niederhauser, 2010; DeStefano and LeFevre, 2007). These additional processes require individuals to not only make a variety of decisions related not only to which links to follow from a respective node, but also to secondary processes involved in navigation and prospective assessment of relevant information. Crucially our capacity to process information in such environments is linked not just to our own working memory capacity, but also to the number of embedded hyperlinks presented in the text. When the individual encounters hypertext that is laden with multiple links per node, there is a residual increase in cognitive load when comparing it to that of normal text (Smart, 2010).

The Use of Technology in Education and Learning

For many of you, this book may have been used as part of your own research or indeed as part of an assessment. The use of digital technology in educational settings is becoming of increasing interest. On the one side, there is the argument that employing the use of digital technology in schools and universities is a step into the future. Many students in higher education experience learning through any number of virtual learning environments (VLEs). These software-based environments help tutors to manage course material for their students, but also present students with the opportunity to access material in their own time. Browne et al. (2006) noted that the VLE had become a universal feature of higher-education establishments, with approximately 95 per cent of institutions using these systems. However, there is a question about the utility of such systems and their impact on learning, with adoption often being driven more by market forces rather than a wish to improve learning (Browne et al. 2006). Brown (2010) presented an argument that the future could be far from bright for the VLE. The discussion focused on the current use of VLEs and the drive to encourage imaginative and creative mechanisms for their use in the context of learning. Rather than these practices being emergent, Brown (2010) argues that they are actually in decline, pointing towards market saturation, declining uptake and a lack of research to demonstrate their effectiveness being at the heart of this. So what does this mean for the future of learning via digital technology? Well, according to Brown (2010) it is the advent of Web 2.0. The advent of Web 2.0 is set to change the way in which we interact with material on the Internet – the change being a fundamental one, with individuals going from being passive recipients of material to being actively involved in the creation and dissemination of information. The concept of Web 2.0 has been conceptualised as:

> a set of economic, social, and technology trends that collectively form the basis for the next generation of the Internet ... characterized by user participation, openness, and network effects (Muser and O'Reilly, 2006: 4).

According to Muser and O'Reilly, the Internet has changed how we view the tools we are interacting with – no longer do we ask about the version number of software, because we are more focused on the services that are being provided. So this process takes the Internet away from being a piece of software and more towards a tool, and a tool that could change the way in which we learn. The mechanisms for learning via Web 2.0 could potentially change the overall way in which we think about learning in any educational environment. Web-based applications (such as YouTube and iTunes) exist to help facilitate the creation of material and its rapid dissemination, bringing ideas to life and allowing a learning process that is as much about the experience as it is about the knowledge we retain. Web 2.0 tools allow the individual to tailor their learning experience through the use of personal learning environments (PLEs) and place the student at the heart of their own learning experience (Rahimi et al., 2015). The flexibility of such learning environments gives the individual access to material without the need to leave their working environment, say to go to the library to find a book, and also removes the time constraints that might also face us when we are trying to source information (e.g. waiting weeks for a book to be returned). It should be noted, however, that the use of PLEs is still very much in its infancy, with a range of issues related to their structure and definition being evident in the literature (Harmelen, 2006; Martindale and Dowdy, 2010; Rahimi et al., 2015).

Schools and universities alike face a broader dilemma in terms of allowing the use of digital technology within the teaching environment. As previously discussed in this chapter, when looking at the use of digital technology in the classroom and the lecture theatre, there appear to be some issues with allowing the free use of such digital devices. Research has noted that there is an impact on the capacity for students to engage in the learning process as well as engage in activities on their smartphones, tablets and laptops. On the flip side the use of digital technology in the classroom invariably offers a number of benefits, particularly in the context of Web 2.0 discussed above. In order to be immersive and interactive, these devices have to be used, but how do we focus their use without the distractions afforded through non-academic use? The evidence shows that individuals who engage in media multitasking whilst learning retain less information and therefore learn less, so it maybe that more careful thought is required when exploring the use of digital technology in the context of education.

During one of my own teaching sessions I brought this issue up with a selection of third-year psychology students. After much discussion, one of the students who had been sitting quietly at the back (engrossed in their smartphone I should add) suddenly became very animated. The central point to the student's argument was that, if we knew (via research) that the use of digital technology in the classroom impacted on education, why did we allow students to use it during teaching? My response was to ask the students what would happen if the university banned the use of such devices, or at the very least tried to implement a policy restricting their use solely for academic purposes. You may want to explore this with a group of your peers and ask them how they would respond if their use of digital technology was curtailed during learning sessions. For many of the students in the room, they saw it as their right to have access to their smartphones wherever they were, and preventing them from using them was just 'not on'. So there has to be a balance, but at the moment we don't know where that balance lies – students need to learn, and students want to learn, and we want to find new and imaginative ways to get students to learn, but then how many times does learning get disturbed by a smartphone ringing, a message alert, or the dreaded 'silent vibration on the desk'?

Summary

So as we have seen, there appears to be a variety of issues related to task switching and dual tasking in the context of education. Some of these issues may be linked directly to the cognitive make-up of the individual, such as individual differences in aspects of attentional control. Similarly, as discussed in earlier chapters of the book, our capacity to do two things at once is pretty limited, and usually if we are doing two things at the same time, one of these will 'give'. This could lead to an error, or more likely the inability to recall specific information that has been presented to us. It has been noted that learning requires focused attention, and only by using this can deeper learning take place. Therefore any activity that serves to distract us and direct our attention elsewhere will interfere with this capacity to learn. If individuals are not paying attention, particularly within the learning environment, memories are not encoded correctly, hence resulting in poorer retention of information – the net result being the inability to recall the information they have been presented with.

However, it isn't all bad for learning with technology and the research would seem to suggest it can work, but only when it is used in a targeted and contextually specific manner. This means that the use of digital technology has to be directly related to the subject matter being introduced. In turn, such media has to be well crafted in its ability to engage the student rather than confuse, disorientate or over-complicate the learning process. Any additional load that comes from trying to figure out how to use an online learning tool or over-complicated program will ultimately result in more time and effort being devoted to this, rather than learning itself. Digital technology can be seen to enhance student engagement, within both the academic environment as well as the non-academic, extra-curricular activities that students participate in. However, there is a paradox here as better learning comes from better student engagement, *but* better student engagement only comes from better, more directed attention.

It would appear that there is a current battle being fought within education establishments across the world. On the one hand educators are constantly faced with the potential for students to be distracted by 'social' use of digital devices. On the other hand there is exploration of how these same such devices could be used as tools to enhance student learning.

9

DECISION-MAKING IN THE ONLINE ENVIRONMENT

CREDIBILITY

Learning Aims and Objectives

- To explore the mechanisms that underlie decision-making in the online digital environment;

- to review the key heuristics used when we are making a judgement of credibility online;

- to understand how making a judgement related to the credibility of information has changed in the light of digital technology.

Overview

In order to introduce this chapter on decision-making in the context of digital technology I need present a quick overview of the background to the area. As discussed in Chapter 2, the notion that humans have a limited capacity for processing information is a central tenet to cognitive psychology (Lang, 2000). This limited capacity places restrictions not only on the amount of time but also the cognitive effort we can spend assessing between available alternatives and reaching a decision. When the individual has no access to an existing decision from past experience, or where the information presented in the pursuit of a decision is incomplete, individuals will often use a fallback 'best guess' heuristic method (Tversky and Kahneman, 1974). A heuristic is seen as a general rule of thumb or mental short cut that, for the majority of the time, will give us an approximate solution. The use of heuristic strategies is linked to other factors, such as the amount of existing information individuals have on the current topic, how well defined the current task is and how easy it is to find information to make a judgement. There are, however, potential pitfalls to the use of these mechanisms related to the very way in which they have been created. As heuristics are based on our own experiences, the frequency of encountering different things can play a critical role in our later decision-making activities. Say, for example, that you have a bad experience with a certain website; this may in turn make you avoid choosing this site when later searching for another piece of information. We don't like to spend a lot of time thinking about decisions that can be defaulted quickly to something we might have experienced previously. The established research in the area of decision-making presents the human as a 'cognitive miser' (Fiske and Taylor, 1991) with an emphasis on maximum gain (in terms of information retrieved) through little expense (in terms of cognitive resources expended).

Wirth (2007) noted a set of theories based in the area of social cognition that are directly relevant to decision-making in the context of cyberspace (Chaiken et al., 1989). Dual-process theories, such as the heuristic-systematic model (HSM; see Chaiken and Trope, 1999; Todorov et al., 2002), make the assertion that individuals can engage in two different modes of information processing. On the one hand, there is a systematic or comprehensive approach to decision-making; in this mode the individual will explore all avenues of information that are seen as being relevant to the task in hand and make decisions based on a comparison with previously stored knowledge. This processing 'mode', according to Todorov et al. (2002), is limited by the resources the individual has available and those associated with the current task demands. In situations where the cognitive resources available are severely limited (possibly due to the complexity of the current task), then an individual will switch to the alternative heuristic mode of processing. This is a non-analytical approach where an individual only focuses on basic information in order to allow them to make a judgement (2002).

According to the HSM model (Chaiken and Trope, 1999; Todorov et al., 2002) the two modes of processing can act simultaneously, with interaction between the two dependent directly on the task requirements and previous experience related to the area of decision-making. In certain instances the two processes can act in a cumulative nature. When this takes place information is obtained independently through the two processes, and where the two processes converge they add more weight to the current decision-making process. A systematic exploration of the reviews for a specific brand name and product can also support our previous experience with a particular brand name. In this instance the evaluative (systematic) aspect of reviewing different brands adds to the experiential (heuristic) processing, therefore giving more strength to the decision made. In the instance where a review of the relevant information leads to an ambiguous situation in which both processes sit in direct opposition according to proposed decision, the information obtained from the systematic approach will cancel out that which is obtained from the heuristic-based processing (Chaiken and Trope, 1999; Wirth, 2007). Essentially, what happens is the information from the heuristic mode of processing is 'turned down' in terms of its perceptual volume, whilst the information gained from the systematic approach is 'turned up' or attenuated.

There have been some attempt made to highlight how these dual-process theories can be applied to information-seeking behaviour, particularly in terms of searching for online health information (Zarro, 2012). The initial work by Zarro (2012) suggested that adopting a dual-process model for way in which users make decisions, could account for the evolution of such a process. An information searcher will begin with limited information about the area they may be searching in, so will engage in the development of a strategy. Feedback from this initial strategy will then inform the current process and help to guide further strategy related to searching for information. From the perspective of searches involving specific health-related issues, individuals may begin with a great deal of motivation but have limited domain-specific knowledge. Here users adopting a strict systematic approach would search for information in a very cognitively demanding way, where new material is analysed and compared with previously held information. In contrast, users opting for a more heuristic-based strategy do not suffer the rigours of such a systematic analysis, have reduced cognitive demands but place an increased demand on personal experience and information held in memory (which could be 'damaged' or biased towards one particular aspect or decision). This process also draws on salient information that may be irrelevant to the task in hand, but which the individual may see as relevant based on their preconceptions. It should be noted that this research is wholly descriptive in nature, and Zarro (2012) presents a detailed exploration of how such research will be conducted in a prospective manner, but to date there is no evidence that such an empirical investigation has been conducted. As such, there is no set reason as to how and why individuals swap between these two distinct processes. Given further evidence from the research into heuristic-based reasoning it could be assumed that such strategies are implemented automatically outside of the direct conscious control of the user.

The internal rules or schemas that govern the use of heuristics (functioning almost like an internal script that individuals follow when they encounter a specific situation) are stored in long-term memory. As such, the ability to use these scripts is governed directly by the same processes that influence our retrieval of any memory of these governed directly by the same processes that would apply to any other memory. Todorov et al. (2002) broadly classified these aspects under three headings:

Availability: Heuristic rules must be available to the individual in order for them to be used; as such, they have to be stored and retained in long-term memory, which assumes that the individual has had some prior experience where these rules have been learned.

Accessibility: This aspect of heuristic processing suggests that the rule itself must be accessible from long-term memory in order for it to be used. Accordingly, the notion of accessibility has two residual implications; notably, if a previous situation in which a heuristic has been used is more memorable, this will in turn influence the likelihood of that mechanism being used again. In contrast, where there is a poor recollection of a previously used mechanism, perhaps due to interference or decay of the memory, then this will reduce the likelihood of such a heuristic being used. As a consequence the accessibility of such resources can be seen to directly influence the application of the most relevant heuristic.

Application: This makes reference to how appropriate the specific heuristic is to the current application; some heuristic strategies are far more useful in certain contexts than others. Where there is a degree of overlap between the subject material on which a decision has to be made and a heuristic existing in long-term memory, this will lead to the increased likelihood of that specific heuristic being used.

Bringing this back into the context of our current discussion, the use of heuristic strategies could lead us to choose the top link from a situation page returned from a search engine. Based on previous experience of such results, individuals may assume that information placed at the top of these searches represents the most accurate and best link available to access the information they need (Wirth et al., 2007). Evidence from Cutrell and Guan (2007) has already shown that individuals are instinctively drawn to the top of a search engine results page, and choose to ignore the information presented lower down in the list of returned results. Granka et al. (2004) also noted that in the context of search engine results users are drawn towards a 'golden triangle' located in the top left corner of the page, paying most attention to the first result and less so to the subsequent results. This heuristic-based strategy is potentially based in a skill that has been learned and where information presented at the top of the results page has yielded the most relevant results (Lorigo et al., 2008).

How Are We Using the Internet in Our Decision-Making?

In order for any decision to be made, we need to gather information so that we can clearly understand all of the various options that lie before us. Similarly we also need to make an assessment of the potential consequences for opting to take one option over another, both for the short and long term. This could include an assessment of what will be affected in the present or perhaps an exploration of how the affects of the decision evolves over a period of time. Similarly, decisions differ in their level of complexity, from deciding which new mobile phone to buy, deciding what future career path you may want to take, or choosing which degree course to enrol on. Irrespective of the magnitude of the decision, the processes that underlie the decision will share some similarities – we may consult our friends, those in authority or those who have specialist knowledge, or we could surf the Internet looking for the answers to our dilemmas.

The Internet has become the most ubiquitous source of information, allowing us to gather relevant information from one place with just a few clicks. In research conducted by the PEW Internet Research Centre (Horrigan and Rainie, 2006) it was noted that 45 per cent of Internet users in the US had used it to help them make major life-changing decisions. The research also detailed what types of decisions individuals had used the Internet for:

- 54 per cent of adults used the Internet to help a significant other cope with a major illness – this increased to 94 per cent when individuals were asked whether the Internet had been used to help themselves cope with a major illness.

- 45 per cent said that the Internet had played a major role in making important financial decisions, such as investments or savings.

- 43 per cent had used the Internet to explore new places to live.

According to the report's authors, the Internet appears to become of critical importance when a decision can be based more directly on advice from what they termed 'non-experts'. For these types of decisions, such as looking for additional training or perhaps choosing a place to study, the need for expert knowledge is seen as less critical than the experiential element. To locate trustworthy information will also place a direct burden on the individual, in terms of not only the cognitive resources that have to be devoted to the task, but also in terms of a time commitment. It becomes easy to understand why individuals take the quick and easy option when looking for information online, and why they place such a heavy reliance on material that can be easily accessed from places such Wikipedia. These sources have the appearance of trustworthiness due to their popularity, which fails to account for the fact that anyone, irrespective of their level of knowledge, can post on such sites (Metzger and Flanagin, 2013).

However, there is one important issue that is often overlooked when we search for information online, and that is the question of *credibility*. As the Internet is seen as a primary source of information for many individuals in today's society, the assessment of credibility is seen as a critical element of web-based literacy (Hargittai and Fullerton, 2010; Schwarz and Morris, 2011). The obvious ramifications for misplaced credibility to online sources can be far reaching, affecting not only our personal lives but also our working lives too. This could include aspects such as basing financial investments on out-of-date or false information or buying a product based on false or incorrect reviews. In the context of credibility judgements online the heuristic mechanism discussed at the start of this chapter is often engaged. Most adult users will browse non-credible websites with the assumption that the popularity of such sites equates directly to the credibility and truthfulness of the material contained on them (Hargittai and Fullerton, 2010). As will be discussed later on in this chapter, this practice is associated with the consensus heuristic and bandwagon heuristic (Sundar, 2008). The use of such heuristics in potentially critical decisions shows how much reliance individuals will place on learned rules and past experiences that may be seriously biased by the behaviour of others.

If we go back to the work presented by Suler (2005) in the first chapter, he talked about the concept of 'net democracy'. In a time before the Internet, if you wanted to get something published or to become an expert in a particular area there were key processes and mechanisms you had to follow. Essentially these processes served to ensure the sanctity of knowledge and expertise, and included processes such as getting a book published, writing a journal article and submitting it for review. However the advent of the Internet changed all of this and made it a lot easier for any individual to voice their opinion, irrespective of their status or expertise. No central group, person or organisation acts as a gatekeeper for the flow of information onto the Internet, so the individual is tasked with two key choices when they use it. Firstly they have to decide whether it is fit for their current purpose and secondly they have to decide if they can accept the risk that the source may not be entirely credible. Researchers such as Flanagin and Metzger (2008) have noted that the rise of digital media may not necessarily be changing the underlying mechanisms that we use in order to assess the credibility of information. Instead they suggested that due to the sheer volume of information contained in the online domain, individuals have to turn to these skills more frequently. Burbules (2001) presented the opposing view that credibility judgements in the context of cyberspace should be viewed as being distinct from other forms of credibility judgements. This view is grounded in the notion that the conventional processes that are used for assessing credibility in the offline environment may not be directly applicable online. Aspects such as speed of website loading, complexity of features, link structure and functionality are all unique to the online digital environment (Burbules, 2001). The common mechanisms that we may have used in the past, such as assessing the reputation of an individual who has presented information, are no longer as reliable as they used to be, and before such individuals would act as intermediaries in our search for information. Metzger and Flanagin (2013) stated that digital media has produced a state of 'disintermediation', a concept that was originally presented by Eysenbach (2007). This is described as a state in which individuals are forced to search for large amounts of information online – by themselves – without the help of such intermediaries. The examples presented include individuals shopping online and buying products without the assistance of a helpful sales person, or perhaps a patient searching for information about an illness online without the input from a medical expert (Metzger and Flanagin, 2013).

How Do We Define Credibility?

For the most part the modern account of credibility includes an element of believability of the sources from which the information originates (Fogg, 2003; Tseng and Fogg, 1999). Self (1996) noted that individuals will often refer to what they view as a credible source in terms of being 'trustworthy' and having some level of 'expertise' in a given area. Hilligoss and Rieh (2008) also noted the interplay between dimensions of trustworthiness and expertise, suggesting that when a source is defined as having expertise individuals are more likely to judge the information originating from that source as also being trustworthy. The individual has to make a judgement about how trustworthy the individual is and the level of expertise they have before they engage in the use of the information obtained from that source (Hovland and Weiss, 1953; Metzger and Flanagin, 2013). Hovland and Weiss (1953) noted very early on that the perceived trustworthiness of the source significantly impacted on the willingness for the participant to accept the message being conveyed. In defining credibility the literature will often focus directly on the credibility of the source, the credibility of the information or message (in instances where there is no reliable information for the source) or these two points taken in combination (Wathen and Burkell, 2002).

Searching for Credibility in the Online Environment

As discussed previously, if you are searching for a credible source in the offline environment there are a variety of things that can help you. First of all, you are faced with a limited number of sources from which to get information from; these might be books written by respected authors, or perhaps an actual discussion with an expert in a particular area. Usually information has to go through a rigorous set of processes to get to the stage where it can be passed on to the general public, so we can usually be assured that this information is, for the most part, credible. Credible sources in the offline environment are also characterised by positions of authority, usually conferred on them through a process of training or education, such as doctors and professors. It is noted that such a process of assigning credibility still exists in contemporary society, but the one key difference is that the capacity for sharing information has removed some of the boundaries and safeguards that were originally in place to ensure that information was credible (Metzger and Flanagin, 2013). The capacity to more easily produce information and distribute it means that more and more information becomes easily accessible, but there is a cost. Researchers have noted that even though such information exists, there is no guarantee that it is credible. The mechanisms that filter out mistakes in the offline world do not exist in the online world, meaning that individuals could be accessing and using material that could be out of date or inaccurate (Flanagin and Metzger, 2003; Metzger and Flanagin, 2013; Metzger et al., 2010; Rieh and Daneilson, 2007).

Modelling Credibility Judgements in the Digital Environment

A variety of researchers have attempted to present frameworks that can be used to encapsulate the processes information seekers are using in order to assess the credibility of something in the digital domain. The aim of this section is to discuss these in more detail and assess their impact on how we search for credible information online.

Fogg's Prominence-Interpretation Theory

Previous research presented by Tseng and Fogg (1999) explored the influence of technology in terms of its capability to persuade the end user into making judgements or decisions. The research highlighted that the end user will assess a wide variety of information in the process of deciding on the credibility of a website:

Presumed credibility: This is based on the assumption made by the individual that certain areas of the Internet are more credible than others. For instance most end users would determine a website with the suffix of *.gov.uk* as being a credible source of information.

Surface credibility: This relates directly to the aesthetic qualities of the website in terms of professionalism and attention to detail. Most users will assess a website's credibility on first impressions, exploring aspects such as layout, spelling and grammar.

Earned credibility: The individual will establish a level of trust associated with a particular website over a period of time or number of visits. Such trust will relate to the ease of use for that particular website and the continuation of information being provided to the individual being of a trustworthy nature.

Reported credibility: An objective assessment of credibility based directly on expert feedback or the provision of certificates/awards being given to that particular website.

The research by Fogg and others (Fogg, 2003; Fogg and Tseng, 1999; Fogg et al., 2003) is important in this context as they noted that the end user places a heavy reliance on the 'look and feel' of information in order to make a direct assessment of credibility. In a similar context, McKnight and Kacmar (2007) also noted that the professional appearance of a website was a key indicator in the perceived credibility of that website (Schwarz and Morris, 2011). Hargittai and Fullerton (2010) noted that the end user is biased towards making decisions of credibility based directly on the popularity of a particular website in the context of using search engines. Many users will consistently misinterpret the notion of higher position in a search engine result as being indicative of higher credibility. Such a notion again links back to the notion of implicit trust that users place on results being presented from search engines.

Fogg (2003) asserted that two things must happen when an individual is making an assessment of credibility online:

1 The user has to notice something (this is the prominence element).

2 The user has to make a judgement about that thing (the interpretation element.

Each of these aspects must be in place in order for a credibility assessment to be made by the individual.

Prominence

Fogg (2003: 722) further elaborated on this element to his framework and suggested that it is the 'likelihood that a Web site element will be noticed or perceived'. Fogg suggested that there are at least five contributing factors that will affect the prominence of elements:

1 *involvement*: the direct involvement of the user within the search environment, including their motivation and ability to study and observe elements of the website;

2   *topic*: whether the website is related to news, entertainment, etc;

3   *task*: the current goal for the user, whether this is directly linked to information seeking, online shopping or more general surfing activities;

4   *experience of the user* in the context of the digital domain as well as in the
context of the current topic;

5   *individual differences* linked to specific elements such as learning styles or
literacy level.

Fogg suggested that one of the key influencers is the determinant of prominence
in the involvement of the user in the activity or task. If the individual has a high
level of motivation when they are approaching specific website, this means they
will be more stimulated and thus notice more elements about the website. Fogg
also links into work conducted by Petty and Cacioppo (1986) and suggested that
both motivation and ability act in conjunction, so when both are high even more
elements will be noticed.

Interpretation

Fogg (2003) defined the process of interpretation as 'a person's judgement about
an element under examination'. This interpretation component to an assessment
of credibility is their own personal evaluation of a particular website element;
so this could include the aesthetics of the website or the presence of misspelt
words or poor grammar. As with prominence, interpretation is also seen to have
a number of contributory factors attached to it, including:

1   *assumption*: those elements that are based in the user's mind, such as their
past experience, which will impact on the way in which the individual
interprets something;

2   *skills and knowledge of the user*: in terms of their level of competency
around the subject matter of the website;

3   *context*: this relates not only to the environment in which the user is
searching for information, but also their current expectations.

According to Fogg's interpretation element, it is suggested that all users will
not see the same website in exactly the same way. He presents the example of
culture and its role in making such decisions: if a particular website contains a
passage from a religious book, some individuals may (based on their cultural
context) be more inclined to see this as a positive and therefore view the website
as more credible; however, this could also work in a negative way, with some

individuals perhaps viewing the presence of such information as being irrelevant, hence not credible.

Sundar's MAIN model

In Sundar's (2008) exploration of credibility judgements he talks about technological affordances that are present in all forms of digital media which, in turn, aid our capacity to make judgements. In simple terms, the concept of an 'affordance' is simply a capacity or capability of something. An example presented by Sundar links into the concept of hypermedia discussed in the previous chapter. One of the affordances presented by hypermedia is that it presents us with a capacity to interact within that website; our capacity to interact could in turn trigger our capacity to make judgements about the credibility of that site through a set of cognitive heuristics (2008).

In his work Sundar noted that there were four key affordances that had shown a significant impact on the capacity for individuals to make a judgement about credibility. These were Modality (M), Agency, (A), Interactivity (I) and Navigability (N). Importantly, Sundar suggested that these affordances are present in some form or other in most aspects of digital media. They in turn have the capacity to trigger the use of particular cognitive heuristics linked directly to the assessment of credibility.

Modality

According to Sundar this is the most structural element of the content as it is the most obvious when examining an interface. For the most part, digital devices have a number of output modalities (or ways in which they can interact with us), these being textual, video and pictorial, each of which have different capacities to trigger heuristics linked to an assessment of credibility. For example, text-based modality is, according to Sundar, the least credible when compared with other modalities such as the auditory or visual. This is partly due to the stages involving the creation and interpretation of the text message, as the sender has to create information about what they have seen or experienced and then the individual receiving that information has to decipher that writing – this leaves the capacity for not only irrelevant material to creep in, but also the possibility of deception as well (Sundar, 2008).

Sundar noted several key heuristics that can be triggered via this modality in the process of judgements for credibility. A selection of these included:

Realism Heuristic: This is the prediction that individuals are more likely to believe information that has a sense of 'real-world' representation about it. For example, Sundar suggested that something communicated through an audio-visual modality is seen as being more trustworthy as its content more closely resembles what we would expect in the real world. Essentially, individuals are more likely to trust information they can see and hear rather than something they can just read.

Old-Media Heuristic: This heuristic is related to the attribution of higher credibility to information that is presented in a more traditional format, something akin to that of newspapers. According to Sundar, these representations trigger a perception of higher-level credibility as they represent a medium that has more stringent policies when it comes to the publication of information.

Being-There Heuristic: This is a by-product of being immersed in the virtual space that comes about as a result of significant advances in the multimodal presentation of digital media (Sundar, 2008). As a result of this it is suggested that an individual is more likely to conclude that information is credible according to the intensity of their experience with such information.

Distraction Heuristic: This heuristic comes about as a result of a drain on the individual's cognitive resources, particularly when an experience contains a great deal of multimodal interaction (Sundar, 2008). The result of the distraction heuristic means that the individual becomes so immersed in the digital environment that they have fewer resources spare to engage in an effortful assessment of the credibility of the presented information.

Agency

This cue relates to how individuals attribute 'agency' (or 'who said this') to information that is being presented online. According to Sundar, attempting to identify the true source of information presented on the Internet and digital media is something of a tricky process. The agency cue presented by Sundar builds upon this potential confusion, and means that we assign the source of information to any number of 'entities' within the communication of material. For example, we could conclude that the information has come from the 'front-end box', which Sundar suggested relates directly to the output device through which we view the information (e.g. the computer, the Ipad, the television; Sundar, 2008). As before, Sundar (2008) noted a number of key heuristics associated with this cue, including:

Bandwagon Heuristic: This is an over-reliance on the opinions of others in an assessment of credibility. Essentially this heuristic suggests that an individual is more likely to trust something if others do, with credibility linked to popularity rather than truthfulness.

Authority Heuristic: In simple terms this heuristic relates directly to the level of perceived authority the source has. This is a common finding from the research in the area of credibility demonstrating that one of the most significant cues for assigning credibility is related to perceived 'officialness' of the source (Sundar, 2008). If an individual views a source as having authority to speak in a particular arena, such as an expert or official body, the message itself will be deemed as being credible.

Social Presence Heuristic: This one is interesting, particularly since the advent of automated help clients that are embedded within websites to offer the individual a point of interaction if they have specific queries or problems. It appears that if the user believes that they are interacting with a human rather than an inanimate object, they are far more likely to attribute credibility to that information. Sundar noted work which demonstrated that humans automatically assume that the 'thing' on the other end of an online interaction is human (Sundar and Nass, 2000). In instances where the interface relaying the information is more human-like, the likelihood of the social presence heuristic being activated is higher.

Interactivity

Sundar, when talking about the concept of interactivity, makes a comparison between more traditional analogue media and those of digital interfaces, with the latter possessing the capacity to instil more interaction. According to Sundar, the level of interaction that is afforded by the interface through which an individual is obtaining information will in turn impact on the perceived level of credibility for that information. The notion of interactivity is embedded in a variety of heuristics presented by Sundar, which include:

Interaction Heuristic: This heuristic relates directly to the level of interaction that is afforded to the end user during their use of digital technology or media. In the instance where there is a higher level of interaction with the system, the individual is able to tailor their experience (and therefore the information they are receiving) more precisely. This in turn will lead the user to assign more credibility to the information they obtain as it is related directly to their current needs and contains little or no irrelevant information.

Choice Heuristic: The level of choice an individual is presented with when engaging in online interaction can also influence the level of credibility both for the information obtained and the website. Choice can be represented in a variety of ways, for example it can be related to the ease of finding information or the level of detail that is presented. In instances where information is really hard to find (and so it is hard to make an informed choice) or when there is a lack of detail, individuals are less likely to see that source as being credible. When we are offered more choice alongside a greater level of detail and flexibility in the system, we are more likely to see the information source as being credible (Sundar, 2008).

Flow Heuristic: When we interact with something, there is a certain 'speed' at which this interaction becomes optimal. If the speed of interaction is too fast or too slow for our own personal preference, then we start to get frustrated with the process and annoyed with the system. This process is operationalised as the concept of 'flow', a psychological concept akin to being 'in the zone' (Csikszentmihalyi, 1990). Where there is a break in the flow of our interaction with a particular system, be this due to poor design, issues with connectivity or interruptions presented by the system, there will be a residual impact on the individual's perception of the credibility of that source and the information associated with it.

Navigability

Linked into the concept of interaction mentioned above, that of navigability is again presented with a contrast between traditional forms of offline media and those online. For the most part print media has a very static and linear level of navigation, with the individual moving from one page to another in order to progress through the information. With the advent of digital technology, the navigability affordance presents the capacity for individuals to engage in parallel processing, escaping from the linearity of presentation. According to Sundar (2008) this is a process that serves to directly emulate the processes that underlie the human memory system, and allows users to navigate from one place to another without having to engage in any number of intermediate steps. The credibility of a site therefore relies directly on its navigational design, in terms of both its flexibility and intuitiveness. As with the other affordances mentioned above, Sundar (2008) specifies a number of key heuristics which are directly associated with navigability, which include:

Browsing Heuristic: In the example presented by Sundar, he suggested that a website that contains a lot of potential to encourage the user to quickly skim through information and investigate the content of various links would engage the use of this heuristic. By engaging the browsing heuristic and allow the individual free and unfettered access to information, the perceived credibility of that site is more likely to be positive. According to Sundar, the freedom to browse at will presents the user with a lack of bias, allows them to verify the information they have found as well as giving them the capacity to explore all of the products/services the website is offering. Barriers to browsing would appear to close off these opportunities, perhaps creating the feeling that there is something to hide or that the source is trying to just show one side of an argument or particular aspect of their product.

Scaffolding Heuristic: In the context of any experience in the online environment individuals have the potential to lose focus or struggle with their navigation of the website. Some websites integrate design elements that help the individual explore different elements, perhaps through clearer organisation or the use of navigational aids (e.g. a site map, site landmarks or a hierarchical structure for links). These aids serve to 'scaffold' the user's experience and by doing so help them, thus making them reflect more positively on the website's credibility.

Sundar's work is important as it shows a more realistic way in which individuals are making a variety of judgements about the credibility of online information. It is clear that the assessment of website credibility is a far more complex and interactive processes in which individuals are seen to be using a variety of heuristic strategies to assess such. More importantly, these processes have evolved to cope with the new media that has emerged as a result of the advent of digital technology. So from this perspective we have evidence that there is a clear difference between those processes used to assess traditional, analogue media (e.g. newspaper, television, books) and those used in the online digital environment.

Cognitive Heuristics for Credibility Assessment

As a result of an extensive period of research, Metzger et al. (2010) distilled five key heuristics that they claimed were used when making an assessment about credibility of an element or source, as follows.

The Reputation Heuristic

According to the findings based on a series of focus groups, Metzger et al. (2010) noted that one mechanism individuals used to assess credibility is to rely on the reputation of the website or source. This is a shortcut, as it essentially means that the individual is placing a heavy reliance on all those people who have gone before them and stated that the product or website is good, rather than the individual investing time and effort to explore these claims. Individuals also transferred credibility between elements, with some assuming that the information contained on a company's website is conferred the same level of credibility as the company due to the presence of the company's brand name. Accordingly the authors suggested that this heuristic has its basis in another, simpler heuristic principle that means individuals will favour a recognised alternative over less familiar ones in order to reduce the amount of cognitive resources being expended (Metzger et al., 2010).

The Endorsement Heuristic

The use of the endorsement heuristic suggests that individuals are often inclined to accept a source or individual as being credible if others also do. Metzger et al. (2010) suggested that the use of endorsement-based heuristics is not something new and has been previously seen in work by Hilligoss and Rieh (2008) and Flanagin and Metzger (2008), and is sometimes referred to as conferred credibility. Wider work has also discussed something called the 'bandwagon heuristic' (Sundar, 2008), which leads people to use peripheral cues to select content based on the popularity of the information rather than the actual content of that information.

The Economic Model of Information Cascade suggests that individuals who make initial selections and Internet choices can in turn influence or inform those individuals coming later to the same search process (Bikhchandani et al., 1992, 1998). Most humans like to think that they are making informed choices when seeking or selecting online content, yet paradoxically want to expend as little cognitive effort as possible in making those choices. There are, however, instances when a person may not have sufficient information to make an informed choice and is therefore reliant on others' votes of confidence, popularity or endorsements (e.g. Bikhchandani et al., 1992, 1998; Choi et al., 2000; De Vany and Lee, 2001). This in turn serves to create a *cascade effect* that grows over time. It also makes items more popular in search engines through the algorithms used by the engines to create a *popularity bias* for these items (e.g. Easley and Kleinberg, 2010). Fu and Sim (2011) suggested that uncertainty reduction escalates the cascade effect, which in turn leads to a bandwagon effect. Here individuals are making an assertion based again on past experiences associated with the notion that popularity of option equates to the most valid or correct choice.

Research has shown that individuals depend on the endorsement heuristic more than on their own knowledge (Metzger et al., 2010) with experimental demonstrations that buyer ratings as well as product reviews are sufficient to create the bandwagon effect in e-commerce (Dholakia and Soltysinski, 2001; Hanson and Putler, 1996; Huang and Chen, 2006; Salganik et al., 2006; Sundar et al., 2009) where higher vote counts and favourable reviews are associated with product purchase or adoption.

In Metzger et al.'s (2010) work they noted that some participants actually overrode their own opinions or views on a product in favour of the comments or reviews of others in order to direct their judgements of credibility. Sundar et al. (2009) had also previously noted that the bandwagon heuristic can also significantly influence individual judgements of credibility, with inflated star ratings or sales rankings being manipulated in order to produce higher band-wagon effects – these in turn produce a higher rating of credibility and as a side result increase the purchase intent for that particular product.

The Consistency Heuristic

When using this heuristic, individuals are seen to go through a process of cross-validation, which may involve comparing information from multiple web-sites in order to assess whether the information they have obtained is consistent. On the surface this process could appear to be quite demanding in terms of the cognitive resources and time being deployed in order to come to a final judge-ment. However, the researchers do note that for the most part the cross-validation process is pretty superficial, with the individual checking just a handful of alter-native sources in an attempt to verify the information as being credible (Metzger et al., 2010). The consistency heuristic can also be seen to share a common root with the others mentioned here, such as the endorsement, bandwagon and con-sensus heuristic – they all operate under a similar mechanism whereby people will believe things if other people do (Metzger et al., 2010).

The Expectancy Violation Heuristic

A large proportion of the participants in the study by Metzger et al. (2010) noted that if a website violated their expectations in terms of the structural elements (appearance, layout, features, functionality, comprehensiveness, etc.) or in the informational content, then they would judge it as not credible. According to Fogg's work, such violations would be brought to the prominence of the indi-vidual and could positively or negatively influence the assessment of credibility for that information. One of the most keenly discussed elements linked to the expectancy violation was linked to a website's appearance and functionality. Participants suggested that certain website features or characteristics acted as critical determinants of credibility, and where they were violated they also detracted from the credibility of that site. These website features included things such as bad grammar and typographical errors, which were flagged as good heuristic indicators for determining the quality and therefore credibility of the website. Both Fogg et al. (2003) and Flanagin and Metzger (2007) had previ-ously noted evidence to suggest that the design of the website often plays a critical role in the individual's assessment of that site's credibility. It would also appear to be the most simple to apply, meaning that the individual is not committing a great deal of cognitive resources to the assessment of credibility (Metzger et al., 2010).

Persuasive Intent Heuristic

The participants in the Metzger et al. (2010) study noted that anything that served to intentionally persuade the individual to do something, such as overt advertising or sales pitch, was seen as a major negative cue for credibility judgements. Flanagin and Metzger (2000) had already noted that the presence of commercial information on webpages caused users to view such websites as less credible. In a similar vein Fogg et al. (2003) noted that users took an almost instant dislike to a website that presented unsolicited commercial information. It would appear that individuals don't like to be interrupted by advertisements or commercial content whilst they are searching for information, and where it does exist it would appear to produce an element of distrust on behalf of the individual, as they may believe the information provider has an ulterior motive for presenting such information. This process will in turn impact negatively on the perceived credibility of that website. The types of adverts we explored in Chapter 4, such as pop-up ads, appear to be the ones that are the most annoying, with the element of intrusion being the critical motivator in creating lower perceived credibility (Sundar, 2008).

How Information Is Presented Can Also Affect Our Credibility Judgements

There has been some research that explores how the way in which information is presented can actually hinder our capacity to make a judgement about the credibility of information. For example, Alexander and Tate (1999) presented some early research that suggested the concept of 'channel convergence' in the context of digital media. In traditional offline media, individuals are presented with boundaries between information and advertising content. One obvious way in which advertisers use this to their best advantage is the use of 'clickbait' (see Figure 9.1). These are usually sponsored links to external websites but are often presented within the main body of the website and appear as real news stories. It is generally very easy to spot an advert in a newspaper or magazine as opposed to the actual news stories, but according to the notion of channel convergence, the split between these two elements becomes blurred. For many websites, the distinction between what is information and what is advertisement is often very hard to discriminate, meaning that the end user may have greater difficulty identifying the 'real' information on which to base a credibility judgement. Burbules (1998) also noted that there is a tendency for information that is presented in a similar style or format to be viewed as the same. This concept of a psychological 'levelling effect' means that information that is placed at the same level of accessibility within the web environment is given the same level of attention and, hence, the same level of credibility. As noted in the previous chapter,

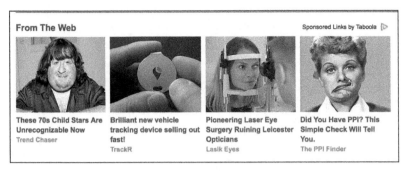

From The Web   Sponsored Links by Taboola ▷

These 70s Child Stars Are   Brilliant new vehicle   Pioneering Laser Eye   Did You Have PPI? This
Unrecognizable Now   tracking device selling out Surgery Ruining Leicester   Simple Check Will Tell
Trend Chaser   fast!   Opticians   You.
                            TrackR   Lasik Eyes   The PPI Finder

Figure 9.1 An example of 'clickbait' adverts taken from a website – these will usually appear in the main body of the website and look like they 'belong' to other news stories that are posted alongside them

the inclusion of hyperlinks and hypermedia can also present something of a challenge for users, particularly in terms of their cognitive processing objectives. If you are asking individuals to navigate from one webpage to another and retain information in order for later evaluation, this will place an increased strain on elements involved in executive function. Research by Eysenbach and Kohler (2002) noted evidence for this, with both source and message information becoming confused and scrambled in the memories of web searchers in the period after they have conducted searches. This means that in essence, the individual could be assigning credibility to information that may have been commercial in nature and vice versa for actual information.

Summary

In the age of digital technology the way in which we view, consume and assign trust to information is changing. Making judgements about the credibility of information has become inherently harder for a variety of reasons, predominantly related to the ease with which anyone, irrespective of their expertise, can have a voice on the Internet. The legitimacy of information in the online digital domain is no longer linked directly to the evidence that is used to support it. Now the credibility of information is associated with popularity, with social networking and viral advertising campaigns seeding the basis for credibility in terms of hits or likes rather than facts and figures. The lack of accepted protocols for regulating the flow of information into the online domain means that we have lost one way of preventing unreliable material being proliferated. This in turn means that individuals are increasingly developing and deploying a set of cognitive rules which have been specifically created to deal with such material. As we have seen, such rules are far from perfect and can often be influenced in ways that lead us to believe that information is credible when indeed it is not.

10

SEARCH STRATEGIES
AND HEURISTICS

Learning Aims and Objectives

- To explore the key ways in which we navigate through cyberspace when searching for information;

- to understand how things such as physical presentation of information affect the way in which we search for information;

- to highlight instances where the framing of the question that acts as the starting point for searching can actually influence the search process;

- to describe the use of 'stop strategies' used as mechanisms preventing us from spending excessive time searching for information online.

Overview

The Internet offers us a plethora of opportunities to search for information on what could be a potentially limitless number of topics. In some instances we are directed to search for specific information (goal-directed), such as the time a particular shop opens, what size shoe Tom Hanks wears (apparently a UK 11) and where all those odd socks go. However, conspiracy theories aside, according to the latter there are other times when we just search for the sake of searching (free browsing), and for which the activity appears to be nothing more than a space-filler or leisure-time activity. Marchionini (1999a, 1999b) suggested that the growth of digital technology had accelerated the transformation of human society into an information society. The concept of the information society is seen as one in which information becomes one of the highest commodities, and pervades economic, political and cultural activities (Karvalics, 2007). Therefore, in order to survive and participate in the information society, an individual needs to be able to adequately identify what information they need from the multitude of sources that are available to them. These skills are captured under the concept of *information literacy* (also referred to as information problem solving; see Eisenberg and Berkowitz, 1990) and include our capacity to locate, analyse and synthesise information from a variety of sources (Marchionini, 1999a, 1999b). According to a number of researchers, information problem solving is a skill that places a high demand on the cognitive resources of the individual (Brand-Gruwel et al., 2005; Walraven et al., 2009). Also, as information problem solving is a skill, we must learn to utilise and perfect what can be seen as a complex set of activities that can take some time to master (Brand-Gruwel et al., 2005).

Some research appeared in the early days of the Internet to explore the actual cognitive processes that people use when searching for information on the Internet. The research itself is, for the most part, still very much in its infancy and there remain a great number of things we still don't know about the cognitive processes that underlie the search processes people engage in online. However, the research focusing on decision-making and information retrieval in the digital environment has noted a distinct difference between those processes being used in an offline context and those being used online. Early research from Jansen et al. (1998) highlighted that the process of collecting information online is seen as being distinct from traditional offline information retrieval.

How Do Information Seekers Use the Web?

White and Iivonen (2001) presented a series of key findings from research that give us an initial starting point to understand how the individual uses the Internet to search for information:

1   *Users navigate cyberspace in a similar way to physical space*: In the context of their online searches, individuals create cognitive maps that bear some resemblance to the physical maps we may use to help us navigate in the physical environment. Some web users will often return to their home page or repeatedly use the back button in order to restart the search process. This process has been symptomatic of the individual experiencing feelings of getting 'lost' in their searches of cyberspace (Fidel et al., 1999; Palmquist and Kim, 2000;White and Iivonen, 2001). Early findings from research also noted that users will often start as well as revisit known sites multiple times throughout the search process (Wang and Tenopir, 1998).

2   *Users will browse for information*: White and Iivonen (2001) suggested that information searchers often use a *browsing* strategy to satisfy their search for information. Our traditional view of 'browsing' may appear to

be random in nature, but in some instances it can be guided through not just the information needs of the searcher but also the support offered by webpages. This support could be in the form of suggestion for alternative webpages or perhaps following hypertext links to alternative sources of information (White and Iivonen, 2001). They also suggested previous research that has shown many users will restrict the scope of their searches and often choose to conduct searches in small domain areas with frequent use of backtracking (Catledge and Pitkow, 1995). Such a process could be seen as being critical in the use of cognitive resources, with restrictions being placed on the scope and depth of searches preventing individuals from entering into negative equity. Fidel et al. (1999) noted that individuals are fast and flexible in their searches, and decisions about which link to follow next are made quickly. White and Iivonen also suggest that the actual pattern of browsing will change depending on the length of the search path as well as the information the individual needs to get from that particular search. This would also suggest that information seekers can modify their search patterns on an ad hoc basis depending on how long they have been searching and also on what the main goal of that search might be.

3   *Reliance on the use of search engines*: A variety of researchers have noted that end users will place a heavy reliance on the use of search engines as a major problem-solving strategy in the context of information retrieval on the Internet. Indeed, the term 'Googlitis' has entered into common language in order to describe what many see as an over-reliance on search engines such as Google (Leibiger, 2011). According to Leibiger (2011), individuals opting to use search engines do so even when better search facilities exist for them to use. For example, citing the work of Griffiths and Brophy (2005), Leibiger noted that 76 per cent of the students in this study used library services to connect directly to the Internet-based search engines rather than using the library resources themselves. Just a small number (10 per cent) actually used information contained in the library catalogue to provide them with the relevant information that they needed. It was also noted that many users display loyalty to a specific search engine and will use these irrespective of better, more effective alternatives (Hawk and Wang, 1999; Veloutsou and McAlonan, 2012). Users will typically be seen to start searches with a search engine, and the general success in the search or the proficiency in web search has been directly related to the skills of the individual user in the utilisation of the web-based search engine (Lazonder, 2000; Lazonder et al., 2000).

However, there is a trade-off between the user's perception of the amount of material they are finding via the use of these search engines and the actual information they are obtaining; most users overestimate the breadth of the material they have found (White and Iivonen, 2001).

4   *Users prefer simple search statements and do not plan searches*: Whilst most users will opt for the strategy of using a search engine to obtain information, this does not necessarily equate to their most efficient use. In most instances the interactivity that is presented by interfaces on the Internet means that most users believe that they do not have to plan a search strategy prior to engaging in them (Fidel et al., 1999). Most web users will employ very few query terms when using a search engine, comparatively lower than those used in more traditional offline information searches (Jansen et al., 2000). Users also avoid the use of complex search statements or engage in the use of Boolean logic-based operators (AND, OR, NOT), which are often seen as being cognitively demanding for the majority of web users (Eysenbach et al., 2016; Jansen and Pooch, 2001; Jansen et al., 2000). Users also typically ignore feedback information from search results that will present associated search terms or possible results that could be of interest (Jansen et al., 2000). Another interesting point is that users readily modify query statements and will easily give up older ones so that they can adopted newer options (Wang and Tenopir, 1998).

5   *Web searchers don't always get it right*: Searching for information and actually succeeding can vary from person to person, usually attributed to the many variables involved in the search process. For instance, we have the interaction between the search system itself and individual differences, as well as differences in the actual mechanisms offered by search engines for information search. In the same regard the cognitive or learning style of the individual will also shape searching, as well as differences between novice and more experienced users (Huang, 2014; Palmquist and Kim, 2000). More able users are better at recalling and finding correct website addresses, but compared with their less experienced counterparts are no more likely to find information they require once they do find the relevant website (Lazonder et al., 2000). However, later research by Brand-Gruwel et al. (2005) noted that both novice and expert searchers used a similar list-link strategy for exploring information. They did, however, point out that expert web searchers spent more time defining the problem related to their search for information in the preliminary stages, perhaps to tap into relevant past experiences (Brand-Gruwel et al., 2005).

6   *Users 'believe' in the 'web'*: It may not be surprising, but according to White and Iivonen (2001) information searchers place a great deal of trust in the information they glean from the Internet. This is viewed in the context maps very neatly onto the discussion in the previous chapter surrounding the credibility of information on the Internet and the lack of measures to protect the individual from incorrect information. Scull et al. (1999) had already noted that both expert and novice information searchers placed a great deal of credibility on information found on the web. Moreover, and perhaps more worrying, is the research by Wang and Tenopir (1998) that indicated that users are generally convinced they have found the correct information even though it is not. Similar findings have also been reported by researchers looking at the use of digital technology in education, with Graham and Metaxas (2003) noting that students have limited critical awareness when it comes to information provided on the Internet.

How Does the Presentation of Information Affect Search Strategy?

An important aspect of searching for information on the Internet relates to how individuals identify and select links on webpages, and how their relevance to the current task influences such decisions. Brumby and Howes (2008) initially suggested that the relevance of labels attached to a link could have a direct impact on the user's choice to select that link. In their work they sought to explore how task, relevance of the link label, and strategies individuals use influence decisions about which links to follow.

Brumby and Howes' (2008) work was based partially on research conducted by Katz and Byrne (2003) as well as being linked into a concept termed 'information scent' (Pirolli, 2005). Now, it might sound a little bit weird to think about information as having a particular smell. However it appears that when we search for information we can elicit details about where it is located based on the design or labelling of links which in turn gives off a 'scent'. The better the information scent of a website, the easier it will be for individuals to find and locate relevant information. Katz and Byrne (2003) presented two studies that showed that the decision to either use a generic search function or use a drop-down menu relied on an interplay between the individual and the website. It was assumed that individuals would choose the search option as this is seen as a faster and more direct route to finding the information that they wanted, but Katz and Byrne (2003) found no evidence that using the search function was faster. It would appear that the participants in their study were not fazed by the potential broadness and depth of the menus presented to them on the test websites used, but only when the information they were looking for was directly evident. The decision as to which option to choose was influenced directly by the information scent of the menu items being presented – for example, if there was a greater match between the thing that the individual was searching for and where it was located in the menus, individuals would more likely use the menu function.

Of key interest for the work of Brumby and Howes (2008) was the follow-on to this work. Essentially they wanted to explore how easy it was for users to discriminate between items that had a direct relevance to the current goal in hand and those aspects that have a high degree of semantic attraction but are not task relevant. There is a possibility that individuals could select more task-irrelevant links, leading to the potential for lost time and the prospect that the required information may never be found. In Brumby and Howes' study they presented a position that contrasted slightly with existing literature in the area. Instead of assuming a more heuristic-based strategy, individuals were seen to employ a more rational and systematic approach. First, individuals were more likely to select an item that presented a high level of information only if other potentially distracting links on the page were less relevant. In addition, where the irrelevant items shared a high degree of similarity with the task-relevant ones, individuals were less likely to select the relevant link on the first visit to the webpage. This process suggested that individuals delayed a decision about the relevance of particular links in order to make a more detailed assessment of *all* links presented. This contrasts directly with a more heuristic approach that would suggest fewer items would be selected in an attempt to reduce cognitive load (Brumby and Howes, 2008). The authors do note that this may be only relevant when individuals are encountering new webpages or new information that could be later incorporated in further heuristic strategies.

How Does the Question We Are Asked Impact on Search Strategy?

White and Iivonen (2001) suggested that there is an important link between the nature of the question being asked of the web user and respective predictions about where this information will be found. Rouet (2003) also noted that when students were asked specific questions they were fast and precise in terms of their searching behaviour with few references back to the question. In contrast, when the question was broader and more ambiguous students took longer to conduct searches and referred back to the question more. White and Iivonen (2001) presented participants with a combination of open and closed-ended questions; closed-answer questions required the user to provide an exact answer with no further input, whereas open-ended questions presented the need for a less direct answer, with a further need for developing an appropriate response. In terms of predictability, a searcher will look for relevant sources where they study and combine this information dependent on its relevance. In some instances the searcher will know an exact website where they can obtain relevant material, which indicates a high level of predictability for the source of the information. In contrast, other questions will require the individual to process the information so that they need to engage in a more extensive search, and the actual location of the answer will not be evident. In the instance of the latter, the individual may have to develop a response to the question based on various sources and developing relevant links to related sites. This aspect is associated directly to the use of heuristic strategies, where the individual has to distribute their resources economically with due consideration to the nature of the question, the importance of the information required and the enormity of the information domain itself.

The study conducted by White and Iivonen (2001) explored the effect of question framing and the way in which this impacts on the initial decision for where to begin the search. In terms of the overall initial stages in the information search, it was noted that participants relied heavily on the use of search engines (43 per cent), followed by the entry of the direct web address (30 per cent) and then directory access or subject directories (such as Online Public Access Catalogues or OPACs; 27 per cent). In further analysis the results showed that for both manipulations of the predictability of the information source there was a predominant use of the direct web address entry strategy to begin the search process. In the instance of the unpredictability of sources, participants are more likely to use a search engine to initiate the initial web search, linked directly to the uncertainty of the location for information.

The work by White and Iivonen is also important as it provides an attempt to classify the reasons provided by participants for their initial choices in their search strategies:

1   *Question-related reasons*: These are related directly to the nature of the question and highlight that the choice by the user is motivated by an attempt to clarify the parameters of the search itself. Here the user may attempt to define some aspects of the question or assess terms in the question and extend these into specific search terms.

2   *Source-related reasons*: This relates directly to the quality of the initial source information and includes aspects of certainty (whether the website will contain information related to the web search), the presence of multiple links from which to extend the search and the reliability of the particular source (in terms of how correct it may be).

3   *Search-strategy-related reasons*: This refers to the actual search process that the end user initiates, and introduces notions of 'browsability'; individuals unable to form tangible searches based on the question's wording instead adopt a strategy of browsing.

In instances where the source of material relevant to answer the question is predictable in nature, individuals are predominantly seen to be placing an emphasis on source-related reasons for making such decisions. This is assumed to be symptomatic of the link between the accessibility of the 'known' information and previous knowledge that suggests to the user a previous source that could provide the information they require. In contrast for users faced with an unpredictability of information source there is an emphasis on search-strategy-related reasons for making initial search choices (White and Iivonen, 2001). Individuals are actively identifying the best pathway for conducting the information search based on how well the search itself can evolve. Such a notion of evolution fits in directly with the aspect of uncertainty related to where the material to answer the question *could be* found rather than where it *will be* found. Such a choice represents the capability of users to modify or change options whilst being able to collect the widest possible selection of sources.

The research by White and Iivonen (2001) presented users as sophisticated decision-makers on the Internet, with the initial move in the search shaping the evolving structure of the continuing search. Here web users are actively engaged in complex forms of information processing, with forward planning for the entire search process being a more systematic approach rather than that of a heuristic-based strategy. The initial step in the search strategy is based directly on the parameters that are outlined in the initial search question, with users presenting reasons for initial search decisions based on an analysis of these parameters. This is clearly a contrast to the generally held view that searchers are conducting information retrieval that is fairly simplistic in nature and lacks cognitive complexity. A clear mediating factor in the choice for the initial search strategy is linked to how predictable the source of the answer to the initial search query will be.

White and Iivonen (2001) highlight some clear implications for this research that are worthy of discussion in the current context. Clearly, there is an impact of question type and question framing on the way in which individuals not only begin their search, but also shapes the whole search process. In this regard, where users are expected to present findings from information retrieval based in the Internet, there is a need to explore the way in which questions are framed, and a suggestion that further research is needed into the overall effect question framing has on the wider search process. There is also an aspect of education and skill development that could be extended to providing users with a series of strengths and weaknesses that could be associated directly with the choice of initial search strategies. Further manipulations of the framing of the question according to complexity, number of stages required in the search process and domain of the search question could also be manipulated to form the basis of future research. This would allow an aggregate picture of how users process information to highlight the best mechanism for searching, and also allow researchers to 'map' question parameters onto the actual shape of the search processes being engaged in.

Heuristics Used in Stopping Search Processes

From the literature reviewed above there is the consistent view that the cognitive resources an individual brings to bear on any given task are limited in nature. Any search that requires analysis of information space, the planning of associated strategies and then conducting the search is seen as mentally effortful (Browne et al., 2007). In this regard it is a waste for the user to expend resources in searches that will yield little or no information at a point of diminishing returns, so research has suggested that individuals need and use mechanisms for stopping the information search process. As Browne et al. (2007) noted, little research has been done, not only on the nature of heuristics in an online context as a whole, but also related directly to the possible stop strategies people are using in information searches. Such processes are seen as being distinct from those that are used in an offline context as the information space presented by the Internet differs along a number of dimensions. These relate directly to the size of the information space that is presented alongside the speed at which such information can be accessed and analysed, with the former being larger and infinite and the latter being faster and more instantaneous.

In general the individual user will terminate the search process once they have assessed the information they have collected and judged it to be sufficient for fulfilling the requirements they have for that particular search. This process then allows the user to move onto the next stage in the search process, so the individual must invoke a stopping rule so that they are not continually trapped in the initial stages of the search (Browne et al., 2007). From a 'normative' view of how it is expected users would invoke such stopping rules, individuals will continue to look for information until they reach a point where the mental cost of acquiring new information exceeds the worth of the prospective information that will be obtained from continuing the search (2007). There is also another associated cost, and that is the trade-off in terms of stopping the search behaviour and the 'expected' value of any additional material that *could be* found after the process has been stopped. However, this presented a very much perfect view of the way in which individuals would stop their search processes, and Browne et al. (2007) noted that end users are not logical in assessing the cost of continuing a search in the light of the additional material they are finding, with most implementing the use of heuristic strategies to satisfy this shortfall.

The literature presented an offline distinction between motivational and cognitive aspects of stopping rules:

1   *Motivational*: These relate directly to the preferences, desires and incentives (both internal and external, e.g. deadlines, costs, professional respect).

2   *Cognitive*: These are a result of the individual processes a user will bring to bear on the information itself and relate directly to the notion of a 'mental model' they have when they are developing the outline for the information search. This will include previous information related to the task and the task environment itself (Browne et al., 2007).

Although it is clear that motivational aspects can have a direct impact on the use of stop strategies, the focus for the current discussion relates directly to those of a cognitive nature. Cognitive stopping rules have been explored according to how they are implemented and how different types are used in stages of the decision-making process (Browne et al., 2007). In the early stages of the information search users are seen to be creating a model of the alternative routes that could be generated as a result of initial decisions. In this instance the use of stopping rules prevents the collection of any additional information so that the user can take stock of the material collected so far. The use of the stopping rule here has a feedback role, where the user will highlight the usefulness of current material collected against the current task parameters. In the later stages of decision-making, the use of stopping rules prevents the searcher from continuing in a cycle of evaluating between distinct alternatives (2007). This has an obviously mediating impact on the amount of cognitive resources being used, but does limit the amount of useful material that could be collected by the individual search.

Browne et al. (2007) suggested five key cognitive stopping rules that are presented in Table 10.1.

In order to develop a framework for understanding the use of cognitive stopping rules in online searches Browne et al. (2007) developed research that explored two

Table 10.1   Cognitive stopping rules for online searches

Rule	Description	Example
Mental list	A person has a mental list of items that must be satisfied before they will stop collecting information.	In searching for information concerning the purchase of a new car, a person will continue to search until all aspects of their mental list have been satisfied, e.g. engine size, colour, make.
Representational stability	The person will search for information until the mental model or internal representation stops moving or changing. The focus here is on maintaining the stability of this representation.	In searching for information online, a person will incorporate findings into their mental model for that particular aspect of information. Where the individual finds that additional information is no longer changing their internal representation, they will cease the information collection.
Difference threshold	A person sets a level of difference prior to engaging in the search to assess when they are not learning anything new from their search. When the individual ceases to learn new information, they will stop the search.	In gathering information for a new project an individual will research information until they determine there is no difference between the information they are now obtaining and what they have learned. At this point the search will be terminated.
Magnitude threshold	The person has a set amount of information they need to satisfy before they will stop searching. Here the focus for the information gatherer is having 'enough' information.	When an individual is reading a webpage, they will skim read the information until they can present an idea about what the webpage is about.
Single criterion	The person decides to search for information that relates to a single facet, and will stop when they have enough information about that criterion.	An individual will search for a particular item that is of a chosen brand; once this item has been found, the search will cease.

Source: Browne et al. (2007: 92)

key aspects in the process. The first one relates to task structure and the second to the overall strategy being used:

1. *Task structure*: Essentially this makes reference to the overall 'shape' of the task itself and how much of the task is familiar to the searcher (Byström and Järvelin, 1995). In the instance of a well-structured task there is a well-defined shape to the task environment. The user is aware of the problem statement, what is needed in order to provide a solution and what is needed in terms of the final answer. In direct contrast, the notion of a poorly defined problem has limited information related to all of the previously highlighted aspects, particularly in relation to what the individual can do or needs to do en route to find an end point for process.

2. *Strategy used*: This is seen as how the individual approaches the actual nature of the problem. It can be further divided into two distinct strategies according to the way in which the user analyses the problem. In the use of a decomposition strategy, the user essentially pulls apart the problem allowing it to be 'decomposed' into its individual constituent parts. This could include an interpretation of task elements (related to task domain) and the criteria for the search (what needs to be found). In contrast, a holistic strategy provides a more integrated and overall representation of the task, providing a general 'gist' of the problem environment (Browne et al., 2007).

According to research reviewed by Browne et al. (2007) both the complexity of the task and the experience of the user can influence the adoption of the above strategies. The notion of complexity in the context of web-based searching has its foundations in the expenditure of cognitive resources, where increased deployment of these indicates a higher perceived complexity of the task (Vakkari, 1998, 1999). In the instance where the information-processing capabilities are overwhelmed by the needs of the task then there is a performance breakdown with users suffering from reduced mental focus (Grisé and Gallupe, 1999), demonstrated more so in the context of online environments (Miranda and Saunders, 2003). There is a residual knock-on effect of this that relates directly to the capability of the user to devote resources to identifying individual components of the task. In high load conditions, there will a reduced likelihood of adopting a decomposition strategy. As Browne et al. (2007) noted, such a notion highlights a link between the capabilities of the individual (in terms of individual differences and processing abilities) and the complexity of the task in the ability to adopt a particular strategy, which then in turn serves to influence the use of particular stop strategies.

Results from Browne et al. (2007) highlighted that task complexity and task structure influence the stopping heuristics in information search. When we have a decent structure to the problem, where there is the ability to pull that problem apart into its individual elements and the complexity of the task is low, individuals are more likely to use mental lists and single criterion strategies. This is assumed to link to the ability of the individual to highlight individual aspects of the task environment. In contrast, where tasks are poorly defined and are of higher over-all complexity, the search is terminated through the use of magnitude threshold or representational stability rules that represent the evolving strategies that are symptomatic of such a process.

Such research not only highlights the limited scope of empirical research in this area, with these two papers being the only ones being returned in a search on the area, but also presents some interesting foundations for future research. There is a clear demonstration that individuals are not only using heuristics in an attempt to limit online information searching, but also that there are a variety of options they have open to them. However, the research is very much a post hoc discussion of the strategies that are being used in the context of online information searching, with no real way of predicting how and why individuals will adopt such strategies apart from a notion that complexity will have an impact. The notion of task complexity and previous task knowledge serve as a basis for this, and link back again to individuals as information processors with limited resources who have to use the most cost-effective strategy. However, there is no associated discussion in the research literature of the associated trade-off between the prospective cost of the individual stopping such a search and how this impacts on future searches. If individuals are ceasing information-gathering activities prematurely, there must be a residual impact on how this cessation in the search process affects the development of more finely tuned and refined stop strategies, with the wealth of information presented on the Internet perhaps leading individuals to believe they have attained more information than they actually have done in reality.

Stop strategies are obvious mechanisms that are being used in online informa-tion- seeking activities. A deeper analysis of the interaction of these with website choices that individuals are making could highlight why particular websites are more favoured and retain more users. If, for instance, a website provides the user with all the information that they require to fulfil a mental list or single criterion-based stop strategy, then clearly the user is going to opt for this website over all others. As highlighted by Browne et al. (2007), there is a need for further research in this area, and as with much of the literature most of it is very dated and does not take into account more recent developments in hypermedia and web-based decision-making, particularly in the context of social media. There is a need to explore how individuals

175

structure and prioritise aspects of their mental lists or determine the nature of the single criterion and how these fit into the underlying information-processing strategies governing search and stop procedures. The research by Browne et al. (2007) placed a distinct emphasis on exploring the use of these strategies in the context of online shopping and e-commerce, but there are a variety of further avenues this could be applied to. For instance, there is an aspect of online searching that has not been answered directly by this research related to why searchers 'make do' with the information they find. Subsequently this may also impact on the individual's assessment of the material they have obtained, but more importantly what material is missed or not encountered in their search. Aspects of stop strategies may terminate a search prematurely, with further research needed to examine how these processes link to previous experience, cognitive styles as well as the structure of the websites.

Previous Experience Effects Decision-Making Online

Again there is a symptomatic lack of literature that explores the effects of the individual's previous experience in terms of how the strategies are biased. The literature in terms of traditional decision-making presents a clear notion that individuals are easily swayed towards a particular choice based on information contained in memory and life experiences. In the only research of this nature found during my review of the literature, Lau and Coiera (2007) explored the effects of cognitive biases on decision-making processes. They explored four key biases:

1   *Anchoring effect*: This occurs when a prior belief exerts a direct influence on how new information is processed. Where information is in direct opposition to the existing information, individuals are far more likely to reject this and stick to their original view or assertion.

2   *Order effect*: The temporal order of when information is introduced affects the final judgement. This follows a common pattern from the literature in cognitive psychology known as the primacy/recency effect. In the context of primacy, events occurring temporally closer to the beginning of the sequence are better remembered, and therefore have a more direct influence on decision-making. In contrast, the notion of recency refers to the effect temporally recent items will have on decision-making. A variety of studies have demonstrated that individuals can make different decisions when presented with the same information at different positions in a sequence (Cromwell, 1950; Luchins, 1957)

3   *Exposure effect*: The level of exposure to information serves to affect the final judgement. The duration of exposure, the spread of experiences over time

and the time between presentation episodes all have a direct influence on an individual's impression formation, and therefore bias decision-making.

4   *Reinforcement effect*: Repeated exposure to information can influence the way in which beliefs and decisions are formed. Increased exposure to a stimulus is correlated with an enhanced attitude towards that stimulus, an effect that is demonstrated regardless of the stimulus type itself.

Lau and Coiera (2007) presented support for the use of all four cognitive biases in an information-seeking activity conducted online. Individuals were more likely to retain a pre-search answer even when newer and correct information was presented. Individuals were fulfilling the anchoring bias, being more resilient to changing their initial preconceptions or beliefs even in the light of information that suggested this information may be incorrect. There was also an influence of item position on the nature of the decision-making, with material being presented either earlier on in the search process or later having a direct impact on the answers presented by individuals. The effect of exposure to a particular stimulus was also apparent, with the amount of time spent on a particular webpage influencing the degree of concurrency between the answers presented by the individual and the information presented on the website. Finally, the reinforcement effect was also evident, where an increase in the frequency of accessing a particular document or website again influenced the concurrency between participants' post-search answers and those presented on that particular website.

Overall these results present interesting, although somewhat limited findings. The authors highlight the point that the measures used in the research may not have been sensitive enough to measure the underlying phenomenon. There is also no further exploration of how the four biases outlined above interact to influence decision-making online, and if they do, whether such an effect is cumulative in nature or whether one bias serves to override the presence of the other one. This research is, however, presented in isolation as the only study of its type exploring the effects of cognitive biases in online decision-making. There are nonetheless other biases that could be explored, and it is clear that there are many other ways in which this material could be explored.

Summary

As you can see from the research reviewed here, searching for information on the Internet isn't simply a case of banging in a random query to Google. The processes that are involved in our attempts to find material that is relevant to our needs without expending excessive amounts of those valuable cognitive resources. From the research explored above we begin to see a picture of how individuals engage in web-based searching for information. We see that they utilise a number of mechanisms that are very similar to those being used to navigate around the physical environment. Individuals also have a tendency to browse for information in more targeted ways when searching online. This more restrictive browsing in turn also allows for the conservation of valuable cognitive resources that can then be devoted to other elements of the task. People also rely very heavily on search engines to help them find information and often fail to understand these might not be returning the full results. Planning web searching appears to be non-existent for the most part, with users being more ad hoc in their approaches, often using very simplified one- or two- word search terms. Furthermore, the way in which material is presented, as well as the question that is asked of the individual, can also be seen to have a direct impact on the way in which we search for information. We do not search for information in an isolated bubble that is protected from our previous interactions and experiences with the Internet, and it is these very experiences that can enhance or bias our capacity to search for information.

11

TECHNOLOGY ADDICTIONS
AND COGNITION

Learning Objectives

- To explore the concept of technology addiction and present an overview of the literature in the area;

- to introduce some key addictions to technology and examine how they can impact on human cognition;

- to highlight some of the key issues inherent in using broad labels for technology addictions.

Digital Addictions and the Impact on Human Cognition

One key area of research that is featured heavily in the cyberpsychology literature is the potential for individuals to become addicted to digital technology. The important question we need to start to ask ourselves is if we do become addicted, how does this addiction start to affect our capacity to focus on normal daily activities? There has been some discussion of aspects of technology addiction in other chapters of this book, with some links to the residual impact these behaviours may have on cognition. However, research that specifically focuses on evidence for addiction to digital technology and how such disorders could have an impact on our daily functioning is limited (Hadlington, 2015). In this chapter the aim is to present a very broad overview of the current state of research in the area of technology addiction. Throughout the chapter the links between these behavioural addictions and the potential impact on cognition will be established, reviewing some of the material that has already been discussed in other chapters of the book. Hopefully, you will see that there is a distinct gap in the literature in this area, and it presents great potential for further research.

The Emergency of Behavioural Addictions

Previous conceptualisations of addictions have focused, for the most part, on substance abuse for things such as drugs and alcohol (Griffiths, 1998). These addictions involve the direct action of ingesting something that alters our experiences via a chemical process. However, in the 1990s a growing area of research suggested that individuals could equally become addicted to activities without the direct need to ingest drugs (Brown, 1993; Griffiths, 1996, 1998). Previous research has highlighted a number of these behavioural addictions including obsessive-compulsive disorder (OCD), compulsive spending and gambling, overeating and kleptomania to name just a few (Marks, 1990). What is apparent from the earlier work on behavioural addiction is that there is some considerable overlap to that of substance addiction. For example a 'repeated urge to engage in a particular behaviour sequence that is counterproductive' and 'mounting tension until the sequence is completed' could easily fit into any number of behavioural addictions, but which are included in the World Health Organization's definition of substance addiction (Marks, 1990).

Brown (1993, 1997) outlined a four-point checklist, later adopted by Griffiths (1996), which can be used to identify whether a particular behaviour falls into the category of an addiction:

1 *Salience*: This is where the activity that is the focus of the addiction becomes the most important activity for the individual; in this instance that activity will be seen to dominate aspects of thought, emotion and behaviour.

2 *Mood modification*: This relates to the subjective experience the individual has as a result of engaging in the activity that is the focus of the addiction – this element links directly to the reported feelings of elation or 'high' that individuals may experience (Griffiths, 1998, 2010).

3 *Tolerance*: An individual must engage in increasing levels of engagement in the particular activity in order to experience the same level of gratification as before; so this might be increasing the amount of time spent on the Internet or increasing the amount of money being spent on clothes.

4 *Symptoms of withdrawal*: In the absence of doing the activity that is the focus of the addiction, or attempting to cut down on the activity, the individual will experience unpleasant feelings such as mood swings, irritability and anxiety.

In the context of this chapter, the behavioural addictions we will focus on are those that fall under the heading of technology addictions (Griffiths, 1996, 1998).

This broad term is used to cover a variety of addictions that have a technology-enabled element, and can include (but are not limited to) online gaming the Internet, smartphone/mobile phone, pornography, online shopping, social networking and email. For our current discussion the focus will fall mainly on aspects that have received the most attention from research, namely the Internet, social networking sites and smartphone/mobile phone addiction.

Mobile Phone and Smartphone Addiction

In recent findings from the Pew Research Centre (Lenhart and Page, 2015) it was noted that 24 per cent of US teens aged between 13 and 17 were classified as being online 'almost constantly'. This phenomenon was partially attributed to the availability of mobile technology, with 70 per cent of teenagers in the study having access to smartphone technology. Those teens that have no mobile access to the Internet are online less frequently, with 68 per cent reporting being online at least daily in comparison with 94 per cent of those who have access to mobile technology such as smartphones. The OfCom (2015) report noted that smartphone users, irrespective of age group, now spend an average of two hours accessing the Internet on these devices. The same report also noted that smartphones are now the most widely owned Internet-enabled device in advance of laptops, with smartphones present in 66 per cent of UK households. There has been a substantial shift in the way individuals are now accessing digital media, including the Internet, hence the importance of exploring how excessive use is impacting on the end user. The additional functionality that the smartphone platform offers also means there is a greater propensity for instantaneous gratification and connectivity, which in turn could mean a higher potential for individuals to become addicted to their use. Thornton et al. (2014) suggested that when aspects of 'cognitive salience', where the smartphone becomes the dominant feature of their thoughts or focus of attention, are paired with 'behavioural salience', in which there is a constant need to check the smartphone for messages and alerts, we have the primary symptoms of a behavioural addiction. Thornton et al. (2014) noted that simply the presence of a smartphone device during tasks was enough to affect performance. It was noted that this effect only occurred for more complex activities, potentially due to greater demands being placed on attentional resources, but importantly this decrement was due to the phone simply being in the same space as the individual!

Prior to the rise and dominance of the smartphone some researchers had begun to explore aspects of problematic mobile phone use. For the purposes of our current discussion, let us make the assumption that the key difference between mobile phones and smartphones is that of functionality – the predominant factor being that of connectivity. For the most part, mobile phones were simply a tool for sending text messages (SMS) and making voice calls, with some later models having rudimentary browsers allowing individuals the capacity to search for information. The smartphone takes this connectivity one step further, and offers the users a wider variety of pathways to explore all in one handset, including the Internet, online shopping, dedicated applications for fitness, teaching, learning and so on. The rapid rise in the use of mobile phones in the early years of the 2000s was not associated with a similar rise in the amount of research being conducted to explore their use (excessive or otherwise) on aspects of human cognition. Much of the earlier research had a tendency to focus on the social elements associated with mobile phone use, including when and where they were used and how individuals were seen to obtain gratification from their use (e.g. Leung and Wei, 2000).

Further work by Bianchi and Phillips (2005) explored the potential for a link between excessive (or problematic) mobile phone use and a variety of psychological constructs. The research employed the use of the Mobile Phone Problematic Use Scale (MPPUS) that included 27 items such as 'I lose sleep due to the time I spend on my mobile phone', 'I can never spend enough time on my mobile phone' and 'I have frequent dreams about the mobile phone'. Elements of the MPPUS tie in directly to underlying elements of cognition, including aspects of distraction alongside an inability to focus or concentrate. The research paired the MPPUS with a variety of other measures, including one that explored the psychological construct of self-esteem and another that examined personality factors. Bianchi and Philips (2005) found that those individuals who scored more highly on a measure of extraversion and lower on measures of self-esteem were more likely to report higher levels of problematic mobile phone use. In follow-up research conducted by Ha et al. (2008) it was noted that excessive levels of mobile phone use were linked directly to symptoms of depression, issues with expressing emotions and higher levels of interpersonal anxiety (related to being in social situations and meeting new people), as well as scoring lower on measures of self-esteem. The latter point supports the earlier work by Bianchi and Philips (2005), with lower levels of self-esteem previously being linked to addictive behaviours (Ha et al., 2008).

However, this research solely focuses on the personality factors that *predict* problematic mobile phone use, and there has been very little in the way of research focusing on the impact excessive mobile phone use has on human cognition. In order to fill this void, my own research has presented an exploration of how problematic mobile phone use could indeed impact on our capacity to focus attention on a daily basis. The research asked 210 participants to complete a series of measures, including the MPPUS (Bianchi and Philips, 2005) discussed above, followed by a measure of Internet addiction (the Online Cognition

Scale – OCS; see Davis et al., 2002) and the Cognitive Failures in Daily Life Questionnaire (CFQ; see Broadbent et al., 1982). The CFQ is an interesting scale that asks participants to indicate whether they have experienced any 'cognitive failures' in a preceding six-month period prior to the completion of the study. These cognitive failures relate to lapses in both attention and memory, and can include things such as not remembering names or forgetting what you went into a room for. The results from the study were both interesting and a little bit shocking, showing that those individuals who scored more highly on the MPPUS experienced significantly more cognitive failures in their daily life in comparison with those who scored lower. It was not possible to conclude whether such failures were directly the result of individuals being engaged on their mobile phone more, but it did present one of the first findings linking the use of such devices to a potential impact on human cognition. It could be that individuals who are experiencing higher levels of mobile phone use are also easily distracted or have a lower level of attentional control, hence are more likely to miss things within their daily spheres of activity (Hadlington, 2015).

As with problematic mobile phone use, there is also a lack of research exploring how excessive or addictive levels of smartphone use can impact on aspects of cognition. There have been some attempts to map the impact of smartphone addiction onto the well-being of individuals that could, as a consequence, also have an impact on cognition. In one of the first studies attempting to explore the factors and impacts underlying smartphone addiction, Kwon et al. (2013) presented the Smartphone Addiction Scale (SAS), which highlighted six key factors:

1   'Daily-life disturbances' included elements such as missing work-related activities, issues of focusing attention, physical stress and sleep disturbance. This aspect of smartphone addiction links into the impact on human cognition, and as we have seen in other chapters, issues related to focusing attention, physical stress and lack of sleep can all have negative impacts on human cognition.

2   'Positive anticipation' is viewed as the emotive component that is linked to the excitement and sense of stress relief that is afforded to the smartphone user. Kwon et al. (2013) suggested that the smartphone is viewed not just as a device with which to make calls and send text messages, but also aids the relief of exhaustion – plus being a point of safety.

3   'Withdrawal' is conceptualised as generalised feelings of anxiety or intolerance due to being prevented from using a smartphone or being interrupted whilst using the device.

4   'Cyberspace-orientated relationship' is associated with feelings of increased intimacy with relationships that are mediated through a smartphone above that experienced in offline relationships. This is also linked to a sense of loss when the individual is unable to connect with their friends due to restricted access to their smartphone, which has direct links to the phenomenon of fear of missing out (FoMO; see Przybylski et al., 2013).

5   'Overuse' is viewed as the element of compulsion attached to the individual's use of smartphone technology as it is associated with an element of uncontrollability (Kwon et al., 2013).

6   'Tolerance' was the final factor included in the scale produced by Kwon et al. (2013). This element is typified by the user acknowledging that they have an issue with excessive smartphone use and making an attempt to curb it, but the end result is a failure to do so.

These factors presented by Kwon et al. (2013) also presented some cross-over to those which are proposed to underlie the Internet addiction. These aspects have included such things as the smartphone presenting a mechanism for social comfort, the presence of compulsive behaviours (such as the need to constantly check for messages), withdrawal from daily activities and the negative impact of use on everyday activities (Young, 1999).

In later research, Lin et al. (2014) presented the development of the Smartphone Addiction Inventory (SPAI), which was heavily based on the Chinese Internet Addiction Scale (CIAS) originally developed by Chen et al. (2003). The adapted SPAI essentially substituted the focus of the original CIAS by replacing the word 'Internet' with that of 'Smartphone' and making some other minor adjustments. The scale by Lin et al. (2014) included four distinct factors:

1   *Compulsive behaviour*: According to Lin et al. (2014), this is a critical element and has been seen at the core of a number of addictions including alcohol dependence (Gau et al., 2005) and Internet addiction (Lin and Gau, 2013). Neuropsychological studies have also noted that those individuals who exhibit addictions also have deficits in the activation of brain areas that are related to the inhibition of behaviour (Lubman et al., 2004).

2   *Functional impairment*: This factor relates directly to physiological symptoms of excessive use as well as impact on motivation and work-related performance. This can include elements such as eye strain, muscle fatigue and the individual experiencing actual injuries as a result of their smartphone through a lack of attention, such as walking into things or tripping over.

3   *Withdrawal*: This factor presents itself as both a lack of connectivity and emotional loss and is experienced when individuals become separated from their smartphones. This factor shares some similarities to that of the 'cyberspace orientated relationship' included in the scale by Kwon et al. (2013), as well as being closely linked to the concept of FoMO.

4   *Tolerance*: Again, this is a feature of the smartphone scale as noted in Kwon et al.'s original study. It was, however, noted by Liu et al. (2014) that this factor was one of the more poorly represented ones and warranted further expansion in later scales. This is presented as the need for the individual to engage in ever increasing engagement with their smartphones in order to maintain their current level of gratification.

We spent some time looking at the excessive use of smartphones and its potential to interfere with basic aspects of cognition when examining the impact this has on education in Chapter 8. The findings from much of the research in this area have suggested that there are clearly some negative relationships between excessive levels of smartphone use and overall educational attainment (Judd, 2014; Junco and Cotten, 2012; Rosen et al., 2013). Some have seen the link between poor educational attainment and excessive smartphone use as one based on diverted attention and the increased load on already stretched cognitive resources (Mayer and Moreno, 2003). Others have surmised that problematic smartphone use actively blocks cognitive resources that are essential for learning to take place successfully (Hawi and Samaha, 2016; Samaha and Hawi, 2016). Finally, the other way in which smartphones can impact on our capacity to learn is their capacity to distract and disrupt within the context of any learning environment. In order for anything to be learned, engagement in the subject matter is essential if the necessary memory traces are to be laid down correctly. If there is a sudden shift in attention from the academic to the non-academic (e.g. checking Pinterest on their smartphones) then there is going to be a decrement in the amount of information that will be retained (Just et al., 2001). Obviously when we enter into the level of problematic or addicted levels of use, these issues are simply going to be exacerbated further, hence the need to clearly identify how learning is affected in a more systematic way.

In an unpublished study designed as a follow-on from the research conducted on mobile phone use I changed the focus away from mobile phone use and instead looked at smartphone use and cognitive failures. The findings from the study that used an adapted version of the SPAI produced by Lin et al. (2014) again noted a significant correlation between levels of smartphone addiction and cognitive failures in daily life. The results from this research appeared to show that current developments in smartphone technology are also linked to the levels of cognitive failures individuals are experiencing in their daily lives. Again, as before, the conclusion from this research cannot be causative in nature – we cannot say with certainty that addiction to smartphones leads to an increase in cognitive failures, as there is no prior measure from which to make a comparison. If we had a group of participants who had never been subjected to smartphone technology, and asked them to start to use said technology, we may be able to make this link. However, trying to find such a group in today's modern society is something of a challenge, so the conclusions we can make from this research are pretty speculative in nature. Excessive levels of both mobile phone and smartphone use are linked to significantly higher levels of cognitive failures. Building on evidence from previous research, it is suggested that those individuals who find themselves engaged in excessive levels of smartphone use have limited working memory capacity and also poorer attentional control (Kane et al., 2007; Ophir et al., 2009; Unsworth et al., 2012). Unsworth et al. (2012) noted that individuals who had poorer attentional control suffered from an inability to prevent a spontaneous shift towards task-irrelevant information. As attentional control is linked to working memory capacity, the logic here would suggest that issues with working memory in turn lead to a deficit in attentional control. In terms of those who are addicted to the use of smartphones, the capacity to be distracted and engage in activities on the smartphone, and not pay attention to elements within their daily sphere of activity, would provide a neat explanation for the rise in experiencing increased levels of cognitive errors. However, as detailed before, such a notion is purely conjectural in nature and we really need to get more research conducted in this area in order for us to understand the process involved in these findings.

Internet Addiction

The fundamentals of Internet addiction and the plethora of research that has been conducted in this area would take an entire book rather than part of a chapter to discuss. For now we are going to be focusing directly on the impact Internet addiction (whether it exists or not) has upon the individual and, in turn, human cognition. For those of you wishing to explore the literature on Internet addiction further I will include some at the end of the chapter. For the most part, the research exploring the psychological impact of Internet addiction has focused predominantly on aspects of social functioning and well-being (see Kuss et al., 2013, for an excellent review of this research). What remains is a gap, and that gap is the exploration of how excessive use of the Internet impacts on aspects of human cognition. Internet addiction, as we have seen with smartphone addiction, has been associated with poor academic performance in adolescent populations

(Mythily et al., 2008; Odaci, 2011; Yang and Tung, 2007). The root cause of this would appear to share similarities with technology addiction overall, where individuals are spending their time engaged in activities that disrupt learning. These processes could be linked directly to aspects of interference or distraction, or could also be associated with fatigue as individuals engage in online activities at the expense of sleep (Kubey et al., 2001). Poor sleep patterns have already been previously linked to poorer academic performance (e.g. Dewald et al., 2010), with excessive use of digital technology also having an impact on delayed sleep (Brunborg et al., 2011; Suganuma et al., 2007).

Other research has noted that those individuals who exhibit symptoms of impulsivity and hyperactivity are more likely to fall into an Internet-addicted classification (Yoo et al., 2004). The authors of this research concluded that the presence of ADHD symptoms in children could present an early predictor for Internet addiction, but there was no suggestion that Internet addiction has actually caused such symptoms. Other researchers have also noted a relationship between Internet addiction and symptoms of ADHD, including Yen et al. (2007, 2009).

In my own research (Hadlington, 2015) Internet addiction had a similar effect on cognitive failures to mobile phone addiction. Those individuals who scored higher on the measure of Internet addiction demonstrated a higher propensity to experience cognitive failures in daily life. Again, as with the findings for mobile phone addiction, there is an issue with the attribution of causality – we cannot say that Internet addiction *causes* higher levels of cognitive failures, but we can say that those people who are addicted to the Internet experience more of these failures. The underlying causes – again this could be due to individual differences in working memory and attention control, meaning that those people who are more likely to be distracted and miss things in their daily lives are less likely to be able to inhibit their use of the Internet. One thing that is very clear is that research in this area is clearly lacking and we need to do more in order to understand these effects. It may take several years for the effects of the Internet, as with any form of digital technology, to show clear and precise impacts on human cognition.

Social Network Addiction?

There is a delightful case study presented by Karaiskos et al., 2010. They presented a 24-year-old woman who, according to them, expressed issues with excessive use of social networking, much to the detriment of her day-to-day functioning. She had been taken to the clinic as she had been spending in excess of five hours per day checking her Facebook account. In the preceding eight months she had accumulated over 400 friends, and had also ceased many of her normal daily activities. She had lost her job as a waitress in a local café as she repeatedly left to find the nearest Internet access in order to check her Facebook page. They also noted that, even during the examination, the woman repeatedly took out her smartphone in order to establish an Internet connection so that she could check her page. After closer examination she was found to exhibit signs of mild anxiety as well as frequent sleep disturbances. The authors concluded that the patient had previously been using the Internet for the preceding seven years prior to getting a Facebook page and had showed no signs of Internet addiction, suggesting that addiction to social networks could present another sub-category of technology related addictions.

Of what limited research there has been in the context of cognition and something that could be loosely termed as social network addiction has come from (Frein et al., 2013). In Frein et al.'s research they explored the key differences in memory recall for those individuals who were typified as high and low users of Facebook. Forty-four participants were split into two groups according to their level of Facebook use, and then asked to complete a free recall task in which they had to remember 72 random words. In this instance, the role of distraction and misguided attention was eliminated as participants were directly prevented from using any form of electronic device in order to access Facebook. The results proved to be rather interesting, showing that those who spent more than one hour per day on Facebook also scored significantly lower on the test of memory in comparison with those in the lower-use Facebook group. The authors of this study make a conclusion based on previous research from Small and Vorgan, 2008, who noted that actively engaging in activities on the Internet served to change the brain activation of participants who had never used the Internet before. They in turn suggested that it is plausible that the use of Facebook has also created a significant underlying change in the mechanisms participants use to process and later access information. The study presents its limitations, as there is no comparison between those individuals who have never used Facebook before and those who were more experienced users. In a similar respect, we cannot directly say that *high* levels of Facebook use are the same as an *addictive* level of use, so the link here between the two is tenuous at the least. However, it does give us the basis to start to do more research into the area and highlights a difference according to memory and level of engagement with social networking sites such as Facebook.

Technology Addiction: With Caveats

To say that someone is suffering from a particular type of addiction, such as Internet, smartphone or social networking, is something of an oversimplification in its own right. As Griffiths (Griffiths, 1998, 2012; Widyanto and Griffiths, 2007) noted, the actual *overall* addiction (particularly in the instance of smartphone and

Internet typologies) tends to mask the true underlying addiction. For example, let us take an example of a person who is spending an excessive amount of time online shopping. The compulsive behaviour here is potentially the need to spend money online and acquire something new, irrespective of whether they need that thing or not (see Rose and Dhandayudham, 2014, for a really good discussion of online shopping addiction). However, the tool used in order to gain access to the primary addiction of shopping online is that of the Internet. It would therefore appear to be pretty logical to assume that such an individual will of course exhibit signs of Internet addiction. As you can see, the addiction to online shopping is being masked, overlooked or overshadowed by the overarching connection to the Internet, which poses the question of how best we view such addictions to technology. For the most part, researchers such as Widyanto and Griffiths (2007) have argued that true Internet addidction (as supposedly that of smartphone addiciton) does not truly exist. Griffiths (2000) presented this distinction very succintly when he suggested a degree of caution when attributing the focus of addiction – is the addiction *to* the Internet or an addiction *on* the Internet? It is useful to have this question in your mind when exploring research looking at aspects of addiction to technology, especially those such as Internet and smartphone.

Summary

It could be the case that over the coming years, as we spend more time with technology, such 'addictions' will become the norm and a level of use we currently see as being excessive will be the status quo. As research methodologies and the development of more sensitive scales progress, there could be a point at which diagnostic tools are presented that give us the capacity to strip out the Internet from the underlying addiction, perhaps to highlight Internet-enabled addictions. When I first started writing this book, I was never entirely sure that a chapter on addiction to technology would fit, given that much of the research focuses very heavily on links to personality factors. However, when delving a little bit deeper into the underlying consequences of excessive technology use, it becomes clear that incidences of cognitive functioning being impaired are a common feature of the research. In the studies that have been reviewed above, individuals report aspects of being unable to focus on their work, are distracted, or suffer from fatigue due to lengthy periods of use or lack of sleep. These aspects all show potential for impaired cognition, especially where individuals are spending more time thinking about the focus of the addiction rather than the thing they should be doing! Research of my own shows that there is a link between technology addiction and the incidence of cognitive failures in daily life, but caution is advised when interpreting these results. We cannot say for sure that addiction to technology is the direct cause of these cognitive failures, as there may be an underlying link to individual differences in attentional control – which in turn means people are more likely to be addicted to digital technology are also more likely to be prone to cognitive failures. As has been made clear throughout this book, the only way to explore this further is – you've guessed it – more research!

12

THE END

WHERE DO WE GO FROM HERE?

As we have seen throughout this book, the use (and mere presence) of digital technology can have an influence on human cognition. Although I have attempted to strike a balance between both the positives and the negatives, some readers may come away with the notion that it is all doom and gloom. This isn't the case and there are some really good examples where digital technology can aid individuals in their day-to-day lives. Smartphones present individuals with newer and more innovative ways of recording, transferring and presenting information, and allow this material to be accessed by an increasingly wider audience. Likewise, those individuals or environments that were previously isolated, whether due to geography, physical disability or social barriers, can now engage in a wealth of activities that would have otherwise remained outside their experience.

The end of any book always appears to have some form of finality to it, but in this instance I am going to challenge the reader to take the material discussed here further. The story that has been told throughout the chapters of this book remains far from a complete one, and a great deal of work still remains if we are to gain a greater understanding of whether and how digital technology is changing the way in which we think. I make no apologies for constantly bombarding the reader with the need to do more research into this area, and the material that has made up the substantive part of this book still remains the tip of the iceberg. It is only over the coming years, as humans spend increasingly more and more time engaged in new and more immersive forms of digital technology, that the impact on human cognition will become clearer. Moreover, we will start to gain a better understanding of *how* humans are using existing cognitive skills in their interactions with digital technology, and by doing so will be able to design better and more useful experiences, particularly in the fields of education, information presentation and entertainment.

One key point that we have to remember is that the development of digital technology is a contextually recent thing within the history of the human race. We don't really know how or whether the digital technology we are using today will change the way in which we think, and it is perhaps far too early to make such massive assertions based on what is perhaps less than a quarter of a century of being exposed to such. However, some writers have suggested that the speed at which technology is being adopted is increasing, pointing to the history of technology adoption over the past hundred years. For example, Michael DeGusta, writing for the *MIT Technology Review* (2012), noted that whilst it took 30 years for electricity to reach a 10 per cent adoption rate, and that for telephones it was 25 years, it has taken smartphones 10 years to reach a 40 per cent adoption rate (taking 2002 as the shipment date of the first BlackBerry device). Although the data used by DeGusta is solely based on US market data, it does present an interesting snapshot of how quickly some areas of the globe are adopting digital technology. Such notions are echoed by earlier suggestions by Felton (2008), who, writing for the *New York Times*, also noted that more recent technological innovations such as the computer and the Internet have been adopted more quickly than the older, analogue technology. So will this meteoric surge in the adoption of new technologies map onto a similar rise in changes to human cognition? Again, only time and more research will tell.

REFERENCES

Adachi, P. J. C., and Willoughby, T. (2013). More than just fun and games: The longitudinal relationships between strategic video games, self-reported problem solving skills, and academic grades. *Journal of Youth and Adolescence, 42*(7), 1041–1052.

Adamczyk, P. D., and Bailey, B. P. (2004). If not now when? The effects of interruption at different moments within task execution. *Proceedings of the SIGCHI Conference on Human Factors in Computing Systems, 6*(1), 271–278.

Adler, R. F., and Benbunan-Fich, R. (2012). Juggling on a high wire: Multitasking effects on performance. *International Journal of Human Computer Studies, 70*(2), 156–168.

Alexander, J. E., and Tate, M. A. (1999). *Web wisdom: How to evaluate and create information quality on the web.* Mahwah, NJ: Erlbaum.

Alloway, T., Horton, J., Alloway, R., and Dawson, C. (2013). Social networking sites and cognitive abilities: Do they make you smarter? *Computers and Education, 63*, 10–16.

Allport, A. (1989). Visual attention. In M. I. Posner (Ed.), *Foundations of cognitive science* (pp. 631–682). Cambridge, MA: The MIT Press.

Altmann, E., and Trafton, J. (2004). Task interruption: Resumption lag and the role of cues. *Proceedings of the 26th Annual Conference of the Cognitive Science Society* (pp. 43–48). Retrieved from http://oai.dtic.mil/oai/oai?verb=getRecord&metadata Prefix=html&identifier=ADA480333

Altmann, E. M., and Trafton, J. G. (2002). *Memory for Goals: An Activation-Based Model. Cognitive Science* (Vol. 26). http://doi.org/10.1016/S0364-0213(01)00058-1

Alzahabi, R., and Becker, M. W. (2013). The association between media multitasking, task-switching, and dual-task performance. *Journal of Experimental Psychology: Human Perception and Performance, 39*(5), 1485–1495. http://doi.org/10.1037/a0031208

Anderson, C. (2008). The end of theory: The data deluge makes the scientific method obsolete. *Wired Magazine, 16*(7).

Anderson, J. R. (1995). *Learning and memory: An integrated approach* (2nd ed.). New York: John Wiley and Sons, Inc.

Anderson, J. R., Bothell, D., Byrne, M. D., Douglass, S., Lebiere, C., and Qin, Y. (2004). An integrated theory of the mind. *Psychological Review, 111*(4), 1036–1060. http://doi.org/10.1037/0033-295X.111.4.1036

Andrade, J. (2009). What does doodling do? *Applied Cognitive Psychology, 24*, 100–106. http://doi.org/10.1002/acp

Anguera, J. A., Boccanfuso, J., Rintoul, J. L., Al-Hashimi, O., Faraji, F., Janowich, J., … Gazzaley, A. (2013). Video game training enhances cognitive control in older adults. *Nature, 501*(7465), 97–101. http://doi.org/10.1038/nature12486

Antonenko, P. D., and Niederhauser, D. S. (2010). Computers in human behavior: The influence of leads on cognitive load and learning in a hypertext environment. *Computers in Human Behavior, 26*(2), 140–150. http://doi.org/10.1016/j.chb.2009.10.014

Appelbaum, L. G., Cain, M. S., Darling, E. F., and Mitroff, S. R. (2013). Action video game playing is associated with improved visual sensitivity, but not alterations in visual sensory memory. *Attention, Perception and Psychophysics*, *75*, 1161–1167. http://doi.org/10.3758/s13414-013-0472-7

Ashcraft, M. H., and Radvansky, G. A. (2013). *Cognition* (6th ed.). London: Pearson.

Astin, A. W. (1984). Student involvement: A developmental theory for higher education. *Journal of College Student Development*, *25*(4), 518–529. http://doi.org/10.1016/0263

Ayres, P., and Sweller, J. (2005). *The split-attention principle in multimedia learning. The Cambridge handbook of multimedia learning.*

Bacon, W. F., and Egeth, H. E. (1994). Overriding stimulus-driven attentional capture. *Perceptionand Psychophysics*, *55*(5), 485–496. http://doi.org/10.3758/BF03205306

Baddeley, A. D. (2000a). The episodic buffer: A new component of working memory? *Trends in Cognitive Sciences*, *4*(11), 417–423. http://doi.org/10.1016/S1364-6613(00)01538-2

Baddeley, A. D. (2000b). The phonological loop and the irrelevant speech effect: Some comments on Neath. *Psychonomic Bulletin and Review*, *7*(3), 544–549. Retrieved from http://www.ncbi.nlm.nih.gov/pubmed/11082863

Bailey, B., and Iqbal, S. (2008). Understanding changes in mental workload during execution of goal-directed tasks and its application for interruption management. *ACM Transactions on Computer-Human Interaction*, *14*(4), 21–28.

Bailey, B. P., Konstan, J. A., and Carlis, J. V. (2000). Measuring the effects of interruptions on task performance in the user interface. *SMC 2000 Conference Proceedings (2000 IEEE International Conference on Systems, Man and Cybernetics: "Cybernetics Evolving to Systems, Humans, Organizations, and Their Complex Interactions")* (Cat. No.00CH37166), *2*, 757–762. http://doi.org/10.1109/ICSMC.2000.885940

Barnett, S. M., and Ceci, S. J. (2002). When and where do we apply what we learn? A taxonomy for far transfer. *Psychological Bulletin*, *128*(4), 612–637. http://doi.org/10.1037/0033-2909.128.4.612

Bartram, L., Ware, C., and Calvert, T. (2003). Moticons: Detection, distraction and task. *International Journal of Human-Computer Studies*, *58*(5), 515–545. http://doi.org/10.1016/S1071-5819(03)00021-1

Basak, C., Boot, W. R., Voss, M. W., and Kramer, A. F. (2008). Can training in a real-time strategy video game attenuate cognitive decline in older adults? *Psychology and Aging*, *23*(4), 765–777. http://doi.org/10.1037/a0013494

Basoglu, K. A., Fuller, M. A., and Sweeney, J. T. (2009). Investigating the effects of computer mediated interruptions: An analysis of task characteristics and interruption frequency on financial performance. *International Journal of Accounting Information Systems*, *10*(4), 177–189. http://doi.org/10.1016/j.accinf.2009.10.003

Baumeister, R. F., Twenge, J. M., and Nuss, C. K. (2002). Effects of social exclusion on cognitive processes: Anticipated aloneness reduces intelligent thought. *Journal of Personality and Social Psychology*, *83*(4), 817–827. http://doi.org/10.1037/0022-3514.83.4.817

Bawden, D., and Robinson, L. (2008). The dark side of information: Overload, anxiety and other paradoxes and pathologies. *Journal of Information Science*, *35*(2), 180–191. http://doi.org/10.1177/0165551508095781

Bayles, M. E. (2002). Designing online banner advertisements: Should we animate? In *Proceedings of the SIGCHI Conference on Human Factors in Computing Systems* (pp. 363–366). http://doi.org/10.1145/503376.503441

Becker, M., Alzahabi, R., and Hopwood, C. (2013). Media multitasking is associated with symptoms of depression and social anxiety. *Cyberpsychology, Behavior and Social Networking, 16*(2), 132–135. http://doi.org/10.1089/cyber.2012.0291

Bellotti, F., Kapralos, B., Lee, K., Moreno-Ger, P., and Berta, R. (2013). Assessment in and of serious games: An overview. *Advances in Human-Computer Interaction, 2013*, 1–2. http://doi.org/10.1155/2013/136864

Benbunan-Fich, R., Adler, R. F., and Mavlanova, T. (2011). Measuring multitasking behavior with activity-based metrics. *ACM Transactions on Computer-Human Interaction, 18*(2), 1–22. http://doi.org/10.1145/1970378.1970381

Bennett, S., Maton, K., and Kervin, L. (2008). The "digital natives" debate: A critical review of the evidence. *British Journal of Educational Technology, 39*(5), 775–786. http://doi.org/10.1111/j.1467-8535.2007.00793.x

Benway, J. P. (1999). *Banner blindness: What searching users notice and do not notice on the World Wide Web*. Houston, TX: Rice University.

Bianchi, A., and Phillips, J. G. (2005). Psychological predictors of problem mobile phone use. *CyberPsychology and Behavior: The Impact of the Internet, Multimedia and Virtual Reality on Behavior and Society, 8*(1), 39–51. http://doi.org/10.1089/cpb.2005.8.39

Biggs, J. (2003). *Aligning teaching for constructing learning*.

Bikhchandani, S., Hirshleifer, D., and Welch, I. (1992). A theory of fads, fashion, custom, and cultural change as informational cascades. *Journal of Political Economy, 100*(5), 992. http://doi.org/10.1086/261849

Bikhchandani, S., Hirshleifer, D., and Welch, I. (1998). Learning from the behavior of others: Conformity, fads, and informational cascades. *Journal of Economic Perspectives, 12*(3), 151–170. http://doi.org/10.1257/jep.12.3.151

Bishop, J. (2014). Representations of "trolls" in mass media communication: A review of media-texts and moral panics relating to "internet trolling." *International Journal of Web Based Communities, 10*(1), 7. http://doi.org/10.1504/IJWBC.2014.058384

Blair, K. S., Smith, B. W., Mitchell, D. G. V, Morton, J., Vythilingam, M., Pessoa, L., … Blair, R. J. R. (2007). Modulation of emotion by cognition and cognition by emotion. *NeuroImage, 35*(1), 430–440. http://doi.org/10.1016/j.neuroimage.2006.11.048

Bliuc, A. M., Ellis, R., Goodyear, P., and Piggott, L. (2010). Learning through face-to-face and online discussions: Associations between students' conceptions, approaches and academic performance in political science. *British Journal of Educational Technology, 41*(3), 512–524. http://doi.org/10.1111/j.1467-8535.2009.00966.x

Bluedorn, A. C., Kaufman, C. F., and Lane, P. M. (1992). How many things do you like to do at once? An introduction to monochronic and polychronic time. *The Executive, 6*(4), 17–26.

Blumberg, F. C., Rosenthal, S. F., and Randall, J. D. (2008). Impasse-driven learning in the context of video games. *Computers in Human Behavior, 24*(4), 1530–1541. http://doi.org/10.1016/j.chb.2007.05.010

Boot, W. R., Blakely, D. P., and Simons, D. J. (2011). Do action video games improve perception and cognition? *Frontiers in Psychology*, *2*(September), 226. http://doi.org/10.3389/fpsyg.2011.00226

Boot, W. R., Kramer, A. F., Simons, D. J., Fabiani, M., and Gratton, G. (2008). The effects of video game playing on attention, memory, and executive control. *Acta Psychologica*, *129*(3), 387–398. http://doi.org/10.1016/j.actpsy.2008.09.005

Brand-Gruwel, S., Wopereis, I., and Vermetten, Y. (2005). Information problem solving by experts and novices: Analysis of a complex cognitive skill. *Computers in Human Behavior*, *21*(3), 487–508. Retrieved from http://www.sciencedirect.com/science/article/pii/S0747563204001591

Brenner, V. (1997). Psychology of computer use: XLVII. Parameters of Internet use, abuse and addiction: The first 90 days of the Internet Usage Survey. *Psychological Reports*, *80*, 879–882. http://doi.org/10.2466/pr0.1997.80.3.879

Breuer, J. J., and Bente, G. (2010). Why so serious? On the relation of serious games and learning. *Eludamos: Journal for Computer Game Culture*, *4*(1), 7–24. Retrieved from http://www.eludamos.org/index.php/eludamos/article/view/vol4no1-2

Broadbent, D. E. (1957). A mechanical model for human attention and immediate memory. *Psychological Review*, *64*(3), 205–215.

Broadbent, D. E. (1971). *Decision and stress*. New York: Academic Press.

Broadbent, D. E., Cooper, P. F., FitzGerald, P., and Parkes, K. R. (1982). The Cognitive Failures Questionnaire (CFQ) and its correlates. *The British Journal of Clinical Psychology*, *21*, 1–16. http://doi.org/10.1111/j.2044-8260.1982.tb01421.x

Brooking, J. B., and Damos, D. L. (1991). Individual differences in multiple-task performance. In D. L. Damos (Ed.), *Mutiple-task performance* (pp. 363–386). London: Taylor & Francis.

Brown, J. S. (2000). Growing up digital. *Change*, *32*(2), 10–20.

Brown, R. I. F. (1993). Some contributions of the study of gambling to the study of other addictions. In W. R. Eadington and J. A. Cornelius (Eds.), *Gambling behavior and problem gambling* (pp. 241–272). Reno, NV: University of Nevada Press.

Brown, R. I. F. (1997). A theoretical model of the behavioural addictions – Applied to offending. In J. E. Hodge, M. McMurran, and C. R. Hollin (Eds.), *Addicted to crime?* (pp. 13–65). Chichester: John Wiley.

Brown, S. (2010). From VLEs to learning webs: The implications of Web 2.0 for learning and teaching. *Interactive Learning Environments*, *18*(1), 1–10.

Browne, G., Pitts, M., and Wetherbe, J. (2007). Cognitive stopping rules for terminating information search in online tasks. *MIS Quarterly*, *31*(1), 89–104. Retrieved from http://dl.acm.org/citation.cfm?id=2017333

Browne, T., Jenkins, M., and Walker, R. (2006). A longitudinal perspective regarding the use of VLEs by higher education institutions in the United Kingdom. *Interactive Learning Environments*, *14*(2), 177–192. http://doi.org/10.1080/10494820600852795

Brumby, D. P., and Howes, A. (2008). Strategies for guiding interactive search: An empirical investigation into the consequences of label relevance for assessment and selection. *Human–Computer Interaction*, *500*(23), 1–46. Retrieved from http://www.tandfonline.com/doi/abs/10.1080/07370020701851078

Brunborg, G. S., Mentzoni, R. A., Molde, H., Myrseth, H., Skouverøe, K. J. M., Bjorvatn, B., and Pallesen, S. (2011). The relationship between media use in the bedroom, sleep habits and symptoms of insomnia. *Journal of Sleep Research*, *20*(4), 569–575. http://doi.org/10.1111/j.1365-2869.2011.00913.x

Bruner, G. C., and Kumar, A. (2000). Web commerical and advertising hierarchy-of-effects. *Journal of Advertising Research*, *40*(1–2), 35–42.

Buitenweg, J. I. V., Murre, J. M. J., and Ridderinkhof, K. R. (2012). Brain training in progress: A review of trainability in healthy seniors. *Frontiers in Human Neuroscience*, *6*(June), 183. http://doi.org/10.3389/fnhum.2012.00183

Burbules, N. C. (2001). Paradoxes of the Web: The ethical dimensions of credibility. *Library Trends*, *49*(3), 441–453.

Burke, M., Hornof, A., Nilsen, E., and Gorman, N. (2005). High-cost banner blindness: Ads increase perceived workload, hinder visual search, and are forgotten. *ACM Transactions on Computer-Human Interaction*, *12*(4), 423–445. http://doi.org/10.1145/1121112.1121116

Burnett, S., Sebastian, C., Cohen Kadosh, K., and Blakemore, S. J. (2011). The social brain in adolescence: Evidence from functional magnetic resonance imaging and behavioural studies. *Neuroscience and Biobehavioral Reviews*, *35*(8), 1654–1664. http://doi.org/10.1016/j.neubiorev.2010.10.011

Buser, T., and Peter, N. (2012). Multitasking. *Experimental Economics*, *15*(4), 641–655. http://doi.org/10.1007/s10683-012-9318-8

Byström, K., and Järvelin, K. (1995). Task complexity affects information seeking and use. *Task Information Processing and Management*, *31*(2), 191–213. http://doi.org/10.1016/0306-4573(95)80035-R

Cain, M. S., Landau, A. N., and Shimamura, A. P. (2012). Action video game experience reduces the cost of switching tasks. *Attention, Perception and Psychophysics*, *74*(4), 641–647. http://doi.org/10.3758/s13414-012-0284-1

Cain, M. S., and Mitroff, S. R. (2011). Distractor filtering in media multitaskers. *Perception*, *40*(10), 1183–1192. http://doi.org/10.1068/p6939

Cain, M. S., Prinzmetal, W., Shimamura, A. P., and Landau, A. N. (2014). Improved control of exogenous attention in action video game players. *Frontiers in Psychology*, *5*(Feb.). http://doi.org/10.3389/fpsyg.2014.00069

Carr, N. (2010). *The shallows: How the Internet is changing the way we think, read and remember*. London: Atlantic Books.

Carrier, L. M., Cheever, N., Rosen, L. D., Benitez, S., and Chang, J. (2009). Multitasking across generations: Multitasking choices and difficulty ratings in three generations of Americans. *Computers in Human Behavior*, *25*(2), 483–489. http://doi.org/10.1016/j.chb.2008.10.012

Carrillo, M. C., Dishman, E., and Plowman, T. (2009). Everyday technologies for Alzheimer's disease care: Research findings, directions, and challenges. *Alzheimer's and Dementia*, *5*(6), 479–488. http://doi.org/10.1016/j.jalz.2009.09.003

Castellanos, F. X., Sonuga-Barke, E. J. S., Milham, M. P., and Tannock, R. (2006). Characterizing cognition in ADHD: Beyond executive dysfunction. *Trends in Cognitive Sciences*, *10*(3), 117–124. http://doi.org/10.1016/j.tics.2006.01.011

Catledge, L. D., and Pitkow, J. E. (1995). Characterising browsing strategies in the World Wide Web. *Computer Networks and ISDN Systems*, *27*(95), 1065–1073.

Cattell, R. B. (1963). Theory of fluid and crystallized intelligence: A critical experiment. *Journal of Educational Psychology*, *54*(1), 1–22. http://doi.org/10.1037/h0046743

Chaiken, S., Liberman, A., and Eagly, A. H. (1989). Heuristic and systematic information processing within and beyond the persuasion context. In J. S. Uleman and J. A. Bargh (Eds.), *Unintended thought* (pp. 212–252). New York: Guilford Press.

Chaiken, S., and Trope, Y. (1999). *Dual-process theories in social psychology*. New York: Guilford Press. Retrieved from http://books.google.it/books?id=5X_auIBx99EC

Chan, P. A., and Rabinowitz, T. (2006). A cross-sectional analysis of video games and attention deficit hyperactivity disorder symptoms in adolescents. *Annals of General Psychiatry*, *5*, 16. http://doi.org/10.1186/1744-859X-5-16

Chang, Y.-J., and Tang, J. C. (2015). Investigating mobile users' ringer mode usage and attentiveness and responsiveness to communication. *17th International Conference on Human-Computer Interaction with Mobile Devices and Services, MobileHCI 2015*, (pp. 6–15). http://doi.org/10.1145/2785830.2785852

Chen, S.-H., Weng, L.-J., Su, Y.-J., Wu, H.-M., and Yang, P.-F. (2003). Development of a Chinese internet addiction scale and its psychometric study. *Chinese Journal of Psychology*. http://doi.org/10.6129/CJP

Chen, Y.-F., and Peng, S. S. (2008). University students' internet use and its relationships with academic performance, interpersonal relationships, psychosocial adjustment, and self-evaluation. *CyberPsychology and Behavior*, *11*(4), 467–469. http://doi.org/10.1089/cpb.2007.0128

Cheong, P. (2008). The young and techless? Investigating internet use and problem-solving behaviors of young adults in Singapore. *New Media and Society*, *10*(5), 771–791. http://doi.org/10.1177/1461444808094356

Cheung, L. M., and Wong, W. S. (2011). The effects of insomnia and internet addiction on depression in Hong Kong Chinese adolescents: An exploratory cross-sectional analysis. *Journal of Sleep Research*, *20*(2), 311–317. http://doi.org/10.1111/j.1365-2869.2010.00883.x

Choi, C. J., Dassiou, X., and Gettings, S. (2000). Herding behaviour and the size of customer base as a commitment to quality. *Economica*, *67*(267), 375–398. http://doi.org/10.1111/1468-0335.00214

Choi, K., Son, H., Park, M., Han, J., Kim, K., Lee, B., and Gwak, H. (2009). Internet overuse and excessive daytime sleepiness in adolescents: *Psychiatry and Clinical Neurosciences*, *63*(4), 455–462. http://doi.org/10.1111/j.1440-1819.2009.01925.x

Chou, C., and Hsiao, M.-C. (2000). Internet addiction, usage, gratification, and pleasure experience: The Taiwan college students' case. *Computers and Education*, *35*(1), 65–80. http://doi.org/10.1016/S0360-1315(00)00019-1

Choudhury, S., and McKinney, K. A. (2013). Digital media, the developing brain and the interpretive plasticity of neuroplasticity. *Transcultural Psychiatry*, *50*(2), 192–215. http://doi.org/10.1177/1363461512474623

Chun, M. M., Golomb, J. D., and Turk-Browne, N. B. (2011). A taxonomy of external and internal attention. *Annual Review of Psychology*, *62*, 73–101.

Clark, J. E., Lanphear, A. K., and Riddick, C. C. (1987). The effects of video game playing on the response selection of elderly adults. *Journal of Gerontology*, *42*(1), 82–85.

Cochrane, S. (2006). *The Memory Recall of Pop-Up Advertisements amongst Experienced Internet Users*. Dublin: Dun Laoghaire Institute of Art, Design and Technology.

Cohen, S. (1980). After effects of stress on human performance and social behavior: A review of research and theory. *Psychological Bulletin*, *88*(1), 82. http://doi.org/10.1037/0033-2909.88.1.82

Cooke, L., Taylor, A. G., and Canny, J. (2008). How do users search web home pages? An eye-tracking study of multiple navigation menus. *Technical Communication*, *55*(2), 176–194.

Coraggio, L. (1990). *Deleterious effects of intermittent interruptions on the task performance of knowledge workers: A laboratory investigation*. Tucson, AZ: University of Arizona.

Cowan, N., Nugent, L. D., Elliott, E. M., Ponomarev, I., and Saults, J. S. (1999). The role of attention in the development of short-term memory: Age differences in the verbal span of apprehension. *Child Development*, *70*(5), 1082–1097. http://doi.org/10.1111/1467-8624.00080

Cromwell, H. (1950). The relative effect on audience attitude of the first versus the second argumentative speech of a series. *Communications Monographs*, *17*(2), 105–122.

Cropper, A. G., and Evans, S. J. W. (1968). Ergonomics and computer display design. *Computer Bulletin*, *12*(3), 94.

Csikszentmihalyi, M. (1990). *Flow: The psychology of optimal performance. Optimal experience: Psychological studies of flow in consciousness*. New York: Cambridge University Press.

Cutrell, E., Czerwinski, M., and Horvitz, E. (2001). Notification, disruption, and memory: Effects of messaging interruptions on memory and performance. *INTERACT '01*, 263–269. Retrieved from http://citeseerx.ist.psu.edu/viewdoc/summary?doi=10.1.1.26.418

Cutrell, E., and Guan, Z. (2007). An eye-tracking study of information usage in Web search: Variations in target position and contextual snippet length. In *Proceedings of the SIGCHI Conference on Human Factors in Computing Systems* (pp. 407–416). ACM. Retrieved from http://www.divinewrite.com.au/downloads/MS_eye_tracking_study.pdf

Czerwinski, M., Cutrell, E., and Horvitz, E. (2000). Instant messaging: Effects of relevance and time. In S. Turner and P. Turner (Eds.), *People and Computers XIV: Proceedings of HCI 2000*, Vol. 2, British Computer Society (pp. 71–76).

Czerwinski, M., Horvitz, E., and Wilhite, S. (2004). A diary study of task switching and interruptions. *CHI '04 Proceedings of the SIGCHI Conference on Human Factors in Computing Systems*, *6*(1), 175–182. http://doi.org/10.1145/985692.985715

Czerwinski, M., and Larson, K. (2003). Cognition and the Web: Moving from theory to Web design. *Human Factors and Web Development*, 147–165. Retrieved from https://books.google.co.uk/books?hl=en&lr=&id=sKvi5fVL-uAC&oi=fnd&pg=PA147&dq=czwerinski+2000++cognition+web&ots=j6YMu6GCFt&sig=YVdLL4JUtiDrJWAuSN43tDMgakE

Dabbish, L., Mark, G., and Gonzalez, V. (2011). Why do I keep interrupting myself? Environment, habit and self-interruption. *Chi*, 3127–3130. http://doi.org/10.1145/1978942.1979405

Dahl, R. (2011). Understanding the risky business of adolescence. *Neuron, 69*(5), 837–839. http://doi.org/10.1016/j.neuron.2011.02.036

Dahlin, E., Nyberg, L., Bäckman, L., and Neely, A. S. (2008). Plasticity of executive functioning in young and older adults: Immediate training gains, transfer, and long-term maintenance. *Psychology and Aging, 23*(4), 720–730. http://doi.org/10.1037/a0014296

David, P., Xu, L., Srivastava, J., and Kim, J. H. (2013). Media multitasking between two conversational tasks. *Computers in Human Behavior, 29*(4), 1657–1663. http://doi.org/10.1016/j.chb.2013.01.052

Davis, R., Flett, G., and Besser, A. (2002). Validation of a new scale for measuring problematic Internet use: Implications for pre-employment screening. *CyberPsychology and Behavior, 5*(4), 331–345. Retrieved from http://online.liebertpub.com/doi/abs/10.1089/109493102760275581

De Vany, A., and Lee, C. (2001). Quality signals in information cascades and the dynamics of the distribution of motion picture box office revenues. *Journal of Economic Dynamics and Control, 25*(3–4), 593–614. http://doi.org/10.1016/S0165-1889(00)00037-3

Deary, I. J., Strand, S., Smith, P., and Fernandes, C. (2007). Intelligence and educational achievement. *Intelligence, 35*(1), 13–21. http://doi.org/10.1016/j.intell.2006.02.001

DeGusta, M. (2012). Are Smart phones spreading faster than any technology in human history? *MIT Technology Review.*

Delbridge, K. A. (2000). *Individual differences in multi-tasking ability: Exploring a nomological network.* Ann Arbor, MI: University Of Michigan.

Dennison, P. E., and Dennison, G. E. (1994). *Brain Gym® teacher's edition – revised.* Ventura, CA: Edu-Kinesthetics.

DePompei, R., Gillette, Y., Goetz, E., Xenopoulos-Oddsson, A., Bryen, D., and Dowds, M. (2008). Practical applications for use of PDAs and smartphones with children and adolescents who have traumatic brain injury. *NeuroRehabilitation, 23*(6), 487–499. Retrieved from http://search.ebscohost.com/login.aspx?direct=true&db=psyh&AN=2008-19368-005&site=ehost-live\nhttp://content.ebscohost.com/ContentServer.asp?T=P&P=AN&K=358218 51&S=L&D=a9h&EbscoContent=dGJyMMvl7ESeprA4y9fwOLCmr02eprVSsKu4S-K+WxWXS&ContentCustomer=dGJyMPGptE

DeStefano, D., and LeFevre, J. (2007). Cognitive load in hypertext reading: A review. *Computers in Human Behavior, 23*(3), 1616–1641. http://doi.org/10.1016/j.chb.2005.08.012

Dewald, J. F., Meijer, A. M., Oort, F. J., Kerkhof, G. A., and Bögels, S. M. (2010). The influence of sleep quality, sleep duration and sleepiness on school performance in children and adolescents: A meta-analytic review. *Sleep Medicine Reviews, 14*, 179–189. http://doi.org/10.1016/j.smrv.2009.10.004

Dholakia, U. M., and Soltysinski, K. (2001). Coveted or overlooked? The psychology of bidding for comparable listings in digital auctions. *Market Letters, 12*(3), 225–237.

Diao, F., and Sundar, S. S. (2004). Orienting response and memory for web advertisements: Exploring effects of pop-up window and animation. *Communication Research, 31*(5), 537–567. http://doi.org/10.1177/0093650204267932

DiMaggio, P., and Hargittai, E. (2001). From the "digital divide" to "digital inequality": Studying internet use as penetration increases. Princeton, NJ: Center for Arts and Cultural Policy Studies, Princeton University, 15, 1–23. Retrieved from http://www. maximise-ict.co.uk/WP15_DiMaggioHargittai.pdf

Dinet, J., Chevalier, A., and Tricot, A. (2012). Information search activity: An overview. *European Review of Applied Psychology*, *62*(2), 49–62. http://doi.org/10.1016/j. erap.2012.03.004

DiVita, J., Obermayer, R., Nugent, W., and Linville, J. M. (2004). Verification of the change blindness phenomenon while managing critical events on a combat information display. *Human Factors*, *46*(2), 205–218.

Dooley, J. J., Pyżalski, J., and Cross, D. (2009). Cyberbullying versus face-to-face bullying. *Zeitschrift Für Psychologie/Journal of Psychology*, *217*(4), 182–188. http://doi. org/10.1027/0044-3409.217.4.182

Dorval, M., and Pépin, M. (1986). Effect of playing a video game on a measure of spatial visualization. *Perceptual and Motor Skills*, *62*, 159–162.

Drews, F. A., Yazdani, H., Godfrey, C. N., Cooper, J. M., and Strayer, D. L. (2009). Text messaging during simulated driving. *Human Factors: The Journal of the Human Factors and Ergonomics Society*, *51*(5), 762–770. http://doi.org/10.1177/0018720809353319

Dreze, X., and Hussherr, F. (2003). Internet advertising: Is anybody watching? *Journal of Interactive Marketing*, *17*(4), 8–23. Retrieved from http://www.sciencedirect.com/science/article/pii/S1094996803701431

Duncan, J. (1984). Selective attention and the organization of visual information. *Journal of Experimental Psychology: General*, *113*(4), 501–17. http://doi.org/10.1037/0096-3445.113.4.501

Durlach, P. (2004). Army digital systems and vulnerability to change blindness. *US Army Research Institute for the Behavioural and Social Sciences*. Retrieved from http://oai. dtic.mil/oai/oai?verb=getRecord&metadataPrefix=html&identifier=ADA433072

Durlach, P. J., and Chen, J. (2003). Visual change detection in digital military displays. In *Proceedings of the Interservice/Industry Training, Simulation, and Education Conference 2003,* Orlando FL: IITSEC.

Dutton, W. H., and Helsper, E. J. (2007). *Oxford internet survey 2007 report: The internet in Britain*. Oxford: Oxford Internet Institute, University of Oxford.

Dzubak, C. M. (2007). Multitasking: The good, the bad and the unknown. *Association for the Tutoring Profession*, *53*(9), 1689–1699. http://doi.org/10.1017/CBO9781107415324.004

Easley, D., and Kleinberg, J. (2010). *Networks, crowds, and markets: Reasoning about a highly connected world*. Cambridge: Cambridge University Press.

Eichenbaum, A., Bavelier, D., and Green, C. (2014). Play that can do serious good. *American Journal of Play*, *7*(1), 50–72.

Eisenberg, M. B., and Berkowitz, R. E. (1990). *Information problem solving: The Big Six skills approach to library and information skills instruction*. Norwood, NJ: Ablex Publishing Corporation.

Englander, F., Terregrossa, R. A., and Wang, Z. (2010). Internet use among college students: Tool or toy? *Educational Review*, *62*(1), 85–96. http://doi.org/10.1080/0013 1910903519793

Ernst, M., and Fudge, J. L. (2009). A developmental neurobiological model of motivated behavior: Anatomy, connectivity and ontogeny of the triadic nodes. *Neuroscience and Biobehavioral Reviews*, *33*(3), 367–382. http://doi.org/10.1016/j.neubiorev.2008.10.009

Evenden, J. L. (1999). Varieties of impulsivity. *Psychopharmacology*, *146*(4), 348–361. http://doi.org/10.1007/PL00005481

Eyrolle, H., and Cellier, J.-M. (2000). The effects of interruptions in work activity: Field and laboratory results. *Applied Ergonomics*, *31*, 537–543.

Eysenbach, G. (2007). From intermediation to disintermediation and apomediation: New models for consumers to access and assess the credibility of health information in the age of Web2. 0. *Studies in Health Technology and Informatics*, *129*(1), 162.

Eysenbach, G., and Köhler, C. (2016). How do consumers search for and appraise health information on the world wide web? Qualitative study using focus groups, usability tests, and in-depth interviews. *BMJ*, *324*(June), 573–577. http://doi.org/10.1136/bmj.324.7337.573

Eysenck, M., Derakshan, N., Santos, R., and Calvo, M. (2007). Anxiety and cognitive performance: Attentional control theory. *Emotion*, *7*(2), 336–353.

Facer, K., and Furlong, R. (2001). Beyond the myth of the 'cyberkid': Young people at the margins of the information revolution. *Journal of Youth Studies*, *4*(4), 451–469. http://doi.org/10.1080/1367626012010190

Felton, M. (2008). How Americans spend their money. *New York Times*. Retrieved from http://www.nytimes.com/imagepages/2008/02/10/opinion/10op.graphic.ready.html

Feng, J., Spence, I., and Pratt, J. (2007). Playing an action video game reduces gender differences in spatial cognition. *Psychological Science*, *18*(10), 850–5. http://doi.org/10.1111/j.1467-9280.2007.01990.x

Fidel, R., Davies, R. K., Douglass, M. H., Holder, J. K., Hopkins, C. J., Kushner, E. J., … Toney, C. D. (1999). A visit to the information mall: Web searching behavior of high school students. *Journal of the American Society for Information Science*, *50*(1), 24–37.

Fiske, S. T., and Taylor, S. E. (1991). *Social cognition* (2nd ed.). London: McGraw-Hill.

Flanagin, A., and Metzger, M. (2000). Perceptions of Internet information credibility. *Journalism and Mass Communication Quarterly*, *77*(3), 515–540. Retrieved from http://jmq.sagepub.com/content/77/3/515.short

Flanagin, A. J., and Metzger, M. J. (2003). The perceived credibility of personal Web page information as influenced by the sex of the source. *Computers in Human Behavior*, *19*(6), 683–701. http://doi.org/10.1016/S0747-5632(03)00021-9

Flanagin, A. J., and Metzger, M. J. (2007). The role of site features, user attributes, and information verification behaviors on the perceived credibility of web-based information. *New Media and Society*, *9*(2), 319–342. http://doi.org/10.1177/1461444807075015

Flanagin, A. J., and Metzger, M. J. (2008). The credibility of volunteered geographic information. *GeoJournal*, *72*(3–4), 137–148. http://doi.org/10.1007/s10708-008-9188-y

Fodor, J. (1980). Methodological solipsism considered as a research strategy in cognitive psychology. *Behavioral and Brain Sciences*, *3*(1), 63. http://doi.org/10.1017/S0140525X00001771

Fogg, B. J. (2003). Prominence-interpretation theory: Explaining how people assess credibility online. In *CHIEA '03 Extended Abstracts on Human Factors in Computing Systems* (pp. 722–723). ACM. Retrieved from http://dl.acm.org/citation.cfm?id=765951

Fogg, B. J., Marshall, J., Kameda, T., Solomon, J., Rangnekar, A., Boyd, J., and Brown, B. (2001). Web credibility research: A method for online experiments and early study results. *CHIEA '01 Extended Abstracts on Human Factors in Computing Systems* (pp. 295–296). http://doi.org/10.1145/634067.634242

Fogg, B. J., Soohoo, C., Danielson, D. R., Marable, L., Stanford, J., and Tauber, E. R. (2003). How do users evaluate the credibility of Web sites? *Proceedings of the 2003 Conference on Designing for User Experiences* (pp. 1–15). http://doi.org/10.1145/997078.997097

Fogg, B. J., and Tseng, H. (1999). The elements of computer credibility. *Proceedings of the SIGCHI Conference on Human Factors in Computing*, May (pp. 80–87). Retrieved from http://dl.acm.org/citation.cfm?id=303001

Folk, C. L., and Remington, R. (1998). Selectivity in distraction by irrelevant featural singletons: Evidence for two forms of attentional capture. *Journal of Experimental Psychology: Human Perception and Performance*, *24*(3), 847–858. http://doi.org/10.1037/0096-1523.24.3.847

Franceschini, S., Gori, S., Ruffino, M., Viola, S., Molteni, M., and Facoetti, A. (2013). Action video games make dyslexic children read better. *Current Biology*, *23*(6), 462–466. http://doi.org/10.1016/j.cub.2013.01.044

Franconeri, S. L. and Simons, D. J. (2003). Moving and looming stimuli capture attention. *Attention, Perception and Psychophysics*, *65*(7): 999–1010.

Franconeri, S. L., Hollingworth, A., and Simons, D. J. (2005). Do new objects capture attention? *Psychological Science*, *16*(4), 275–281. http://doi.org/10.1111/j.0956-7976.2005.01528.x

Franken, R. E., Gibson, K. J., and Rowland, G. L. (1992). Sensation seeking and the tendency to view the world as threatening. *Personality and Individual Differences*, *13*(1), 31–38. http://doi.org/10.1016/0191-8869(92)90214-A

Frederiksen, J. R., and White, B. Y. (1989). An approach to training based upon principled task decomposition. *Acta Psychologica*, *71*(1–3), 89–146. http://doi.org/10.1016/0001-6918(89)90006-1

Frein, S. T., Jones, S. L., and Gerow, J. E. (2013). When it comes to Facebook there may be more to bad memory than just multitasking. *Computers in Human Behavior*, *29*(6), 2179–2182. http://doi.org/10.1016/j.chb.2013.04.031

Fu, W., and Sim, C. (2011). Aggregate bandwagon effect on online videos' viewership: Value uncertainty, popularity cues, and heuristics. *Journal of the American Society for Information Science and Technology*, *62*(12), 2382–2395. http://doi.org/10.1002/asi

Gau, S. S. F., Liu, C., Lee, C., Chang, J.-C., Chang, C.-J., Li, C., … Cheng, A. T. A. (2005). Development of a Chinese version of the Yale-Brown Obsessive Compulsive Scale for Heavy Drinking. *Alcoholism: Clinical and Experimental Research*, *29*(7), 1172–1179. http://doi.org/10.1097/01.ALC.0000172167.20119.9F

Geary, D. C., Saults, S. J., Liu, F., and Hoard, M. K. (2000). Sex differences in spatial cognition, computational fluency, and arithmetical reasoning. *Journal of Experimental Child Psychology*, *77*(4), 337–353. http://doi.org/10.1006/jecp.2000.2594

Gentile, D. A., Swing, E. L., Lim, C. G., and Khoo, A. (2012). Video game playing, attention problems, and impulsiveness: Evidence of bidirectional causality. *Psychology of Popular Media Culture*, *1*(1), 62–70. http://doi.org/10.1037/a0026969

Gifford, E. (2008). It's 3 A.M. – are you checking your email again? *Businesswire*. Retrievedfromhttp://www.businesswire.com/news/home/20080730005282/en/3-A.M.---Checking-Email

Gigerenzer, G. (2004). Fast and frugal heuristics: The tools of bounded rationality. In D. Koehlerand N. Harvey (Eds.), *Blackwell handbook of judgment and decision making* (pp. 62–88). Oxford: Blackwell. http://doi.org/10.1002/9780470752937.ch4

Goldstein, D., McAfee, R., and Suri, S. (2013). The cost of annoying ads. In *Proceedings of the 22nd International Conference on World Wide Web* (pp. 459–469). ACM. Retrieved from http://dl.acm.org/citation.cfm?id=2488429

González, V., and Mark, G. (2004). Constant, constant, multi-tasking craziness: Managing multiple working spheres. In *CHI '04 Proceedings of the SIGCHI Conference on Human Factors in Computing Systems* (April 24–29 pp. 113–120). ACM. Retrieved from http://dl.acm.org/citation.cfm?id=985707

Gopher, D., Well, M., and Bareket, T. (1994). Transfer of skill from a computer game trainer to flight. *Human Factors: The Journal of the Human Factors and Ergonomics Society*, *36*(3), 387–405. http://doi.org/10.1177/001872089403600301

Gorman, N., Burke, M., Hornof, A., and Nilsen, E. (2005). High-cost banner blindness: Ads increase perceived workload, hinder visual search, and are forgotten. *ACM Transactions on Computer-Human Interaction*, *12*(4), 423–445. Retrieved from http://dl.acm.org/citation.cfm?id=1121116

Grabe, M., and Christopherson, K. (2005). Evaluating the advantages and disadvantages of providing lecture notes: The role of internet technology as a delivery system and research tool. *The Internet and Higher Education*, *8*(4), 291–298.

Graham, L., and Metaxas, P. T. (2003). "Of course it's true; I saw it on the Internet!" Critical thinking in the internet era. *Communications of the ACM*, *46*(5), 70–75. http://doi.org/10.1145/769800.769804

Granka, L. A., Joachims, T., and Gay, G. (2004). Eye-tracking analysis of user behavior in WWW search. In *Proceedings of the 27th Annual International ACM SIGIR Conference on Research and Development in Information Retrieval* (pp. 478–479). http://doi.org/10.1145/1008992.1009079

Green, C. S., and Bavelier, D. (2003). Action video game modifies visual selective attention. *Nature*, *423*(6939), 534–537. http://doi.org/10.1038/nature01647

Green, C. S., and Bavelier, D. (2006a). Effect of action video games on the spatial distribution of visuospatial attention. *Journal of Experimental Psychology: Human Perception and Performance*, *32*(6), 1465–1478. http://doi.org/10.1037/0096-1523.32.6.1465

Green, C. S., and Bavelier, D. (2006b). Enumeration versus multiple object tracking: The case of action video game players. *Cognition*, *101*(1), 217–245. http://doi.org/10.1016/j.cognition.2005.10.004.Enumeration

Green, C. S., and Bavelier, D. (2007). Action video game experience alters the spatial resolution of vision. *Psychological Science*, *18*(1), 88–94. http://doi.org/10.1016/j.bio techadv.2011.08.021.Secreted

Greitzer, F. L., Kuchar, O. A., and Huston, K. (2007). Cognitive science implications for enhancing training effectiveness in a serious gaming context. *Journal on Educational Resources in Computing*, *7*(3), 2–16. http://doi.org/10.1145/1281320.1281322

Griffiths, J. R., and Brophy, P. (2005). Student searching behaviour and the web: Use of academic resources and google. *Library Trends*, *53*(4), 539–554. http://doi.org/Article

Griffiths, M. (1996). Behavioural addiction: An issue for everybody? *Journal of Workplace Learning*, *8*(3), 19–25. http://doi.org/10.1108/13665629610116872

Griffiths, M. (1998). Internet addiction: Does it really exist? In J. Gackenbach (Ed.), *Psychology and the internet: Intrapersonal, interpersonal, and transpersonal implications* (pp. 61–75). San Deigo, CA: Academic Press. Retrieved from http://search.ebscohost.com/login.aspx?direct=true&db=psyh&AN=1998-06638-003&site=ehost-live

Griffiths, M. (1999). Violent video games and aggression. *Aggression and Violent Behavior*, *4*(2), 203–212. http://doi.org/10.1016/S1359-1789(97)00055-4

Griffiths, M. (2000). Internet addiction – time to be taken seriously? *Addiction Research*, *8*(5), 413. http://doi.org/10.3109/16066350009005587

Griffiths, M. (2010). Internet abuse and internet addiction in the workplace. *Journal of Workplace Learning*, *22*(7), 463–472. http://doi.org/10.1108/13665621011071127

Griffiths, M. D. (2012). Facebook addiction: Concerns, criticism, and recommendations – A response to Andreassen and collegues. *Psychological Reports*, *110*(2), 518–520. http://doi.org/10.2466/01.07.18.PR0.110.2.518-520

Grisé, M.-L., and Gallupe, R. B. (1999). Information overload: Addressing the productivity paradox in face-to-face electronic meetings. *Journal of Management Information Systems*, *16*(3), 157–185. http://doi.org/10.1080/07421222.1999.11518260

Gupta, A., Li, H., and Sharda, R. (2013). Should I send this message? Understanding the impact of interruptions, social hierarchy and perceived task complexity on user performance and perceived workload. *Decision Support Systems*, *55*(1), 135–145. http://doi.org/10.1016/j.dss.2012.12.035

Gupta, A., and Sharda, R. (2008). SIMONE: A Simulator for Interruptions and Message Overload in Network Environments. *International Journal of Simulation and Process Modelling*, *4*(4/4), 237–247.

Gupta, A., Sharda, R., and Greve, R. A. (2011). You've got email! Does it really matter to process emails now or later? *Information Systems Frontiers*, *13*(5), 637–653. http://doi.org/10.1007/s10796-010-9242-4

Ha, J. H., Ph, D., Chin, B., Park, D., Ryu, S., and Yu, J. (2008). Characteristics of excessive cellular phone use in Korean adolescents. *CyberPsychology and Behavior*, *11*(6), 783–785. http://doi.org/10.1089/cpb.2008.0096

Hadlington, L. J. (2015). Cognitive failures in daily life: Exploring the link with Internet addiction and problematic mobile phone use. *Computers in Human Behavior*, *51*, 75–81. http://doi.org/10.1016/j.chb.2015.04.036

Hadlington, L. J., Attrill, A., and Scase, M. O. (2013). *Cognitive and behavioural concepts of cyber activities: Information processing of online content*. Technical Report for TIN 3.040 Task 3.

Hahn, B., Wolkenberg, F. A., Ross, T. J., Myers, C. S., Heishman, S. J., Stein, D. J., ... Stein, E. A. (2008). Divided versus selective attention: Evidence for common processing mechanisms. *Brain Research*, *1215*, 137–146. http://doi.org/10.1016/j.brainres.2008.03.058

Hair, M., Renaud, K. V., and Ramsay, J. (2007). The influence of self-esteem and locus of control on perceived email-related stress. *Computers in Human Behavior*, *23*(6), 2791–2803. http://doi.org/10.1016/j.chb.2006.05.005

Hanson, W. A., and Putler, D. S. (1996). Hits and misses: Herd behavior and online product popularity. *Marketing Letters*, *7*(4), 297–305. http://doi.org/10.1007/BF00435537

Hardaker, C. (2010). Trolling in asynchronous computer-mediated communication: From user discussions to academic definitions. *Journal of Politeness Research*, *6*(2), 215–242. http://doi.org/10.1515/JPLR.2010.011

Harel, I. (2002). Learning new-media literacy: A new necessity for the Clickerati Generation. *Telemedium Journal of Media Literacy*.

Hargittai, E., and Fullerton, L. (2010). Trust online: Young adults' evaluation of web content. *International Journal of Communication*, *4*, 468–494. Retrieved from http://megafotos.ru/-NZaWpvYy5vcmc.ZN-ojs/index.php/ijoc/article/viewPDFInterstitial/636/423

Harmelen, M. Van. (2006). Personal learning environments. *Sixth International Conference on Advanced Learning Technologies (ICALT'06)*, 1–2. http://doi.org/10.1109/ICALT.2006.1652565

Hawi, N. S., and Samaha, M. (2016). To excel or not to excel: Strong evidence on the adverse effect of smartphone addiction on academic performance. *Computers and Education*, *98*, 81–89. http://doi.org/10.1016/j.compedu.2016.03.007

Hawk, W. B., and Wang, P. (1999). Users' interaction with the World Wide Web: problems and problem-solving. *Proceedings of the ASIS Annual Meeting*, *36*, 256–270.

Hazelhurst, S., Johnson, Y., and Sanders, I. (2011). What clever hominids browse: An empirical analysis of the relationship between web usage and academic performance in undergraduate students. *Proceedings of the Annual Conference of the South African Computer Lecturers' Association*, July (pp. 29–37).

Helsper, E. J., and Eynon, R. (2010). Digitalnatives: Where is the evidence? *British Educational Research Journal*, *36*(3), 503–520. http://doi.org/10.1080/0141192090 2989227

Hidi, S. E. (1995). A reexamination of the role of attention in learning from text. *Educational Psychology Review*, *7*(4), 323–350.

Hilligoss, B., and Rieh, S. Y. (2008). Developing a unifying framework of credibility assessment: Construct, heuristics, and interaction in context. *Information Processing and Management*, *44*(4), 1467–1484. http://doi.org/10.1016/j.ipm.2007.10.001

Hong, W., Thong, J. Y. L., and Tam, K. Y. (2004). Does animation attract online consumers' attention? The effect of flash on information search performance and perceptions. *Information Systems Research*, *15*(1), 60–86. http://doi.org/10.1287/isre.1040.0017

Horrigan, J., and Rainie, L. (2006). *The internet's growing role in life's major moments.* Pew Internet and American Life Project (April), 1–11.

Horvath, P., and Zuckerman, M. (1993). Sensation seeking, risk appraisal, and risky behavior. *Personality and Individual Differences*, *14*(1), 41–52.

Hovland, C., and Weiss, W. (1953). The influence of source credibility on communication effectiveness. *Educational Technology Research and Development*, *1*(2), 635–650. http://doi.org/10.1007/BF02716996

Huang, C. (2014). Understanding novice users' help-seeking behavior in getting started with digital libraries: Influence of learning styles. *ProQuest Dissertations and Theses*. Retrieved from http://search.proquest.com/docview/1640735564?accountid=14643\nhttp://mlbsfx.sibi.usp.br:3410/sfxlcl41?url_ver=Z39.88-2004&rft_val_fmt=info:ofi/fmt:kev:mtx:dissertation&genre=dissertations+&+theses&sid=ProQ:ProQuest+Dissertations+&+Theses+Global&atitl

Huang, J.-H., and Chen, Y.-F. (2006). Herding in online product choice. *Psychology and Marketing*, *23*(5), 413–428. http://doi.org/10.1002/mar

Hyman, I., Boss, M., Wise, B., McKenzie, K., and Caggiano, J. (2010). Did you see the unicycling clown? Inattentional blindness while walking and talking on a cell phone. *Applied Cognitive Psychology*, *24*, 597–607. http://doi.org/10.1002/acp

Ishizaka, K., Marshall, S. P., and Conte, J. M. (2001). Individual differences in attentional strategies in multitasking situations. *Human Performance*, *14*(4), 339–358.

Jackson, T., Dawson, R., and Wilson, D. (2001). The cost of email interruption. *Journal of Systems and Information Technology*, *5*(1), 81–92. Retrieved from http://www.emeraldinsight.com/journals.htm?articleid=1718383&show=abstract

Jackson, T., Dawson, R., and Wilson, D. (2002). Case study: Evaluating the effect of email interruptions within the workplace. *Conference on Empirical Assessment in Software Engineering, Keele University (EASE) 2002*, Keele, UK (April), 3–7. Retrieved from https://dspace.lboro.ac.uk/2134/489

Jacobsen, W. C., and Forste, R. (2011). The wired generation: Academic and social outcomes of electronic media use among university students. *Cyberpsychology, Behavior and Social Networking*, *14*(5), 275–280. http://doi.org/10.1089/cyber.2010.0135

Jaeggi, S. M., Buschkuehl, M., Jonides, J., Shah, P., Morrison, A. B., and Chein, J. M. (2011). Short- and long-term benefits of cognitive training. *Proceedings of the National Academy of Sciences*, *108*(25), 46–60. http://doi.org/10.1073/pnas.1103228108

James, W. (1890). *The Principles of Psychology* (Vols. 1 and 2). New York: Henry Holt and Company. http://doi.org/10.1037/10538-000

Jansen, B. J., and Pooch, U. (2001). A review of Web searching studies and a framework for future research. *Journal of the American Society for Information Science and Technology*, *52*(3), 235–246. http://doi.org/10.1002/1097-4571(2000)9999:9999<::AID-ASI1607>3.0.CO;2-F

Jansen, B. J., Spink, A., Bateman, J., and Saracevic, T. (1998). Real life information retrieval: A study of user queries on the web. *SIGIR Forum (ACM Special Interest Group on Information Retrieval)*, *32*(1), 5–17. http://doi.org/10.1145/281250.281253

Jansen, B. J., Spink, A., and Saracevic, T. (2000). Real life, real users, and real needs: A study and analysis of user queries on the Web. *Information Processing and Management*, *36*(2), 207–227. http://doi.org/10.1016/S0261-5177(02)00005-5

Jensen, M. S., Yao, R., Street, W. N., and Simons, D. J. (2011). Change blindness and inattentional blindness. *Wiley Interdisciplinary Reviews: Cognitive Science*, *2*(5), 529–546. http://doi.org/10.1002/wcs.130

Jin, J., and Dabbish, L. A. (2009). Self-interruption on the computer: A typology of discretionary task interleaving. *Proceedings of the 27th International Conference on Human Factors in Computing Systems, CHI 2009* (pp. 1799–1808). http://doi.org/10.1145/1518701.1518979

Johnson-Laird, P. N. (1983). *Mental models.* Cambridge: Cambridge University Press.

Jonides, J., and Yantis, S. (1988). Uniqueness of abrupt visual onset in capturing attention. *Perception and Psychophysics, 43*(4), 346–354. http://doi.org/10.3758/BF03208805

Joy, S., and Kolb, D. A. (2009). Are there cultural differences in learning style? *International Journal of Intercultural Relations, 33*(1), 69–85. http://doi.org/10.1016/j.ijintrel.2008.11.002

Judd, T. (2014). Making sense of multitasking: The role of Facebook. *Computers and Education, 70,* 194–202. http://doi.org/10.1016/j.compedu.2013.08.013

Junco, R. (2012). The relationship between frequency of Facebook use, participation in Facebook activities, and student engagement. *Computers and Education, 58*(1), 162–171. http://doi.org/10.1016/j.compedu.2011.08.004

Junco, R., and Cotten, S. R. (2011). Perceived academic effects of instant messaging use. *Computersand Education, 56*(2), 370–378. http://doi.org/10.1016/j.compedu.2010.08.020

Junco, R., and Cotten, S. R. (2012). No A 4 U: The relationship between multitasking and academic performance. *Computers and Education, 59*(2), 505–514. http://doi.org/10.1016/j.compedu.2011.12.023

Junco, R., Heiberger, G., and Loken, E. (2011). The effect of Twitter on college student engagement and grades. *Journal of Computer Assisted Learning, 27*(2), 119–132. http://doi.org/10.1111/j.1365-2729.2010.00387.x

Just, M. A., Carpenter, P. A., Keller, T. A., Emery, L., Zajac, H., and Thulborn, K. R. (2001). Interdependence of nonoverlapping cortical systems in dual cognitive tasks. *NeuroImage, 14*(2), 417–426. http://doi.org/10.1006/nimg.2001.0826

Kahneman, D. (1973). Attention and effort. *The American Journal of Psychology 88*(2), 339–340. http://doi.org/10.2307/1421603

Kalyanaraman, S., Ivory, J., and Maschmeyer, L. (2005). Interruptions and online information processing: The role of interruption type, interruption content, and interruption frequency. In *Proceedings of the 2005 Annual Meeting of International Communication Association* (pp. 1–32). Retrieved from http://scholar.google.com/scholar?hl=en&btnG=Search&q=intitle:Interruptions+and+Online+Information+Processing:+the+role+of+in terruption+type,+interruption+content+and+interruption+frequency#2

Kalyanaraman, S., and Sundar, S. (2006). The psychological appeal of personalized content in web portals: Does customization affect attitudes and behavior? *Journal of Communication, 56*(1), 110–132. http://doi.org/10.1111/j.1460-2466.2006.00006.x

Kane, M. J., Brown, L. H., McVay, J. C., Silvia, P. J., Myin-Germeys, I., and Kwapil, T. R. (2007). For whom the mind wanders, and when. *Psychological Science, 18*(7), 614–621. http://doi.org/10.1111/j.1467-9280.2007.01948.x

Karaiskos, D., Tzavellas, E., Balta, G., and Paparrigopoulos, T. (2010). Social network addiction: A new clinical disorder? *European Psychiatry, 25*(1), 855–856. http://doi.org/10.1016/S0924-9338(10)70846-4

Karbach, J., and Kray, J. (2009). How useful is executive control training? Age differences in near and far transfer of task-switching training. *Developmental Science, 12*(6), 978–990. http://doi.org/10.1111/j.1467-7687.2009.00846.x

Karvalics, L. Z. (2007). Information society – what is it exactly? (The meaning, history and conceptual framework of an expression). In R. Pinter (Ed.), *Information society. From theory to political practice* (Vol. 29). Budapest: Library of Congress Cataloging-in-Publication Data.

Katz, M. A., and Byrne, M. D. (2003). Effects of scent and breadth on use of site-specific search on e-commerce Web sites. *ACM Transactions on Computer-Human Interaction, 10*(3), 198–220.

Kensinger, E. A. (2007). Negative emotion enhances memory accuracy. *Current Directions in Psychological Science, 16*(4), 213–218.

Kessler, S. (2011). 38% of college students can't go 10 minutes without tech [STATS]. Retrieved from http://mashable.com/2011/05/31/college-tech-device-stats/

Kiewra, K. A. (1984). Acquiring effective notetaking skills: An alternative to professional notetaking. *Journal of Reading, 27,* 299–302.

Kirschner, P. A., and Karpinski, A. C. (2010). Facebook® and academic performance. *Computers in Human Behavior, 26*(6), 1237–1245. http://doi.org/10.1016/j.chb.2010.03.024

Koch, I., Gade, M., Schuch, S., and Philipp, A. M. (2010). The role of inhibition in task switching: A review. *Psychonomic Bulletin and Review, 17*(1), 1–14. http://doi.org/10.3758/PBR.17.1.1

Kolikant, Y. B.-D. (2010). Digital natives, better learners? Students' beliefs about how the Internet influenced their ability to learn. *Computers in Human Behavior, 26*(6), 1384–1391. http://doi.org/10.1016/j.chb.2010.04.012

Kubey, R. W., Lavin, M. J., and Barrows, J. R. (2001). Internet use and collegiate academic performance decrements: Early findings. *Journal of Communication, 51*(2), 366–382. http://doi.org/10.1093/joc/51.2.366

Kushlev, K., and Dunn, E. W. (2015). Checking email less frequently reduces stress. *Computers in Human Behavior, 43*(February), 220–228. http://doi.org/10.1016/j.chb.2014.11.005

Kushlev, K., Proulx, J., and Dunn, E. W. (2016). "Silence your phones": Smartphone notifications increase inattention and hyperactivity symptoms. *Proceedings of the 2016 Conference on Human Factors in Computing Systems*, pp. 1011–1020. http://doi.org/10.1145/2858036.2858359

Kuss, D., Rooij, A. Van, and Shorter, G. (2013). Internet addiction in adolescents: Prevalence and risk factors. *Computers in Human Behavior, 29*(5), 1987–1996. http://doi.org/10.1016/j.chb.2013.04.002

Kuznekoff, J. H., and Titsworth, S. (2013). The impact of mobile phone usage on student learning. *Communication Education, 62*(3), 233–252. http://doi.org/10.1080/03634523.2013.767917

Kwon, M., Lee, J.-Y., Won, W.-Y., Park, J.-W., Min, J.-A., Hahn, C., … Kim, D.-J. (2013). Development and validation of a Smartphone Addiction Scale (SAS). *PLoS ONE, 8*(2), e56936. http://doi.org/10.1371/journal.pone.0056936

Lang, A. (2000). The limited capacity model of mediated message processing. *Journal of Communication*, 46–70. http://doi.org/10.1111/j.1460-2466.2000.tb02833.x

Lau, A., and Coiera, E. (2007). Do people experience cognitive biases while searching for information? *Journal of the American Medical Informatics Association, 14*(5), 599–608. http://doi.org/10.1197/jamia.M2411.Introduction

Lavie, N., Hirst, A., de Fockert, J. W., and Viding, E. (2004). Load theory of selective attention and cognitive control. *Journal of Experimental Psychology: General, 133*(3), 339–354. http://doi.org/10.1037/0096-3445.133.3.339

Lavie, N., Ro, T., and Russell, C. (2003). The role of perceptual load in processing distractor faces. *Psychological Science, 14*(5), 510–515.

Lazonder, A. W. (2000). Exploring novice users' training needs in searching information on the WWW. *Journal of Computer Assisted Learning, 16*(4), 326–335. http://doi.org/10.1046/j.1365-2729.2000.00145.x

Lazonder, A. W., Biemans, H. J. A., and Wopereis, I. G. J. H. (2000). Differences between novice and experienced users in search information on the World Wide Web. *Journal of the American Society for Information Science, 51*(6), 576–581.

Lee, M. J., and Tedder, M. C. (2003). The effects of three different computer texts on readers' recall: Based on working memory capacity. *Computers in Human Behavior, 19*(6), 767–783.

Leibiger, C. (2011). "Google reigns triumphant"? Stemming the tide of Googlitis via collaborative, situated information literacy instruction. *Behavioral and Social Sciences Librarian, 30*(4), 187–222.

Leiva, L., Böhmer, M., Gehring, S., and Krüger, A. (2012). Back to the app: The costs of mobile appication interruptions. *Proceedings of the 14th International Conference on Human-Computer Interaction with Mobile Devices and Services – MobileHCI '12* (pp. 291–294).

Lenhart, A. (2010). *Teens, cell phones and texting: Text messaging becomes centerpiece communication.* Washington, DC. Retrieved from http://pewresearch.org/pubs/1572/teens-cell-phones-text-messages.

Lenhart, A., and Page, D. (2015). Report: *Teens, social media and technology overview 2015.* Pew Research Center, April.

Leung, L., and Wei, R. (2000). More than just talk on the move: Uses and gratifications of the cellular phone. *Journalism and Mass Communication Quarterly, 77*(2), 308–320. http://doi.org/10.1177/107769900007700206

Levitas, D. (2013). *Always connected. How smartphones and social keep us engaged.*

Li, H., Edwards, S. M., and Lee, J.-H. (2002). Measuring the intrusiveness of advertisements: Scale development and validation. *Journal of Advertising, 31*(2), 37–47. http://doi.org/10.1080/00913367.2002.10673665

Lin, Y.-H., Chang, L.-R., Lee, Y.-H., Tseng, H.-W., Kuo, T. B. J., and Chen, S.-H. (2014). Development and validation of the Smartphone Addiction Inventory (SPAI). *PloS One, 9*(6), e98312. http://doi.org/10.1371/journal.pone.0098312

Lin, Y.-H., and Gau, S. S.-F. (2013). Association between morningness–eveningness and the severity of compulsive Internet use: The moderating role of gender and parenting style. *Sleep Medicine, 14*(12), 1398–1404. http://doi.org/10.1016/j. sleep.2013.06.015

Logan, G. D., Schachar, R. J., and Tannock, R. (1997). Impulsivity and inhibitory control. *Psychological Science, 8*(1), 60–64. http://doi.org/10.1111/j.1467-9280.1997. tb00545.x

LoPresti, E., Bodine, C., and Lewis, C. (2008). Assistive technology for cognition: Understanding the needs of persons with disabilities. *IEEE Engineering in Medicine and Biology Magazine, 27*(2). http://doi.org/10.1109/EMB.2007.907396

Lorigo, L., Haridasan, M., Brynjarsdottir, H., Xia, L., Joachims, T., Gay, G., … Pan, B. (2008). Eye tracking and online search: Lessons learned and challenges ahead. *Journal of the American Society for Information Science and Technology, 59*(7), 1041–1052. http://doi.org/10.1002/asi

Lubman, D. I., Yüeel, M., and Pantelis, C. (2004). Addiction, a condition of compulsive behaviour? Neuroimaging and neuropsychological evidence of inhibitory dysregulation. *Addiction, 99,* 1491–1502. http://doi.org/10.1111/j.1360-0443.2004.00808.x

Luchins, A. S. (1957). Experimental attempts to minimize the impact of first impressions. In C. I. Hovland (Ed.), *The order of presentation in persuasion* (pp. 62–75). New Haven, CT: Yale University Press.

Madden, M., Fox, S., Smith, A., and Vitak, J. (2007). *Digital footprints: Online identity management and search in the age of transparency.* Pew Internet and American Life Project, December. Retrieved from http://scholar.google.com/ scholar?hl=en&btnG=Search&q=intitle:Digital+Footprints+Online+identity+ management+and+search+in+the+age+of+transparency+Findings#0

Madden, M., Lenhart, A., and Cortesi, S. (2013). *Teens, social media, and privacy.* Pew Internet and American Life Project. Washington DC: Pew Research Centre.

Maglio, P. P., and Barrett, R. (1997). On the trail of information searchers. In *Proceedings of the Nineteenth Annual Conference of the Cognitive Science Society* (pp. 466–471). Lawrence Erlbaum Associates.

Maglio, P. P., and Campbell, C. S. (2000). Tradeoffs in displaying peripheral information. In *Proceedings of the SIGCHI Conference on Human Factors in Computing Systems CHI 00* (pp. 241–248). ACM. http://doi.org/10.1145/332040.332438

Mané, A., and Donchin, E. (1989). The space fortress game. *Acta Psychologica, 71,* 17–22. http://doi.org/10.1016/0001-6918(89)90003-6

Marchionini, G. (1999a). Augmenting library services: Toward the sharium. *Proceedings of International Symposium on Digital Libraries. Symposium on Digital Libraries,* March (pp. 40–47).

Marchionini, G. (1999b). Educating responsible citizens in the information society. *Educational Technology Magazine, 39*(2), 17–26. Retrieved from http://scholar. google.com/scholar?hl=en&btnG=Search&q=intitle:Educating+Responsible+Citi zens+in+the+Information+Society#0

Marci, C. (2012). A (biometric) day in the life: Engaging across media. Paper presented at *Re:Think 2012,* 28 March, New York.

Mark, G., Gonzalez, V., and Harris, J. (2005). No task left behind? Examining the nature of fragmented work. *Proceedings of the SIGCHI Conference on Human Factors in Computing Systems* (pp. 321–330). Retrieved from http://dl.acm.org/citation.cfm?id=1055017

Mark, G. J., Voida, S., and Cardello, A. V. (2012). A pace not dictated by electrons: An empirical study of work without email. *Proceedings of the SIGCHI Conference on Human Factors in Computing Systems* May 5–10 (pp. 555–564). http://doi.org/10.1145/2207676.2207754

Marks, I. (1990). Behavioural (non-chemical) addictions. *British Journal of Addiction, 85*(11), 1389–1394. http://doi.org/10.1111/j.1360-0443.1990.tb01625.x

Martindale, T., and Dowdy, M. (2010). Personal learning environments. In G. Veletsianos (Ed.), *Emerging technologies in distance education*, (pp. 177–193). Edmonton, AB: Athabasca University Press.

Marulanda-Carter, L., and Jackson, T. W. (2012). Effects of e-mail addiction and interruptions on employees. *Journal of Systems and Information Technology, 14*(1), 82–94. http://doi.org/10.1108/13287261211221146

Mayer, R., and Moreno, R. (2003). Nine ways to reduce cognitive load in multimedia learning. *Journal of Educational Psychology, 38*(1), 43–52. http://doi.org/10.1207/S15326985EP3801_6

McCormick, E. J. (1970). *Human factors engineering* (3rd ed.). New York: McGraw-Hill.

McCoy, S., and Galletta, D. F. (2004). A study of the effects of online advertising: A focus on pop-up and in-line ads.

McFarlane, D. (2002). Comparison of four primary methods for coordinating the interruption of people in human-computer interaction. *Human-Computer Interaction, 17*(1), 63–139. http://doi.org/10.1207/S15327051HCI1701_2

McKnight, D. H., and Kacmar, C. J. (2007). Factors and effects of information credibility. In *Proceedings of the Ninth International Conference on Electronic Commerce* (pp. 423–432). ACM. http://doi.org/10.1145/1282100.1282180

McLeod, P. (1977). A dual task response modality effect: Support for multiprocessor models of attention. *Quarterly Journal of Experimental Psychology, 29*(4), 651–667. http://doi.org/10.1080/14640747708400639

Metzger, M. J., and Flanagin, A. J. (2013). Credibility and trust of information in online environments: The use of cognitive heuristics. *Journal of Pragmatics, 59*, 210–220. http://doi.org/10.1016/j.pragma.2013.07.012

Metzger, M. J., Flanagin, A. J., and Medders, R. B. (2010). Social and heuristic approaches to credibility evaluation online. *Journal of Communication, 60*(3), 413–439. http://doi.org/10.1111/j.1460-2466.2010.01488.x

Miller, D. J., and Robertson, D. P. (2010). Using a games console in the primary classroom: Effects of "Brain Training" programme on computation and self-esteem. *British Journal of Educational Technology, 41*(2), 242–255. http://doi.org/10.1111/j.1467-8535.2008.00918.x

Miller, G. A. (1956). The magical number seven, plus or minus two: Some limits on our capacity for processing information. *Psychological Review, 63*, 81–97. http://doi.org/10.1037/h0043158

Minear, M., Brasher, F., McCurdy, M., Lewis, J., and Younggren, A. (2013). Working memory, fluid intelligence, and impulsiveness in heavy media multitaskers. *Psychonomic Bulletin and Review*, *20*, 1274–1281. http://doi.org/10.3758/s13423-013-0456-6

Miranda, S. M., and Saunders, C. S. (2003). The social construction of meaning: An alternative perspective on information sharing. *Information Systems Research*, *14*(1), 87–106.

Mitchell, C. M., Sundstrom, G. A., and Sundström, G. A. (1997). Human interaction with complex systems: Design issues and research approaches. *IEEE Transactions on Systems, Man, and Cybernetics*, *27*(3), 265–273.

Mitchell, E. K. L., James, S., and D'Amore, A. (2015). How learning styles and preferences of first-year nursing and midwifery students change. *Australian Journal of Education*, *59*(2), 158–168. http://doi.org/10.1177/0004944115587917

Monk, C. A, Trafton, J. G., and Boehm-Davis, D. A. (2008). The effect of interruption duration and demand on resuming suspended goals. *Journal of Experimental Psychology. Applied*, *14*(4), 299–313. http://doi.org/10.1037/a0014402

Muntean, C. C. I. (2011). Raising engagement in e-learning through gamification. *The 6th International Conference on Virtual Learning ICVL 2011*, (1), 323–329. Retrieved from http://icvl.eu/2011/disc/icvl/documente/pdf/met/ICVL_ModelsAndMethodologies_paper42.pdf

Murphy, K., and Spence, A. (2009). Playing video games does not make for better visual attention skills. *Journal of Articles in Support of the Null Hypothesis*, *6*(1), 1–20.

Muser, J., and O'Reilly, T. (2006). *Web 2.0: Principles and Best Practices [Excerpt]*.

Mythily, S., Qiu, S., and Winslow, M. (2008). Prevalence and correlates of excessive internet use among youth in Singapore. *Annals of the Academy of Medicine Singapore*, *37*(1), 9–14.

Nasar, J., Hecht, P., and Wener, R. (2008). Mobile telephones, distracted attention, and pedestrian safety. *Accident Analysis and Prevention*, *40*(1), 69–75. http://doi.org/10.1016/j.aap.2007.04.005

Nasar, J. L., and Troyer, D. (2013). Pedestrian injuries due to mobile phone use in public places. *Accident Analysis and Prevention*, *57*, 91–95. http://doi.org/10.1016/j.aap.2013.03.021

Navalpakkam, V., and Itti, L. (2005). Modeling the influence of task on attention. *Vision Research*, *45*(2), 205–231. http://doi.org/10.1016/j.visres.2004.07.042

Niederhauser, D. S., Reynolds, R. E., Salmen, D. J., and Skolmoski, P. (2000). The influence of cognitive load on learning from hypertext. *Journal of Educational Computing Research*, *23*(3), 237–255. http://doi.org/10.2190/81BG-RPDJ-9FA0-Q7PA

Nisbett, R. E., Peng, K., Choi, I., and Norenzayan, A. (2001). Culture and systems of thought: Holistic versus analytic cognition. *Psychological Review*, *108*(2), 291–310. http://doi.org/10.1037/0033-295X.108.2.291

Nouchi, R., Taki, Y., Takeuchi, H., Hashizume, H., Nozawa, T., Kambara, T., … Kawashima, R. (2013). Brain training game boosts executive functions, working memory and processing speed in the young adults: a randomized controlled trial. *PLoS ONE*, *8*(2). http://doi.org/10.1371/journal.pone.0055518

Nouchi, R., Taki, Y., Takeuchi, H., Hashizume, H., Akitsuki, Y., Shigemune, Y., … Kawashima, R. (2012). Brain training game improves executive functions and processing speed in the elderly: A randomized controlled trial. *PLoS ONE, 7*(1), e29676. http://doi.org/10.1371/journal.pone.0029676

O'Neill, T. A., Hambley, L. A., and Bercovich, A. (2014). Prediction of cyberslacking when employees are working away from the office. *Computers in Human Behavior, 34*, 291–298. http://doi.org/10.1016/j.chb.2014.02.015

Oblinger, D., and Oblinger, J. (2005). Is it age or IT: First steps toward understanding the net generation. *Learning, Chapter 2*(2), 2.1-2.20. http://doi.org/Article

Odaci, H. (2011). Academic self-efficacy and academic procrastination as predictors of problematic internet use in university students. *Computers and Education, 57*(1), 1109–1113. http://doi.org/10.1016/j.compedu.2011.01.005

Oei, A. C., and Patterson, M. D. (2013). Enhancing cognition with video games: A multiple game training study. *PLoS ONE, 8*(3), e58546. http://doi.org/10.1371/journal.pone.0058546

Ofcom. (2015). *The Communications Market Report.*

Ofcom. (2016). *Adults' media use and attitudes report.* Retrieved from http://stakeholders.ofcom.org.uk/market-data-research/media-literacy/media-lit-research/adults-2013/

Op de Macks, Z. A., Bunge, S. A., Bell, O. N., Wilbrecht, L., Kriegsfeld, L. J., Kayser, A. S., and Dahl, R. E. (2016). Risky decision-making in adolescent girls: The role of pubertal hormones and reward circuitry. *Psychoneuroendocrinology, 74*, 77–91. http://doi.org/10.1016/j.psyneuen.2016.08.013

Ophir, E., Nass, C., and Wagner, A. D. (2009). Cognitive control in media multitaskers. *Proceedings of the National Academy of Sciences of the United States of America, 106*(37), 15583–15587. http://doi.org/10.1073/pnas.0903620106

Owen, A. M., Hampshire, A., Grahn, J. A., Stenton, R., Dajani, S., Burns, A. S., … Ballard, C. G. (2010). Putting brain training to the test. *Nature, 465*(7299), 775–778. http://doi.org/10.1038/nature09042

Owens, J. W., Chaparro, B. S., and Palmer, E. M. (2011). Text advertising blindness: The new banner blindness? *Journal of Usability Studies, 6*(3), 172–197.

Özdemir, S. (2008). E-learning's effect on knowledge: Can you download tacit knowledge? *British Journal of Educational Technology, 39*(3), 552–554. http://doi.org/10.1111/j.1467-8535.2007.00764.x

Pagendarm, M., and Schaumberg, H. (2006). Why are users banner-blind? The impact of navigation style in the perception of web banners. *Journal of Digital Information, 2*(1).

Palmquist, R. A., and Kim, K.-S. (2000). Cognitive style and on-line database search experience as predictors of Web search performance. *Journal of the American Society for Information Science and Technology, 51*(6), 558–566. http://doi.org/10.1002/(SICI)1097-4571(2000)51:6<558::AID-ASI7>3.0.CO;2-9

Pascarella, E. T., and Terenzini, P. T. (2005). How college affects students: A third decade of research. *The Journal of Higher Education, 63*(3). pp. 355–358. http://doi.org/10.2307/1982025

Pashler, H. (2000). Task switching and multitask performance. In S. Monsell and J. Driver (Eds.), *Control of cognitive processes: Attention and performance XVIII*, (pp. 277–307). Cambridge, MA: MIT Press.

Pashler, H., Johnston, J. C., and Ruthruff, E. (2001). Attention and performance. *Annual Review of Psychology, 52*(1), 629–651.

Pashler, H. E., and Johnston, J. C. (1998). Attentional limitations in dual-task performance. *Attention*, 155–189.

Payne, J. W., and Bettman, J. (2004). Walking with the scarecrow: The information-processing approach to decision research. In D. Koehler and N. Harvey (Eds.), *Blackwell handbook of judgment and decision making* (pp. 110–132). Oxford: Blackwell. http://doi.org/10.1002/9780470752937.ch16

Payne, S. J., Duggan, G. B., and Neth, H. (2007). Discrentionary task interleaving: Heuristics for time allocation in cogntive foraging. *Jounral of Experimental Psychology: General, 136*(3), 370–388. http://doi.org/10.2966/scrip.

Pinker, S. (1997). *How the mind works*. New York: Norton.

Pirolli, P. (2005). Rational analyses of information foraging on the web. *Cognitive Science, 29*(3), 343–373. http://doi.org/10.1207/s15516709cog0000_20

Poposki, E. M., and Oswald, F. L. (2009). Development of a new measure of polychronicity, 182–202.

Posner, M. I., and Rothbart, M. K. (2005). Influencing brain networks: Implications for education. *Trends in Cognitive Sciences, 9*(3, Special Issue), 99–103. http://doi.org/10.1016/j.tics.2005.01.007

Praziale, L., Britt, D., Davis, C., Forrester, J., Liu, W., Matthews, C., and Rosselot, N. (2006). *TCP/IP tutorial and technical overview*. IBM Redbooks. Retrieved from http://pages.cpsc.ucalgary.ca/~ijirasek/courses/cpsc441/tcpip_2001.ps

Prensky, M. (2001a). Digital natives, digital immigrants, Part 1. *On the Horizon, 9*(5), 1–6. http://doi.org/10.1108/10748120110424816

Prensky, M. (2001b). Fun, play and games: what makes games engaging. In *Digital Game-Based Learning* (pp. 1–31). McGraw-Hill. http://doi.org/10.1103/PhysRevB.66.085421

Prensky, M. (2005). Engage me or enrage me. *EDUCAUSE Review, 40*(5), 1–5.

Prensky, M. (2009). H. sapiens digital: From digital immigrants and digital natives to digital wisdom. *Journal of Online Education, 5*(3), 1–9. http://doi.org/www.innovate online.info/index.php?view=article&id=705

Prensky, M. R. (2012). *From digital natives to digital wisdom: Hopeful essays for 21st century learning*. Thousand Oaks, CA: Corwin Press.

Price, J., and Davis, B. (2008). *The woman who can't forget: The extraordinary story of living with the most remarkable memory known to science: A memoir*. New York: Simon and Schuster.

PricewaterhouseCoopers. (2016). *IAB Internet Advertising Revenue Report – 2015 Full Year Results*. Retrieved from http://www.iab.net/media/file/IAB_Full_year_2010_0413_Final.pdf

Przybylski, A. K., Murayama, K., Dehaan, C. R., and Gladwell, V. (2013). Motivational, emotional, and behavioral correlates of fear of missing out. *Computers in Human Behavior, 29*(4), 1841–1848. http://doi.org/10.1016/j.chb.2013.02.014

Quinlan, P., and Dyson, B. (2008). *Cognitive psychology*. New Jersey: Prentice-Hall.

Rabipour, S., and Raz, A. (2012). Training the brain: Fact and fad in cognitive and behavioral remediation. *Brain and Cognition, 79*(2), 159–179. http://doi.org/10.1016/j.bandc.2012.02.006

Rahimi, E., van den Berg, J., and Veen, W. (2015). Facilitating student-driven constructing of learning environments using Web 2.0 personal learning environments. *Computers and Education, 81*, 235–246. http://doi.org/10.1016/j.compedu.2014.10.012

Ralph, B. C. W., Thomson, D. R., Cheyne, J. A., and Smilek, D. (2013). Media multitasking and failures of attention in everyday life. *Psychological Research*, 1–9. http://doi.org/10.1007/s00426-013-0523-7

Ravizza, S. M., Hambrick, D. Z., and Fenn, K. M. (2014). Non-academic internet use in the classroom is negatively related to classroom learning regardless of intellectual ability. *Computers and Education, 78*, 109–114. http://doi.org/10.1016/j.compedu.2014.05.007

Rensink, R. A. (2008). On the applications of change blindness. *Psychologia, 51*(2), 100–106. http://doi.org/10.2117/psysoc.2008.100

Reynolds, R. E. (1992). Selective attention and prose learning: Theoretical and empirical research. *Educational Psychology Review, 4*(4), 345–391.

Rideout, V., Foehr, U., and Roberts, D. F. (2010). Generation M2: Media in the lives of 8 to 18 year-olds. *The Henry J. Kaiser Family Foundation*, 1–79. http://doi.org/P0-446179799-1366925520306

Risko, E. F., Buchanan, D., Medimorec, S., and Kingstone, A. (2013). Everyday attention: Mind wandering and computer use during lectures. *Computers and Education, 68*, 275–283. http://doi.org/10.1016/j.compedu.2013.05.001

Roberti, J. W. (2004). A review of behavioral and biological correlates of sensation seeking. *Journal of Research in Personality, 38*(3), 256–279. http://doi.org/10.1016/S0092-6566(03)00067-9

Roda, C. (2011). *Human attention in digital environments*. Cambridge: Cambridge University Press.

Rohde, T. E., and Thompson, L. A. (2007). Predicting academic achievement with cognitive ability. *Intelligence, 35*(1), 83–92. http://doi.org/10.1016/j.intell.2006.05.004

Rose, S., and Dhandayudham, A. (2014). Towards an understanding of Internet-based problem shopping behaviour: The concept of online shopping addiction and its proposed predictors. *Journal of Behavioral Addictions, 3*(2), 83–89. http://doi.org/10.1556/JBA.3.2014.003

Rosen, C. (2008). The myth of multitasking. *The New Atlantis*, 105–110. Retrieved from http://faculty.winthrop.edu/hinera/CRTW-Spring_2011/TheMythofMultitasking_Rosen.pdf

Rosen, L., Lim, A., Carrier, M., and Cheever, N. (2011). An empirical examination of the educational impact of text message-induced task switching in the classroom: Educational implications and strategies to enhance learning. *Psicología Educativa, 17*, 163–177. Retrieved from http://my.psychologytoday.com/files/attachments/40095/anempiricalexaminationoftheeducationalimpactoftextmessage-inducedtaskswitchingin-theclassroom-educati.pdf

Rosen, L. D., Carrier, L. M., and Cheever, N. (2013). Facebook and texting made me do it: Media-induced task-switching while studying. *Computers in Human Behavior, 29*(3), 948–958. http://doi.org/10.1016/j.chb.2012.12.001

Rouet, J. F. (2003). What was I looking for? The influence of task specificity and prior knowledge on students' search strategies in hypertext. *Interacting with Computers, 15*(3 Special Issue), 409–428. http://doi.org/10.1016/S0953-5438(02)00064-4

Rubinstein, J. S., Meyer, D. E., and Evans, J. E. (2001). Executive control of cognitive processes in task switching. *Journal of Experimental Psychology: Human Perception and Performance, 27*(4), 763–797. http://doi.org/10.1037//0096-1523.27.4.763

Rushkoff, D. (2006). *Screenagers: Lessons in chaos from digital kids*. New York: Hampton Press.

Sahami Shirazi, A., Henze, N., Dingler, T., Pielot, M., Weber, D., and Schmidt, A. (2014). Large-scale assessment of mobile notifications. *Proceedings of the 32nd Annual ACM Conference on Human Factors in Computing Systems – CHI '14* (pp. 3055–3064). http://doi.org/10.1145/2556288.2557189

Salganik, M. J., Dodds, P. S., and Watts, D. J. (2006). Experimental study of inequality and unpredictability in an artificial cultural market. *Science, 311*(5762), 854–856. http://doi.org/10.1126/science.1121066

Salvucci, D. D., and Taatgen, N. A. (2008). Threaded cognition: An integrated theory of concurrent multitasking. *Psychological Review, 115*(1), 101–130. http://doi.org/10.1037/0033-295X.115.1.101

Salvucci, D. D., Taatgen, N. A, and Borst, J. (2009). Toward a unified theory of the multitasking continuum: From concurrent performance to task switching, interruption, and resumption. In *CHI '09: Proceedings of the SIGCHI Conference on Human Factors in Computing Systems*, 1819–1828. http://doi.org/10.1145/1518701.1518981

Samaha, M., and Hawi, N. S. (2016). Relationships among smartphone addiction, stress, academic performance, and satisfaction with life. *Computers in Human Behavior, 57*, 321–325. http://doi.org/10.1016/j.chb.2015.12.045

Sanbonmatsu, D. M., Strayer, D. L., Medeiros-Ward, N., and Watson, J. M. (2013). Who multi-tasks and why? Multi-tasking ability, perceived multi-tasking ability, impulsivity, and sensation seeking. *PLoS ONE, 8*(1). http://doi.org/10.1371/journal.pone.0054402

Sapp, D. A., and Simon, J. L. (2005). Comparing grades in online and face-to-face writing courses: Interpersonal accountability and institutional commitment. *Computers and Composition, 22*(4), 471–489. http://doi.org/10.1016/j.compcom.2005.08.005

Sarter, N. B., and Woods, D. D. (1995). How in the world did we ever get into that mode? Mode error and awareness in supervisory control. *Human Factors: The Journal of the Human Factors and Ergonomics Society, 37*(1), 5–19. http://doi.org/10.1518/001872095779049516

Schumacher, E. H., Seymour, T. L., Glass, J. M., Fencsik, D. E., Lauber, E. J., Kieras, D. E., and Meyer, D. E. (2001). Virtually perfect time sharing in dual-task performance: Uncorking the central cognitive bottleneck. *Psychological Science, 12*(2), 101–108. http://doi.org/10.1111/1467-9280.00318

Schwarz, J., and Morris, M. (2011). Augmenting web pages and search results to help people find trustworthy information online. *Proceedings of the Annual SIGCHI Conference*. Retrieved from http://www.notjulie.com/research/web_credibility/paper.pdf

Schwebel, D. C., Stavrinos, D., Byington, K. W., Davis, T., O'Neal, E. E., and De Jong, D. (2012). Distraction and pedestrian safety: How talking on the phone, texting, and listening to music impact crossing the street. *Accident Analysis and Prevention*, *45*, 266–271. http://doi.org/10.1016/j.aap.2011.07.011

Scull, C., Milewski, A., and Millen, D. (1999). Envisioning the Web: User expectations about the cyber-experience. *Proceedings of the ASIS Annual Meeting*, *36*, 17–24. Retrieved from http://www.scopus.com/inward/record.url?eid=2-s2.0-27844497971&partnerID=tZOtx3y1

Searle, J. R. (1980). Minds, brains, and programs. *Behavioral and Brain Sciences*, *3*, 417–457. http://doi.org/10.1016/B978-1-4832-1446-7.50007-8

Sears, C. R., and Pylyshyn, Z. W. (2000). Multiple object tracking and attentional processing. *Canadian Journal of Experimental Psychology/Revue Canadienne de Psychologie Experimentale*, *54*(1), 1–14. http://doi.org/10.1037/h0087326

Shannon, C. E., and Weaver, W. (1949). *The mathematical theory of communication*. Urbana-Champaign, IL: University of Illinois Press.

Shapiro, A., and Niederhauser, D. (2004). Learning from hypertext: Research issues and findings. *Research on Educational Communications*, 605–620. Retrieved from http://learngen.org/~aust/EdTecheBooks/AECT HANDBOOK 2ND/23.pdf

Shapiro, K. L., Arnell, K. M., and Raymond, J. E. (1997). The attentional blink. *Trends in Cognitive Sciences*, *1*(8), 291–295.

Shaw, C. A., Lanius, R. A., and van den Doel, K. (1994). The origin of synaptic neuroplasticity: Crucial molecules or a dynamical cascade? *Brain Research Reviews*, *19*(3), 241–263.

Shiffrin, R. M., and Schneider, W. (1984). Automatic and controlled processing revisited. *Psychological Review*, *91*(2), 269–276. http://doi.org/10.1037/0033-295X.91.2.269

Shute, V. J., Ventura, M., and Ke, F. (2015). The power of play: The effects of Portal 2 and Lumosity on cognitive and noncognitive skills. *Computers and Education*, *80*, 58–67. http://doi.org/10.1016/j.compedu.2014.08.013

Simola, J., Kuisma, J., Oörni, A., Uusitalo, L., Hyönä, J., Oörni, A., and Hyönä, J. (2011). The impact of salient advertisements on reading and attention on web pages. *Journal of Experimental Psychology: Applied*, *17*(2), 174–190. http://doi.org/10.1037/a0024042

Simon, H. A. (1957). *Models of man; social and rational*. Oxford: Wiley.

Simon, H. A. (1971). Designing organizations for an information-rich world. In M. Greenberger (Ed.), *Computers, communications, and the public interest* (pp. 37–52). Baltimore, MD: The Johns Hopkins University Press.

Skinner, B. F. (1974). *About behaviourism*. New York: Random House.

Slocombe, T., and Bluedorn, A. (1999). Organizational behavior implications of the congruence between preferred polychronicity and experienced work-unit polychronicity. *Journal of Organizational Behavior*, *20*(1), 75–99. Retrieved from http://www.jstor.org/stable/3100205

Slonje, R., Smith, P. K., and Frisén, A. (2013). The nature of cyberbullying , and strategies for prevention. *Computers in Human Behavior*, *29*(1), 26–32. http://doi.org/10.1016/j.chb.2012.05.024

Small, G. W., and Vorgan, G. (2008). Meet your iBrain. *Scientific American, 19*(5), 42–49.

Smart, P. R. (2010). Cognition and the Web. In *1st ITA Workshop on Network-Enabled Cognition: The Contribution of Social and Technological Networks to Human Cognition,* Maryland, USA (pp. 1–41). Retrieved from http://eprints.ecs.soton.ac.uk/21824/

Smith, A., Rainie, L., McGeeney, K., Keeter, S., and Duggan, M. (2015). *U.S. Smartphone Use in 2015.* Pew Research Center. Retrieved from http://www.pewinternet.org/2015/04/01/us-smartphone-use-in-2015/

Smith, J. E. (2010). *Examining the effects of interruptions on processing of online news.*

Smith, S. L., and Goodwin, N. (1971). Blink coding for information display. *Human Factors, 13*(3), 283–290. Retrieved from http://hfs.sagepub.com/content/13/3/283.short

Sokolov, E. N. (1963). Higher nervous functions: The orienting reflex. *Annual Review of Physiology, 25,* 545–580.

Soucek, R., and Moser, K. (2010). Coping with information overload in email communication: Evaluation of a training intervention. *Computers in Human Behavior, 26*(6), 1458–1466. http://doi.org/10.1016/j.chb.2010.04.024

Sparrow, B., Liu, J., and Wegner, D. M. (2011). Google effects on memory: Cognitive consequences of having information at our fingertips. *Science, 333*(6043), 776–778. http://doi.org/10.1126/science.1207745

Speier, C., Vessey, I., and Valacich, J. S. (2003). The effects of interruptions, task complexity, and information presentation on computer-supported decision-making performance. *Decision Sciences, 34*(4), 771–797. http://doi.org/10.1111/j.1540-5414.2003.02292.x

Spence, I., and Feng, J. (2010). Video games and spatial cognition. *Review of General Psychology, 14*(2), 92–104. http://doi.org/10.1037/a0019491

Spinath, B., Spinath, F. M., Harlaar, N., and Plomin, R. (2006). Predicting school achievement from general cognitive ability, self-perceived ability, and intrinsic value. *Intelligence, 34*(4), 363–374. http://doi.org/10.1016/j.intell.2005.11.004

Squire, L. R., Knowlton, B., and Musen, G. (1993). The structure and organization of memory. *Annual peview of Psychology, 44,* 453–495. http://doi.org/10.1073/pnas.70.5.1478

Stavrinos, D., Byington, K. W., and Schwebel, D. C. (2009). Effect of cell phone distraction on pediatric pedestrian injury risk. *Pediatrics, 123*(2), e179-85. http://doi.org/10.1542/peds.2008-1382

Steffner, D., and Schenkman, B. (2012). Change blindness when viewing web pages. *Work: A Journal of Prevention, Assessment & Rehabilitation, 41,* 6098–6102. http://doi.org/10.3233/WOR-2012-1067-6098

Steinkuehler, C., and Duncan, S. (2008). Scientific habits of mind in virtual worlds. *Journal of Science Education and Technology, 17*(6), 530–543. http://doi.org/10.1007/s10956-008-9120-8

Stenfors, I., Morén, J., and Balkenius, C. (2003). Behavioural strategies in web interaction: A view from eye-movement research. In J. Hyönä, R. Radach and H. Deubel (Eds.), *The mind's eye: Cognitive and applied aspects of eye movement research* (pp. 633–644). http://doi.org/10.1016/B978-044451020-4/50033-5

Stern, Y., Blumen, H. M., Rich, L. W., Richards, A., Herzberg, G., and Gopher, D. (2013). Space Fortress game training and executive control in older adults: A pilot intervention. *Aging, Neuropsychology, and Cognitive Development, 18*(6), 653–677. http://doi.org/1 0.1080/13825585.2011.613450.Space

Steuer, J. (1992). Defining virtual reality: Dimensions determining telepresence. *Journal of Communication, 42*(4), 73–93. http://doi.org/10.1111/j.1460-2466.1992. tb00812.x

Stewart, T. F. M. (1976). Displays and the software interface. *Applied Ergonomics, 7*(3), 137–146. http://doi.org/10.1016/0003-6870(76)90202-7

Strayer, D. L., Cooper, J. M., and Drews, F. A. (2004). What do drivers fail to see when conversing on a cell phone? *Proceedings of the Human Factors and Ergonomics Society Annual Meeting, 48*, 2213–2217. http://doi.org/10.1177/154193120404801902

Strayer, D. L., and Drews, F. A. (2006). Multitasking in the automobile. *Attention: From Theory to Practice*, 121–133.

Strayer, D. L., and Drews, F. A. (2007). Cell-phone? Induced driver distraction. *Current Directions in Psychological Science, 16*(3), 128–131. http://doi.org/10.1111/j.1467-8721.2007.00489.x

Strayer, D. L., Drews, F. A., and Johnston, W. A. (2003). Cell phone-induced failures of visual attention during simulated driving. *Journal of Experimental Psychology: Applied, 9*(1), 23–32. http://doi.org/10.1037/1076-898X.9.1.23

Strayer, D. L., and Johnston, W. A. (2001). Driven to distraction: Dual-task studies of simulated driving and conversing on a cellular telephone. *Psychological Science, 12*(6), 462–466. http://doi.org/10.1111/1467-9280.00386

Strayer, D. L., Watson, J. M., and Drews, F. A. (2011). Cognitive distraction while multitasking in the automobile. In B. H. Ross (Ed.), *The Psychology of Learning and Motivation: Advances in Research and Theory* (Vol. 54, pp. 29–58). http://doi. org/10.1016/B978-0-12-385527-5.00002-4

Suganuma, N., Kikuchi, T., Yanagi, K., Yamamura, S., Morishima, H., Adachi, H., ... Takeda, M. (2007). Using electronic media before sleep can curtail sleep time and result in self-perceived insufficient sleep. *Sleep and Biological Rhythms, 5*(3), 204–214. http:// doi.org/10.1111/j.1479-8425.2007.00276.x

Suler, J. (2005). The basic psychological features of cyberspace. In *The Psychology of Cyberspace*. Retrieved from http://truecenterpublishing.com/psycyber/basicfeat .html

Suler, J. (2015). *Psychology of the digital age: Humans become electric*. Cambridge: Cambridge University Press.

Sun, D.-L., Chen, Z.-J., Ma, N., Zhang, X.-C., Fu, X.-M., and Zhang, D.-R. (2009). Decision-making and prepotent response inhibition functions in excessive internet users. *CNS Spectrums, 14*, 75–81.

Sundar, S. (2008). The MAIN model: A heuristic approach to understanding technology effects on credibility. *Digital Media, Youth, and Credibility*, 73–100. http://doi. org/10.1162/dmal.9780262562324.073

Sundar, S. S., and Nass, C. (2000). Source orientation in human-computer interaction. *Communication Research, 27*(6), 683–703.

Sundar, S. S., Xu, Q., and Oeldorf-Hirsch, A. (2009). Authority vs. peer: How interface cues influence users. *CHI '09 Extended Abstract on Human Factors in Computing Systems* (pp. 4231–4236). http://doi.org/10.1145/1520340.1520645

Susi, T., Johannesson, M., and Backlund, P. (2007). Serious games – an overview. *Elearning, 73*(10), 28. http://doi.org/10.1.1.105.7828

Sweller, J. (1994). Cognitive load theory, learning difficulty and instructional design. *Learning and Instruction, 4*, 295–312. Retrieved from http://www.sciencedirect.com/science/article/pii/0959475294900035

Sykes, E. R. (2011). Interruptions in the workplace: A case study to reduce their effects. *International Journal of Information Management, 31*(4), 385–394. http://doi.org/10.1016/j.ijinfomgt.2010.10.010

Tapscott, D. (1998). *Growing up digital: The rise of the net generation.* New York: McGraw-Hill. http://doi.org/10.1177/019263659908360714

Thorndike, E. L. (1898). Animal intelligence: An experimental study of the associative processes in animals. *Psychological Review, 2*(4), 1–107. http://doi.org/10.1097/00005053-190001000-00013

Thornton, B., Faires, A., Robbins, M., and Rollins, E. (2014). The mere presence of a cell phone may be distracting: Implications for attention and task performance. *Social Psychology, 45*(6), 479–488. http://doi.org/10.1027/1864-9335/a000216

Todorov, A., Chaiken, S., and Henderson, M. D. (2002). The heuristic-systematic model of social information processing. In J. P. Dillard and M. Pfau (Eds.), *The persuasion handbook: Developments in theory and practice* (pp. 195–211). Thousand Oaks, CA: SAGE Publications.

Trafton, J. G., Altmann, E. M., Brock, D. P., and Mintz, F. E. (2003). Preparing to resume an interrupted task: Effects of prospective goal encoding and retrospective rehearsal. *International Journal of Human Computer Studies, 58*(5), 583–603. http://doi.org/10.1016/S1071-5819(03)00023-5

Treisman, A. (1991). Search, similarity, and integration of features between and within dimensions. *Journal of Experimental Psychology: Human Perception and Performance, 17*(3), 652–676. http://doi.org/10.1037/0096-1523.17.3.652

Trick, L. M., Jaspers-Fayer, F., and Sethi, N. (2005). Multiple-object tracking in children: The "Catch the Spies" task. *Cognitive Development, 20*(3), 373–387. http://doi.org/10.1016/j.cogdev.2005.05.009

Trojan, S., and Pokorný, J. (1999). Theoretical aspects of neuroplasticity. *Physiological Research, 48*(2), 87–97.

Tseng, S., and Fogg, B. J. (1999). Credibility and computing technology. *Communications of the ACM, 42*(5), 39–44. http://doi.org/10.1145/301353.301402

Tulving, E. (1972). Episodic and semantic memory. In E. Tulving and W. Donaldson (Eds.), *Organization of memory* (Vol. 1, pp. 381–403). New York: Academic Press. http://doi.org/10.1017/S0140525X00047257

Turkle, S., and Papert, S. (1992). Epistemological pluralism and the revaluation of the concrete. *Journal of Mathematical Behavior, 11*(1), 13–33. http://doi.org/citeulike-article-id:513444

Tuten, L., Bosnjak, M., and Bandilla, W. (2000). Banner-advertised Web surveys. *Marketing Research, 11*(4), 16.

Tversky, A., and Kahneman, D. (1974). Judgment under uncertainty: Heuristics and biases. *Science, 185*(4157), 1124–1131. http://doi.org/10.1126/science.185.4157.1124

Unsworth, N., McMillan, B., Brewer, G., and Spillers, G. (2012). Everyday attention failures: An individual differences investigation. *Journal of Experimental Psychology: Learning, Memory, and Cognition, 38*(6), 1765–1772. http://doi.org/10.1037/a0028075

Vakkari, P. (1998). Growth of theories on information seeking: An analysis of growth of a theoretical research program on the relation between task complexity and information seeking. *Information Processing and Management, 34*(2–3), 361–382. http://doi.org/10.1016/S0306-4573(97)00074-5

Vakkari, P. (1999). Task complexity, problem structure and information actions: Integrating studies on information seeking and retrieval. *Information Processing and Management, 35*(6), 819–837. http://doi.org/10.1016/S0306-4573(99)00028-X

van Dijk, J. (2005). *The deepening divide: Inequality in the information society*. Thousand Oaks, CA: SAGE Publications.

van Solingen, R., Berghout, E., and Van Latum, F. (1998). Interrupts: Just a minute never is. *IEEE Software, 15*(5), 97–103. http://doi.org/10.1109/52.714843

Varakin, D. A., Levin, D. T., and Fidler, R. (2004). Unseen and unaware: Implications of recent research on failures of visual awareness for human–computer interface design. *Human-Computer Interaction, 19*(4), 389–422. http://doi.org/10.1207/s15327051hci1904_9

Veloutsou, C., and McAlonan, A. (2012). Loyalty and or disloyalty to a search engine: The case of young Millennials. *Journal of Consumer Marketing, 29*(2), 125–135. http://doi.org/10.1108/07363761211206375

Ventura, M., Shute, V., and Zhao, W. (2013). The relationship between video game use and a performance-based measure of persistence. *Computers and Education, 60*(1), 52–58. http://doi.org/10.1016/j.compedu.2012.07.003

Vitak, J., Crouse, J., and Larose, R. (2011). Personal Internet use at work: Understanding cyberslacking. *Computers in Human Behavior, 27*(5), 1751–1759. http://doi.org/10.1016/j.chb.2011.03.002

Wajcman, J., and Rose, E. (2011). Constant connectivity: Rethinking interruptions at work. *Organization Studies, 32*(7), 941–961. http://doi.org/10.1177/0170840611410829

Wall, D. S. (2007). *Cybercrime: The transformation of crime in the information age*. Cambridge: Polity.

Walraven, A., Brand-Gruwel, S., and Boshuizen, H. P. A. (2009). How students evaluate information and sources when searching the World Wide Web for information. *Computers and Education, 52*(1), 234–246. http://doi.org/10.1016/j.compedu.2008.08.003

Wang, P., and Tenopir, C. (1998). An exploratory study of users' interaction with world wide web resources: Information skills, cognitive styles, affective states, and searching behaviours. *School of Information Sciences – Faculty Publications and Other Works*, 445–454. Retrieved from http://trace.tennessee.edu/utk_infosciepubs/35

Ware, C. (2000). *Information visualization: Perception for design.* New York: Morgan Kaufmann.

Warschauer, M. (2002). Reconceptualizing the digital divide. *First Monday, 7*(7).

Wathen, C. N., and Burkell, J. (2002). Believe it or not: Factors influencing credibility on the Web. *Journal of the American Society for Information Science and Technology, 53*(2), 134–144. http://doi.org/10.1002/asi.10016

Watson, J. B. (1913). Psychology as the behaviourist views it. *Psychological Review, 20*, 158–177. http://doi.org/10.1371/journal.pone.0035056

Watson, J. M., and Strayer, D. L. (2010). Supertaskers: Profiles in extraordinary multitasking ability. *Psychonomic Bulletin and Review, 17*(4), 479–485. http://doi.org/10.3758/PBR.17.4.479

Weatherly, J. N., Gabe, M., and Arthur, E. I. (2003). Providing introductory psychology students access to lecture slides via Blackboard 5: A negative impact on performance. *Journal of Education Technology Systems, 31*(4), 463–474.

Wei, F., Wang, Y.K. and Klausner, M. (2012). Rethinking college students' self-regulation and sustained attention: does text messaging during class influence cognitive learning? *Communication Education, 3*(61), 185–204.

Wertsch, J. (1998). *Mind as action.* New York: Oxford University Press.

White, M. D., and Iivonen, M. (1999). Factors influencing Web search strategies. In *ASIS Annual Conference.*

White, M. D., and Iivonen, M. (2001). Questions as a factor in Web search strategy. *Information Processing and Management, 37*(5), 721–740. http://doi.org/10.1016/S0306-4573(00)00043-1

Whitehead, A. N. (1911). *An introduction to mathematics.* London: Williams and Norgate.

Whittle, D. B. (1997). *Cyberspace: The human dimension.* New York: W.H. Freeman and Co Ltd.

Whitty, M. T. (2013). Anatomy of the online dating romance scam. *Security Journal,* 1–13. http://doi.org/10.1057/sj.2012.57

Whitty, M. T., and Buchanan, T. (2012). The online romance scam: A serious cybercrime. *Cyberpsychology, 15*(3), 181–183. http://doi.org/10.1089/cyber.2011.0352

Wickens, C. D. (1981). *Processing resources in attention, dual task performance, and workload assessment.* Retrieved from http://www.aviation.illinois.edu/avimain/papers/research/pub_pdfs/techreports/EPL-81-3.pdf

Wickens, C. D. (2002). Multiple resources and performance prediction. *Theoretical Issues in Ergonomics Science, 3*(2), 159–177. http://doi.org/10.1080/14639220210123806

Wickens, C. D., and Carswell, C. M. (2006). Information processing. In G. Salvendy (Ed.), *Handbook of human factors and ergonomics* (4th ed., Vol. 42, pp. 111–149). New York: Wiley.

Widyanto, L., and Griffiths, M. (2007). Internet addiction: Does it really exist? (Revisited). *Young,* 127–149.

Wilson, K., and Korn, J. H. (2007). Attention during lectures: Beyond ten minutes. *Teaching of Psychology, 34*, 85–89.

Wirth, W., Böcking, T., Karnowski, V., and Von Pape, T. (2007). The Webnas method: A holistic approach to the analysis of web navigating and search behaviour. *Communication Methods and Measures, 3*(3), 115–146.

Wittmann, M., and Paulus, M. P. (2008). Decision making, impulsivity and time perception. *Trends in Cognitive Sciences, 12*(1), 7–12. http://doi.org/10.1016/j.tics.2007.10.004

Wood, E., Zivcakova, L., Gentile, P., Archer, K., De Pasquale, D., and Nosko, A. (2012). Examining the impact of off-task multi-tasking with technology on real-time classroom learning. *Computers and Education, 58*(1), 365–374. http://doi.org/10.1016/j.compedu.2011.08.029

Xin, Z., Lai, Z. R., Li, F., and Maes, J. H. R. (2014). Near- and far-transfer effects of working memory updating training in elderly adults. *Applied Cognitive Psychology, 28*(3), 403–408. http://doi.org/10.1002/acp.3011

Yang, S. C., and Tung, C.-J. (2007). Comparison of Internet addicts and non-addicts in Taiwanese high school. *Computers in Human Behavior, 23*(1), 79–96. http://doi.org/10.1016/j.chb.2004.03.037

Yantis, S. (2000). Goal-directed and stimulus-driven determinants of attentional control. *Control of Cognitive Processes: Attention and Performance Xviii*, 73–103. http://doi.org/10.2337/db11-0571

Yantis, S., and Jonides, J. (1984). Abrupt visual onsets and selective attention: Evidence from visual search, *Journal of Experimental Psychology: Human Perception and Performance, 10*(5), 601–621.

Yantis, S., and Jonides, J. (1990). Abrupt visual onsets and selective attention: Voluntary versus automatic allocation. *Journal of Experimental Psychology. Human Perception and Performance, 16*(1), 121–134. Retrieved from http://www.ncbi.nlm.nih.gov/pubmed/2137514

Yen, J.-Y., Ko, C.-H., Yen, C.-F., Wu, H.-Y., and Yang, M.-J. (2007). The comorbid psychiatric symptoms of Internet addiction: Attention deficit and hyperactivity disorder (ADHD), depression, social phobia, and hostility. *The Journal of Adolescent Health, 41*, 93–98. http://doi.org/10.1016/j.jadohealth.2007.02.002

Yen, J.-Y., Yen, C.-F., Chen, C.-S., Tang, T.-C., and Ko, C.-H. (2009). The association between adult ADHD symptoms and Internet addiction among college students: The gender difference. *CyberPsychology & Behavior, 12*(2), 187–191. http://doi.org/10.1089/cpb.2008.0113

Yesilada, Y., Jay, C., Stevens, R., and Harper, S. (2008). Validating the use and role of visual elements of web pages in navigation with an eye-tracking study. *Proceedings of the 17th International Conference on World Wide Web WWW 08*, 11. http://doi.org/10.1145/1367497.1367500

Yoo, C. Y. C., Kim, K., and Stout, P. A. (2004). Assessing the effects of animation in online banner advertising: Hierarchy of effects model. *Journal of Interactive Advertising, 4*(2), 49–60. Retrieved from http://jiad.org/download?p=49&a=bi&pagenumber=1&w=100

Yoo, H. J., Cho, S. C., Ha, J., Yune, S. K., Kim, S. J., Hwang, J., ... Lyoo, I. K. (2004). Attention deficit hyperactivity symptoms and internet addiction. *Psychiatry and Clinical Neurosciences, 58*, 487–494. http://doi.org/10.1111/j.1440-1819.2004.01290.x

Young, K., and Regan, M. (2007). Driver distraction: A review of the literature. *Distracted Driving*, 379–405. http://doi.org/10.1201/9781420007497

Young, K. S. (1999). Internet addiction: Symptoms, evaluation and treatment. *Innovations in Clinical Practice: A Source Book*, *17*, 19–31. Retrieved from http://www.netaddiction.com/articles/symptoms.pdf

Zarro, M. (2012). Developing a dual-process information seeking model for exploratory search. *Mikezarro.com*. Retrieved from http://www.mikezarro.com/docs/Zarro_HCIR2012_FINAL.pdf

Zelikovich, D. (2011). The negative effect of e-mails at work. *Journal of Systems and Information Technology*, *14*(1), 82–94

Zhang, P. (2000). The effects of animation on information seeking performance on the World Wide Web: Securing attention or interfering with primary tasks? *Journal of the AIS*, *1*(March). Retrieved from http://dl.acm.org/citation.cfm?id=374128

Zhu, E. (1999). Hypermedia interface design: The effects of number of links and granularity of nodes. *Journal of Educational Multimedia and Hypermedia*, *8*(3), 331–358.

Zuckerman, M., and Kuhlman, D. M. (2000). Personality and risk-taking: Common biosocial factors. *Journal of Personality*, *68*(6), 999. http://doi.org/10.1111/1467-6494.00124

Zyda, M. (2005). From visual simulation to virtual reality to games. *Computer*, *38*(9), 25–32. http://doi.org/10.1109/MC.2005.297

INDEX

Note: Page numbers in *italics* indicate figures and tables.